Notable British Trials Series No. 88

TRIAL OF
ELIZA FENNING

EDITED BY

Kate Clarke

MANGO BOOKS

First edition published 2020

Copyright © Kate Clarke, 2020

The right of Kate Clarke to be identified as the author of this work has been asserted in accordance with the Copyright, Designs & Patents Act 1988.

All rights reserved. No part of this book may be reprinted or reproduced or utilised in any form or by any electronic, mechanical or other means, now known or hereafter invented, including photocopying and recording, or in any information storage or retrieval system, without the prior permission in writing of the publishers.

ISBN: 978-1-911273-87-5 (hardback)
ISBN: 978-1-914277-12-2 (softcover)
ISBN: 978-1-911273-88-2 (ebook)

Notable British Trials imprint ©William Hodge & Company (Holdings) Ltd Used with kind permission.

General Editors:
David Green - M.W. Oldridge - Adam Wood

Published by Mango Books
www.MangoBooks.co.uk
18 Soho Square
London W1D 3QL

Notable British Trials Series No. 88

TRIAL OF
ELIZA FENNING

EDITED BY

Kate Clarke

ELIZA FENNING.

CONTENTS.

Introduction 1
Leading Dates 81

THE TRIAL: TUESDAY 11 APRIL 1815 —
List of the Jury 84

Charlotte Turner	85	John Marshall	95
Orlibar Turner	88	Eliza Fenning	95
Roger Gadsden	90	John Woodderson	96
Margaret Turner	91	Mrs Hutchinson	96
Robert Gregson Turner	92	Mrs Hinson	96
Sarah Peer	92	Richard Maze	96
Orlibar Turner [recalled]	94	John Smith	96
William Thiselton	94	Roger Gadsden [recalled]	97
Joseph Penson	94	William Fenning	98
Sarah Peer [recalled]	95		

Summing Up 98
The Verdict 100

Appendices 101
I. Examination at Hatton Garden 103
II. The Petition for Royal Clemency 107
III. The Coal Merchant's Records 109
IV. Affidavits of Samuel Davis and William Fenning 113
V. 'Effects of Arsenic upon Yeast Dough' and 'Effects of Arsenic upon the Knives' 119
VI. The Opinions of Mr and Mrs Hardy 121
VII. The Letters of Eliza Fenning 129
VIII. 'Written in Newgate.' 153
IX. Extract from F. W. Hackwood's Biography of William Hone 157
X. All the Year Round 161
XI. *La Pie Voleuse.* 175
XII. The Harvard Papers 187
XIII. The Hone Papers 199
XIV. Trial of Henry William Wyatt 203
XV. Trial of Elizabeth Mary Miller 211

Index 219
Notable British Trials Series 225

Fenning's trial and execution was sensational because of the popular perception of her innocence and this view was shared by some in high quarters – as Dickens notes, Samuel Romilly, the advocate of legal and penal reform, demurred from the verdict because no adequate motive for the crime was established. All manner of facts favourable to Fenning were not known to the jury and no appeal system in the modern sense existed so the conviction turned upon flimsy circumstantial evidence. 'Not enough evidence to hang a cat', as one historian puts it.

Tim Marshall, 'Not Forgotten: Eliza Fenning, Frankenstein and Victorian Chivalry'.

———

[On the Recorder of the City of London, Sir John Silvester] Widely known as a randy reprobate – 'Black Jack' he was called – he demanded sexual favours from any lady who came to beg him for mercy or justice. He was also slapdash in his trying, though not alone in this: Old Bailey trials were usually conducted at breakneck pace ... But his was a glaring prejudice and it did not escape notice. Although Romilly held aloof from the case, he noted in private the absence of motive and that the recorder had 'conceived a strong prejudice against the criminal' making 'some very unjust and unfounded observations' against her in his summing-up.

V. A. C. Gatrell, *The Hanging Tree: Execution and the English People, 1770-1868*.

———

This trial and its consequences are of too much importance to the public to be forgotten as one of the passing events of the day. It does not require much sagacity to discover the whole of this mysterious case. I think that, with a little patience and some perseverance, it will be developed: I ask only for a suspension of judgment.

John Watkins (William Hone), *The Important Results of an Elaborate Investigation into the Mysterious Case of Elizabeth Fenning*.

ELIZA FENNING.

INTRODUCTION.

I.

Regency London was the setting for the dramatic but disturbing case of Eliza Fenning and the poisoned dumplings. It was 1815, the year that saw the end of the Napoleonic Wars, and many Londoners took to the streets to celebrate. Though it was an era of great creative energy in architecture, art and literature, it was also a time when society was starkly divided between the idle rich – as epitomised by the decadence of the lifestyle of the Prince Regent and his like – and the working classes: the servants, artisans and labourers who often toiled long and hard in unhealthy conditions to ensure the comfort and wellbeing of their masters.

On 30 January, 1815, Elizabeth Fenning, usually known as Eliza and described as young, petite and extremely pretty,[1] was employed as a cook in the home of twenty-four year old Robert Gregson Turner, an established law stationer, and his twenty-three year old wife, Charlotte, at 68 Chancery Lane, London. The Turners employed three other live-in servants – a housemaid called Sarah Peer (sometimes referred to as Pearse or Pear), and two male apprentices: Roger Gadsden, almost sixteen[2], and eighteen year old Thomas King. Two part-time clerks were also occasionally employed.

At the time Eliza went to work for the Turner family she was twenty-one years old and in a relationship with a young man called Edward whom she hoped to marry. She had been in service since the age of fourteen. Her father, William Fenning, from Suffolk farming stock, had been a soldier in the 15th Regiment of Foot and, whilst stationed in Ireland in 1790, he married Mary Swayne, whose grandfather had been a London silversmith. Three years after the marriage, the regiment was sent to Dominica in the West Indies, where Eliza was born on 10 June 1793. Mary gave birth to ten children, of which only Eliza survived into adulthood. Contrary to some subsequent (and offensively

---

1   In his pamphlet, *An Authentic Narrative of the Conduct of Elizabeth Fenning from the Time that the Warrant Arrived for her Death till her Execution*, Dr Thomas William Wansbrough, who spent many hours visiting Eliza in the condemned cell at Newgate, gives us this description: 'Elizabeth's stature was below the middling size, inclining to *embonpoint* [buxom], and a round full face, with expressive black eyes. Her countenance was indicative of strong feelings …' (Wansbrough, 26).
2   Roger Gadsden was born on 28 March 1799, so would have been fifteen years and eleven months old at the time of the incident. When Charlotte Turner was asked in court the ages of the apprentices, she replied, 'I suppose seventeen or eighteen years old'.

Fenning.

prejudicial) reporting, the Fennings were Baptists, not Roman Catholics, and Eliza was raised in that faith.

William Fenning's regiment returned to Dublin in 1796 or 1797, having incurred many casualties during battles at Martinique and St Lucia; he was by this time a non-commissioned officer, and in 1802 he obtained his discharge with a certificate of good character. He moved to London and worked for three years as a potato dealer with his brother in Red Lion Street, Holborn. His wife, despite bearing so many children, worked as an upholsterer for a number of years and was of good character.[3] At the time, as many ex-soldiers were returning to the capital, the rise in the crime rate was, perhaps unjustly, attributed to some of their number, and this prevailing assumption may have had some bearing on the attitude of members of the Establishment in the case.

The pattern of Eliza's life began to unravel when, on Tuesday 21 March, seven weeks after joining the Turner household, she prepared lunch for the family – a meal that consisted of rump steak, potatoes and dumplings. Those present at the dinner table that day were Robert and Charlotte Turner – who was in an advanced stage of pregnancy at the time – and Robert's father, Orlibar Turner (some press reports refer to him as Haldebart), who, though he lived in Lambeth,[4] was in partnership with his son in the Chancery Lane office.[5] His wife, Margaret, was not present. It was the routine of the house that the servants would eat their meal downstairs in the kitchen at 2.00 pm, whilst the family upstairs were served theirs at 3.00 pm. Soon after eating the dumplings, all three members of the Turner family were taken violently ill with stomach pains and vomiting. Eliza and one of the apprentices, Roger Gadsden, were also seized with the same symptoms, and a local apothecary, Henry Ogilvy, known to the Turners, was called to the house soon after the family became ill (although, controversially, he was not called to give evidence at the subsequent trial).

At 8.45 that evening, a surgeon, John Marshall, was sent for; he lived at Half Moon Street, Piccadilly, and had been a friend of the Turner family for nearly ten years. After further treatment, all those affected soon recovered: all, that is,

---

3   Roughead (86) identifies Mary Fenning's employer as 'one Norris … at 55 High Holborn'.

4   Marshall, J. (21) identifies Orlibar and Margaret Turner's address as Belmont Place (now Nine Elms Lane), Vauxhall.

5   Orlibar Turner was also the author of at least two works detailing the application of the Stamp Act (1712, with subsequent amendments, including one in 1797). The extension of the reach of this Act was controversial as it was interpreted as an attempt by the government to suppress dissenting voices. Eliza Fenning's own case – which pitted a lowly girl of the servant class against an established family – was considered by some to be an exemplar of the dangers to the ruling classes of the wider movement for popular suffrage, representation and rights.

Introduction.

except Eliza, whose illness was more protracted.[6] The other apprentice, Thomas King, may have left the house after his meal but was sent to fetch John Marshall later that evening. He was not, however, mentioned in any of the press reports and was not called later to give evidence in court.

For some reason, Mr Orlibar Turner immediately suspected Eliza of attempting to poison the family and his suspicions were, from the start, focussed on the dumplings. It was well known by everyone in the house that a packet of white arsenic[7] was kept in a drawer in the office to be used to kill mice that might damage the 'parchments and papers of consequence'. It was wrapped in paper and clearly marked: *'Arsenic, deadly poison'* and kept in the same drawer as scraps of spare paper; one of Eliza's jobs was to light the fire in the office each morning, and the apprentices said that she often went to the drawer to find bits of paper to start the fire.

The next morning, apparently intent on incriminating Eliza, Orlibar Turner inspected the residue in the pan that she had used to make the dumplings and when the surgeon, John Marshall, returned to the house, Turner showed it to him. After examining it, Marshall professed that the residue contained arsenic and, after he and Orlibar reported their suspicions to the magistrate, Mr Raynsford, at the Public Office, Hatton Garden, a warrant for Eliza's arrest was issued.[8]

Eliza was found in her attic bedroom, still suffering from sickness.[9] She was arrested by a police officer, William Thiselton, under suspicion of

---

6   John Marshall, surgeon, was a member of the Royal College of Surgeons; he also acted as apothecary to HRH the Duke of Gloucester's family. Apothecaries were not qualified to perform medical procedures; they were basically dispensing remedies – Marshall was scathingly described by John Watkins in a letter to William Hone as a 'compounder of medicine' as opposed to a physician. The title of surgeon – a progression from barber-surgeons – denoted a practitioner with some medical qualifications, but not a surgeon in the modern sense of the word.

7   White arsenic was easily available in 1815 and equally easy to mistake for innocuous substances like flour: for this reason, it was frequently the cause of accidental domestic poisonings. The Sale of Arsenic Regulation Act of 1851 (introduced after the number of cases of poisoning had risen alarmingly) stipulated that arsenic was to be coloured with soot or indigo dye to prevent domestic poisoning accidents. Purchasers of arsenic had to sign a register, give their name and address and provide a guarantor known to them. The Pharmacy and Sale of Poisons Act of 1868 extended the arsenic provisions to cover the sale of other poisons such as strychnine and cyanide. In 1871, when embarking on her poisoning spree, Christiana Edmunds had to follow the rules stipulated in the Act when buying the strychnine she said she needed for killing 'stray cats'.

8   Prior to the development of the Marsh test in 1836 and the more advanced Reinsch test in 1841, there was no reliable method of determining the presence or the quantity of arsenic. John Marshall and the chemist Joseph Hume, who assisted in the testing (he had introduced his 'silver test' in 1809), were therefore not correct in stating unequivocally that arsenic was present in the dumpling mixture.

9   In John Marshall's pamphlet, *Five Cases of Recovery*, he states that while he and Orlibar Turner were reporting their suspicions against Eliza, she, unaware that she was imprisoned in the house, had tried to run away, but fainted. Thomas King, under orders from Orlibar Turner, had locked all the inner and outer doors to prevent her escape. (Marshall, J., 33.)

Fenning.

attempted murder. As she was so ill, a sedan chair was requested to convey her to the Magistrates' Court, Hatton Garden, but as none was available she was transported in a coach. After being charged with attempted murder, she was taken to the infirmary ward at Clerkenwell Prison.[10]

A columnist for *The Globe* was already of the opinion that Eliza was guilty of 'a diabolical attempt' to poison the Turner family, but a subsequent article, published on 27 March, added this telling observation:

> We understand that there is some slight suspicion attached to another person.[11]

On Monday 27 March, Eliza was brought before the magistrate once more. Orlibar, Margaret, Robert and Charlotte Turner,[12] John Marshall, Roger Gadsden, Sarah Peer and William Thiselton gave their depositions (the clerk to the magistrates, Mr Shearman, was a friend of the Turners),[13] after which – at a final hearing on Thursday 30 March – the depositions were read and signed by the witnesses and Eliza Fenning was ordered to stand trial for attempted murder. She was then given the choice of being allowed bail with two sureties of £50 each, a year on remand in Clerkenwell Prison, or a trial at the current Old Bailey sessions. Not wishing to burden her poverty-stricken parents with trying to fund her bail and preferring her ordeal to be over and done with as soon as possible, she chose to stand trial at the Old Bailey and was therefore sent straight to the notorious Newgate prison.[14]

On Tuesday 28 March, Eliza had written to Edward from Clerkenwell,[15]

---

10   John Marshall states that Eliza was taken to Coldbath Fields prison at Clerkenwell, but some of her earliest letters are headed New Clerkenwell Prison. (Marshall, J., 19.)
11   *The Globe*, 25 March 1815; 27 March 1815.
12   According to the evidence of William Thiselton, Charlotte Turner, seven months pregnant and only six days after the poisoning 'showed no appearance of indisposition; she did not complain of any and although she was longer in giving her evidence than the other witnesses, from her remarks and observations being very numerous and spoke more than either of them, she did not appear at all fatigued or inconvenienced'. John Marshall, however, demurred: '… she persevered in the recumbent position for a fortnight afterwards [after the supposed poisoning] which relieved the pain in the loins, and kept off, or lessened, the disposition to the bearing pains of the gravid uterus' (Marshall, J., 15).
13   See Watkins, 112-115, in which he describes later futile attempts to obtain copies of the depositions.
14   Two years earlier the Quaker prison reformer, Elizabeth Fry (1780-1845), had visited the female section of Newgate Gaol and found the conditions appalling – women and children kept in squalid, overcrowded cells, rife with conflict and drunkenness; some prisoners were manacled or wearing leg-irons. In 1817, the Association for the Reformation of the Female Prisoners at Newgate was formed.
15   There is no evidence relating to the identity of Edward, the young man to whom it was said Eliza was engaged to be married. Wansbrough, 9, states that Eliza wrote to 'a young man to whom she was attached, enclosing a lock of her hair'; however, she forgot to enclose the hair as a memento (she did this for her parents, fellow inmates and friends). This was remedied by Mr Newman, the Newgate Chief Gaoler, when he opened the letter to check its content and asked Wansbrough to enclose the lock of hair. The letter was addressed to 'Charles', not Edward – or perhaps pseudonymised before publication.

Introduction.

> I now lay ill at the infirmary sick ward. My mother attends me three times a day, and brings me everything I can wish for; but, Edward, I shall never be right or happy again, to think I ever was in prison.[16]

From Newgate, on 3 April, Eliza wrote again to Edward:

> Thank God I shall stand my trial at the Old Bailey, where I shall have a Counsellor to plead for me, so I have nothing to fear as my conscience tells me I am not guilty.[17]

Though extremely poor, Eliza's parents managed – by, it was said, selling their few items of furniture and even their bedding – to raise the money to pay for their daughter to share a cell with another woman, Mary Ann Clarke, who had been charged with larceny and was also awaiting trial.[18]

II.

The trial took place in the Central Criminal Court of the Old Bailey on Tuesday 11 April 1815, before the Recorder of the City of London, Sir John Silvester[19], and a jury of twelve men. Mr John Gurney K. C.[20] conducted the prosecution on behalf of the Turners. Eliza's parents had managed to raise £5 for her defence, of which a barrister, Mr Peter Alley,[21] was paid £2 2s – two guineas – to watch proceedings on her behalf.

The precise wording of the charge against Eliza Fenning was that she 'feloniously and unlawfully and with malice aforethought did administer to

---

16 Watkins, 196.
17 Watkins, 197.
18 Mary Ann Clarke was arrested on 2 June 1815 and found guilty of theft at the Old Bailey on 21 June. Until Eliza Fenning was named on the Report – the list of those to be hanged – issued on 20 July, she was allowed to share a cell with Mary Ann: however, once the date of her execution was listed, she would have been removed to solitary confinement in the condemned cell at Felons' Side.
19 Sir John 'Black Jack' Silvester (1745-1822): aged 70 at the time of the trial. Ben Wilson (112) describes Silvester as 'a much-maligned magistrate; he was well known as a hanging judge, and was notorious for his prejudice against female defendants'. V. A. C. Gatrell (359) describes Silvester as a 'randy reprobate – he demanded sexual favours from any lady who came to beg him for mercy or justice'. He was also described as 'exceedingly obnoxious by his coarseness, the violence of his temper, and his utter disregard for the rules of courtesy' by Archer Polson (Vol. 2, 164).
20 Sir John Gurney, K. C. (1768-1845). Barrister; prosecuted a number of cases at the Old Bailey, including that of the Cato Street Conspirators in 1820. He was knighted in 1832 and made Baron of the Exchequer.
21 Peter Alley (1769-1834). May (138) describes Alley as of Irish descent and 'hot-tempered'. In 1816, after a trial at the Old Bailey over the alleged theft of two cows from a field in Bermondsey, he and barrister John Adolphus fought a duel with pistols on the beach at Calais; both were injured, but they thereafter became friends. In 1824, he defended Henry Fauntleroy against charges of forgery (see NBT 34).

and cause to be administered to Orlibar Turner, Robert Gregson Turner and Charlotte Turner (his wife) certain deadly poison (to wit, arsenic) with intent the said persons to kill and murder'.

Through the testimony of the witnesses, the events of that fateful day became clear.

Called to give evidence, Mrs Charlotte Turner told the court that she had recently caught Eliza in the apprentices' room in a partly undressed state, and had threatened her with instant dismissal. Eliza later insisted that she had only entered the boys' room to ask for a light for her candle:

> I unfortunately knocked at the door of the boys' bed-room for a light, they opened the door and gave me a light, and began taking liberties I did not approve of; I told them if they dared to insult me, I would call Mrs Turner, which I did, but she not coming at the instant I went to my own room, and, when nearly undressed, Mrs Turner came into the room and asked me what was the matter; I informed her of what had passed, and she said she did not approve of such behaviour.[22]

It was only when Margaret Turner who had, in fact, initially employed her, and stayed in the house in Chancery Lane for two weeks while she settled in, interceded on her behalf that it was agreed that Eliza should keep her job.

Charlotte Turner went on to say that after she had reprimanded Eliza, the girl had been sullen and resentful, and treated her disrespectfully. She also emphasised the fact that, on several occasions, Eliza had specifically asked to be allowed to make dumplings (before the magistrates, Charlotte had remembered Eliza saying, 'You cannot believe how well I can make them').

Mrs Turner usually made dumplings with ready-mixed dough supplied by a local baker, but, on Saturday 18 March, when the brewer – Mr Edmonds, of Gray's Inn Lane – sent his man, Joseph Penson, to deliver some table beer for Robert Turner, Eliza took it upon herself to order some yeast so that she could make her own. On Monday 20 March, the maid, Sarah, took delivery of the yeast from the brewer and gave it to Eliza in a white basin. Charlotte Turner then agreed to let Eliza use it to make dumplings from scratch.

Recalling the events of Tuesday 21 March, Charlotte Turner told the court:

> I told her she might make some, but, before she made the dumplings, to make a beef steak pie for dinner for the young men ... This was about 11.30 am. She carried the pie to the baker's before the kneading of the dough commenced ... I gave her directions about making the dough.

---

22   Fenning, 4.

Introduction.

According to Eliza's account:

> Then I was sent to the butcher's [in Brooks Market], for the steaks; when I came back I went into the back-kitchen to clean a dozen and a half of knives and forks; during the time I was doing them I heard some person in the front kitchen, and thought it was my mistress, but, on my coming out of the back-kitchen, I saw Thomas King, one of the apprentices, coming out: I asked him what he had been doing in the kitchen; he made no answer, but went upstairs. ...[23]

> Mrs Turner told me to be sure not to leave the kitchen, but I did not pay any attention to her in that respect, knowing I must leave it to do the remaining part of my work.[24]

There was clearly some friction over domestic matters – Eliza had been in service for several years and had been employed in nine different positions whereas Charlotte had only recently become mistress of her own household. When Eliza made it clear that she did not need to be supervised whilst making the dumplings, her mistress left her alone in the kitchen and went upstairs; but she went back two or three times during the morning, and, she later confirmed that, although she had nothing to do with the making of the dumplings, it was she who had made the sauce. At this time, the maid, Sarah, was upstairs, in a bedroom, repairing a counterpane.

When questioned further about the dough Eliza had made, Charlotte Turner said that when she came back to the kitchen the mixture was in a covered pan, left by the fire to rise; however, when she inspected the mixture, it looked odd and had not risen at all. When she mentioned this to Eliza, she seemed unconcerned and said it would rise, given time.

The court then heard that, at 3.00 pm, the family sat down to eat their lunch, brought to the table by the housemaid, Sarah Peer, before she left to visit her sister. Charlotte Turner had noticed that the dumplings 'were black and heavy, instead of being white and light' and said as much to Sarah. She testified that after eating a small amount of dumpling, she felt faint and was so stricken with severe stomach pains that she had to leave the room. She was upstairs for about half an hour, vomiting profusely, and when she came back downstairs she found the rest of the family – her husband, Robert, and her father-in-law, Orlibar – also stricken with similar symptoms.

Mr Orlibar Turner was next to be called to the witness box and told the court that he had been taken ill within three minutes of eating some dumpling.

---

23 Fenning, 5.
24 Fenning, 7.

Fenning.

'The effect was so violent,' he said, 'that I hardly had time to get into the back yard before my dinner came up. I felt considerable heat across my stomach and chest, and pain.' When asked if Eliza had offered any assistance, he replied, 'Not in the smallest'. Nor, he insisted, did he see her eat any of the dumplings.

Orlibar's instincts told him that the family had been the victims of a deliberate poisoning. The next morning, he noticed that the remainder of the dumplings 'sticked round the pan' in which they had been mixed. 'I put some water into the pan and stirred it up with a spoon with a view to form a liquid of the whole. I found – upon the pan being set down for a moment or two, or half a minute, upon taking it slowly and in a slanting direction – I discovered a white powder at the bottom of it. I showed it to several persons in the house; I kept it in my custody ... until Mr Marshall came. No person had access to it.'

He then stated that the packet of arsenic, in two paper wrappers, was usually kept in the office drawer and bore the label *'Arsenic, deadly poison'*. Charlotte Turner was asked to testify that Eliza could 'read and write very well', insinuating that she knew perfectly well that the packet contained poison. This supply of arsenic, Orlibar Turner announced, had been missing since 7 March. He then drew from his pocket two blackened knives which he said had been used to cut the dumplings.

Next to give evidence was the apprentice, Roger Gadsden, who confirmed that the packet of arsenic had been missing from the drawer since 7 March. He also told the court that Eliza had made yeast dumplings for the servants' supper the night before – Monday 20 March – and he, Eliza and Sarah had all eaten them. 'They were quite different from these dumplings in point of colour and weight, light and white and very good,' he said.[25]

On Tuesday 21 March, Gadsden went into the kitchen between 3.00 pm and 4.00 pm (he was later more precise, giving the time as 3.20 pm), still feeling hungry despite having eaten not long before: 'I observed there a plate on the table. On it was a dumpling and a half. I took a knife and fork up and was going to cut it, to eat of it.'

Sarah Peer had taken the dumplings upstairs to the Turners' dinner table before leaving the house, so it fell to Eliza to fetch the leftovers, returning with the uneaten dumplings to the kitchen. She sampled them herself and then, when Gadsden came in, she told him not to try them, saying, 'Gadsden, do not eat that! It is cold and heavy. It will do you no good.'

Ignoring her advice, the lad ate a piece of dumpling the size of a walnut and

---

25   Eliza would have made the dumpling mixture with water, not milk, but Charlotte Turner had insisted she also add milk when she made the dumplings for the family the next day which might indicate that there *was*, as Eliza suspected, something wrong with the milk, not the yeast.

Introduction.

then consumed the remains of the sauce, soaking it up with a piece of bread. Within minutes he felt unwell but, nevertheless, was sent to fetch Orlibar's wife, Margaret, from her home in Lambeth. They hastened back to Chancery Lane in a coach, accompanied (although this is not revealed in the transcript of the trial) by her son-in-law, Richard Abbot.[26] Gadsden started vomiting on the southbound journey, and continued to vomit on the way back.

They reached Chancery Lane at about 8.00 pm, and, on entering the house, Margaret Turner said she found her husband, son and daughter-in-law extremely ill. 'Very soon after I was there, [Eliza] was sick and vomiting. ... I exclaimed to her, "Oh, these devilish dumplings!" supposing they had done the mischief. She said, "Not the dumplings, but the milk, ma'am." I asked her what milk she meant. She said, "The halfpennyworth of milk that Sarah had fetched to make the sauce."'

Robert Gregson Turner was called next and gave the briefest of accounts. He was not questioned in any depth, and he merely said that he had eaten some of the dumplings but none of the sauce which his wife had made. He said that he had suffered more than the others as he had eaten more of the dumplings.

The maid, Sarah Peer, testified that on 21 March she went for the milk after she and Eliza had eaten their meal of pie at 2.00 pm; she had served the Turners with the dumplings, potatoes and rump steak at 3.00. Immediately after doing so, she left the house, having been given permission to visit her sister in Hackney.

'I came home at 9.00 pm exactly,' she told the court. 'I ate none of the dumplings myself.' She had eaten some of the crust of the pie, but 'was not at all ill'. In addition, she had eaten 'some dumplings she [Eliza] had made the night before. I never tasted any better. They were all made out of the same flour.'

Sarah admitted that she and Eliza sometimes quarrelled about petty things. At one time, for instance, they fell out when Eliza had 'taken something' – an apron – out of Sarah's drawer 'to use as a duster'. According to Sarah, when Mrs Turner had reprimanded Eliza about the incident in the apprentices' room, Eliza had said that she didn't like Mr and Mrs Turner any more. Finally, the maid said that she had not known about the poison kept in the office drawer; nor had she ever had any reason to go there.

William Thiselton, the police officer from the Hatton Garden police office who had arrested Eliza, told the court that he had asked her whether she thought the flour was to blame for the sickness. She thought not, as she had used the same flour to make a beef steak pie with no ill effects and, in her opinion, it was

---

26 Richard Abbot was married to the Turners' daughter, Mary Elisabeth Turner. Even though he witnessed the agonies of the members of the household soon after they became ill, and then watched Marshall's testing of the pan for evidence of arsenic the following day, he was not mentioned during the trial.

Fenning.

more likely to be the yeast as she had seen a 'red sediment' when she used it to make the dumplings. At the magistrates' court, Thiselton had stated that Eliza had suggested that Sarah Peer might have put something in the milk she had fetched that morning, as she was 'sly and artful' – but this important detail did not, apparently, emerge at the Old Bailey. Whereas in later cases – Victorian and onwards – there is typically a great deal of correspondence between witnesses' depositions (given in the lower courts) and their examination in chief in the higher courts, the scant records of the proceedings before the magistrate in Eliza's case suggest considerable divergence in the details given by the prosecution witnesses between hearings. Even apparently significant snippets like Eliza's denunciation of Sarah Peer do not appear to have survived the transition to the Central Criminal Court, getting lost somewhere east of Hatton Garden.

Mr John Marshall, the surgeon who attended the family, told the court that 'on the evening of Tuesday 21 March, I was sent for to Mr Turner's family in a great hurry. I got there about 8.45 pm.'[27]

'All the symptoms attending the family,' Marshall asserted, 'were such as would be produced by arsenic. I have no doubt of it, by the symptoms.[28] The prisoner was also ill – by the same, I have no doubt.' The next morning, Marshall inspected the dish which Orlibar Turner had found so suspicious. 'I washed it with a tea-kettle of warm water,' said Marshall. 'I first stirred it and let it subside. I decanted it off. I found half a teaspoonful of white powder. I washed it a second time. I decidedly found it to be arsenic.' Then there were the blackened knives: would the blades of knives become discoloured if they were used to cut an arsenical foodstuff? Marshall's view was absolute: 'I have no doubt of it'. And what of the yeast? 'There was not a grain of arsenic there; and I examined the flour tub – there was no arsenic there.'[29]

---

27 The fact that John Marshall was only sent for nearly six hours after the family became ill was a matter of curiosity for Watkins (45): 'How did it happen that Mr Marshall, of Half Moon Street, Piccadilly, the only medical man whom it was deemed proper to examine on this most important trial, should not have seen the family till five or six hours after the affair? How did it happen that Mr Ogilvy, of Southampton Buildings, Chancery Lane, was *not* a witness on the trial?'

28 In her book, *The Secret Poisoner*, Linda Stratmann describes the symptoms of Robert Turner thus: 'The muscles of Turner's abdomen and viscera were contracting spasmodically, and so powerful were these movements that basins of his yellowish-green vomit included faecal matter driven up from the intestines. Turner was also suffering from violent diarrhoea, and his motions were a homogenous bright green like paint'. (Stratmann, 6-7.) These and other symptoms were described by John Marshall.

29 Before the trial, Marshall, unwilling to rely on his own observations alone, had also taken the precaution of contacting Joseph Hume, a scientist (before the word itself was coined) who had experience in testing for arsenic. Starting with the white powder collected by Marshall from the pan, Hume undertook a byzantine experiment which ended with the deposition of 'a copious precipitate' in the bottom of a phial; this 'in the course of a few hours turned to a dark brown'. Marshall reported that this 'beautiful and highly satisfactory experiment infallibly proved the powder to be white arsenic'. (Marshall, J., 28).

Introduction.

That was the case for the prosecution, conspicuous for its brevity and the lack of significant interrogation of witnesses by Peter Alley, who had been paid £2 2s to defend Eliza Fenning against the extremely serious allegations which she faced. When Eliza was asked if she had anything to say in her own defence, she said this:

> I am truly innocent of the whole charge, as God is my witness. I am innocent; indeed I am! I liked my place. I was very comfortable. ... As to my master saying I did not assist him, I was too ill. I had no concern with that drawer at all: when I wanted a piece of paper, I always asked for it.

Five witnesses to Eliza's character were then called to vouch for her sobriety, cheerfulness, integrity and humanity. However, when one of these witnesses testified that Eliza had told him, a few days before the Turner household became ill, that she was extremely happy in her work and liked her master and mistress, the Recorder stopped him, saying his testimony could not be accepted as evidence.

Nor did he accept the evidence of Eliza's father, William Fenning, who handed over a piece of paper to Mr Alley on which was written a statement to the effect that, on the evening of 21 March, he had gone to the Turners' house to see his daughter and was told by Sarah Peer that Eliza had been sent on an errand by Charlotte Turner when, in fact, she was being violently sick at the time. He had gone away none the wiser. The Recorder looked briefly at the piece of paper when it was handed to him by Mr Alley, but then totally disregarded it.

Between these hopeless, disorganised attempts to construct a meaningful defence, Eliza had requested one of the apprentices to be called to the witness box; however, when Roger Gadsden was brought into the court, she vehemently protested that it was the older of the two apprentices, Thomas King, whom she wanted to question, not Gadsden. Only Thomas King, she insisted, could testify that she never went to the office drawer where the arsenic was kept. In fact, whenever she needed spare paper for the fire, he always gave it to her. Her request was dismissed by the Recorder and, when asked, Roger Gadsden said that both he and Thomas King had seen Eliza go to the drawer for spare paper to light the fire many times.

At this point, Mr Alley, counsel for the prisoner, left the court, not even bothering to listen to the Recorder's address to the jury. Clearly, he felt that he had done all that he could in the circumstances – and he was probably right. Basil Montagu (to whom we will return) lamented the legal ties that bound the hands of Mr Alley: 'Why is a prisoner indicted for a capital offence deprived of the privilege to which every British subject is, in every other case, entitled to resort – the privilege of counsel to address the jury?'[30]

The Recorder's summing-up was basically a brief direction to convict, and the jury returned a verdict of guilty after no more than a few minutes' deliberation. She was sentenced to death.[31] Eliza's composure broke at the door of the court, 'and she fell senseless to the ground, after which she was seized with hysteric fits'.[32]

Eliza later said: 'When I was on my trial I did not know I was to answer at all, as I had Mr Alley; but when I heard Mrs Turner speak falsely of me, being in the boys' bedroom, I contradicted her, knowing it to be false; and when Mr Turner said I never assisted them when they were ill, I was going to speak, but everything seemed in such confusion that I was not heard to speak, and I not knowing the ways of the trial, I did not know hardly what to say, for everyone's eyes were on me, as if I was the greatest criminal on earth.'[33]

III.

After her conviction, Eliza was taken back to Newgate Prison to await her fate. From there, she wrote hopefully to Edward, whom she regarded as her fiancé. Perhaps the death sentence would be revoked; perhaps the whole thing would be resolved by a short term of imprisonment:

> They have, which is the most cruellest thing in this world, brought me in guilty … I may be confined most likely six months at least.[34]

Her letters, first from New Clerkenwell Prison and then from Newgate, illustrate the anguish of a young woman embroiled in a catastrophic situation, sentenced to execution and incarcerated, awaiting the terror of a hideous public death. Added to this, as illustrated by extracts from some of her letters, was the agony of losing the love of her young man. She wrote this from New Clerkenwell

---

30 Harvard Law School Library, MSS HLS MS 4130 (237). It was not until the Prisoners' Counsel Act of 1836 that a summing-up speech on behalf of the defence was allowed.
31 The crime of attempted murder remained a capital offence until 1861. Silvester, therefore, on the strength of the jury's verdict and regardless of the inadequacy of the trial, had no option but to sentence Eliza Fenning to death. It was, however, within his power to petition the Prince Regent for a reprieve or commutation of the death sentence to one of imprisonment or transportation – a plea for mercy he chose not to entertain. Murder of a husband, master or mistress by a servant was classed as petty treason. In 1726, Catherine Hayes was charged with petty treason for the murder of her husband and burned at the stake at Tyburn.
32 *Chester Chronicle*, 21 April 1815.
33 Fenning, 8.
34 Watkins, 198.

Introduction.

Prison on 29 March:

> Dear Edward,
>
> You may be truly surprised at me for not writing or sending to you; but, no doubt, you have heard what has happened to me, for I now lay ill at the infirmary sick ward at the New Clerkenwell Prison; for on last Tuesday week I had some yeast dumplings to make, and there was something in which I can't answer for, and they made four of us, including myself, dangerously ill; and because I made them, they suspect me that I have put something in them, which I assure you I am innocent of; but I expect I shall be cleared on Thursday, if in case I can attend. My mother attends me three times a day, and brings me every thing I can wish for; but, Edward, I shall never be right or happy again to think that I was ever in prison; but if I was to die, I still should be happy to think I die innocent. If it be no trouble to you, I wish you would answer this quick though I am in a prison, and send directly.
>
> Yours truly,
> Eliza Fenning.[35]

Two days later, on 31 March, she wrote to Edward again:

> This is the second time that I have wrote to you, and I feel very unhappy at your not answering my letters: but, I suppose, as you have heard what has happened to me, you don't care to take any notice of me now; but I never should disgrace you, as I suffer innocent; but I trust in God I shall get the better of my enemies yet: but I assure you, never did I suffer so much in all my life as I do now …[36]

Having been transferred to Newgate, she wrote another letter to 'Dearest Edward' at the beginning of April, in which she told him that she expected her trial to begin on Monday:

> It was my full intention of writing to you, as I wish to inform you of every particular that will happen; for if I had not been removed from Clerkenwell prison, I should have been confined in there most likely a twelve-month; but thank God I shall stand my trial at the Old Bailey, where I shall have a Counsellor to plead for me; so I have nothing to fear, as my conscience tells me that I am not guilty. …
>
> But I have been informed that you got acquainted with another young woman; but I am not apt to be jealous, therefore I shall think no more about it; but I firmly believe you are still true and faithful to me; and as to me, I have fixed my mind

---

[35] Watkins, 195-196.
[36] Watkins, 196.

Fenning.

and heart entirely on you.

Pray send me a line or two on Friday, if you can spare time.

I am, dearest Edward,
Your affectionate and true
Eliza Fenning.[37]

Her next letter, written on Tuesday 11 April:

I attended my trial on Tuesday and they have, which is the most cruellest thing in this world, brought me in guilty, because I had the fire to light in the office where the arsenick was kept, and my master said that I went often into the office for things, and so, on that account, they suppose that I must have taken the arsenick out of the drawer, which is the most horrid thing I ever can think of; for was I to die this instant I am sure I should be happy in thinking I am innocent. But God reward them for all they have done towards me: but I can't tell my fate as yet as the sessions won't be over till Saturday, and then I shall know on Monday. But, Edward, let me advise you to for ever forget me, as most likely you will often have it thrown up in your face, for I am, Edward, I believe, now for ever shut from the world. I still have some comfort left, when I can see my parents as yet; but pray make your mind happy, and get some one else that will never bring any reflection on you. I shall never think of marrying any person excepting yourself; but I must for ever give up any thought of such, as it may hurt your character; but I still love and respect you. Pray write soon.

From your much injured and afflicted
Eliza.
Don't forget.[38]

On Thursday 13 April, she wrote to say that she could not accept a visit from his mother as she had no clothes to 'appear respectable in'. She also asked him not to be unhappy 'as you very well know how much I love and respect you, for no young woman can ever love you more than I do; and I am certain, at least I think so, that I have yours in return'.[39]

By the time she wrote again on Sunday 23 April, the hoped-for reprieve had decisively failed to arrive. Eliza assured Edward that she was 'making my peace with God, and hope to be in a better world, as I shall leave this world innocent of a crime that's alleged against me: but its [sic] dreadful to think what I suffer at such a thing being laid against me, when my conscience is thoroughly clear'.[40]

---

37   Watkins, 197.
38   Watkins, 198.
39   Watkins, 199.
40   Watkins, 200.

Introduction.

Writing on the night of 25 April, she makes arrangements for Edward to visit her in Newgate and adds:

> Do not disappoint me, as you may easily believe where my affection is placed; but I hope you will find another that will make you happy when I am no more. But I don't wish to hurt your feelings but as little as I can, but I hope we shall meet in a better world, where no one can separate us: and I trust when you read this, that you will make your mind more composed concerning me, for you alone have often made my mind unhappy ...[41]

Unfortunately, Edward did not visit her as planned and, on 4 May, she sent him this reproach:

> You are the last person that I should think would behave to me as you do now; for I fully expected you on Sunday; but most likely you have other places to go to much better than to come and see me, though I am in Newgate. Other young men and women come and see me, and are surprised when I inform them that you seldom come near, or even send to me. Was you in my place, I never should have slighted you: but God bless you and yours as long as you live, is the prayer of Eliza, who once was yours, but now never shall be; for was the Lord to spare my life, though I have no hopes, I don't think I should ever like a man that would forget me, because I can't help myself now. Once more, God bless you! – Adieu! – from
> Eliza Fenning.
> You may answer this, just as you please.[42]

The following day, she wrote in reply to a letter Edward had sent her:

> I received your letter, and am surprised at your thinking that I wish to quarrel with you; but I think I have a just right to speak, when you promised me that you would come and see me, and then to disappoint me when there was no excuse; for you well know that my life is at stake, and one would suppose that a person that respected another should feel happy in seeing them as often as time could permit them. ...
>
> I have not seen my father since, therefore I don't know any thing of your being with him, but I am glad that he is in such good friendship with you, for you can spend many hours with them, when I am no more – and pray make them as happy as you can, for, should I suffer, it shall be my last prayer for you to go as often as you can; and I am certain that they will always respect you on the account of

---

41　Watkins, 200.
42　Watkins, 201.

Fenning.

their daughter. Pray don't send any note with farewell again to me; for, though we never shall meet in the world again, it's cruel to say adieu as yet. God bless you, dear Edward, and all your friends, and may you never feel the pangs of a broken heart. You say you shan't be out till Sunday week, and so I suppose I shall not see you any more, as I expect the report [the announcement of the date set for her execution] will be down every day – and now I wait with impatience to know my fate.

From your unhappy and forsaken,

Eliza Fenning.

Once more write when you can spare time.[43]

It would appear that this was the last letter that Eliza wrote to Edward, and from then on she turned her full attention to comforting her distraught parents and writing letters to various officials – probably guided by her supporters and religious advisers. These letters chart the shift from her initial optimism, her attempts to prove her innocence and, finally, the acceptance of her fate.

April the 16th, 1815. Newgate.

Dearest and beloved Father and Mother,

This is from your poor and only, unhappy child, who is going to suffer: but be happy, as I told you that I am innocent. O mother! believe me for the last time, that I die innocent of the crime I am charged with: but I entreat you to bury me with my two brothers; and likewise another request I have, that is, to put Edward's picture in the coffin with me: don't refuse, as I never shall rest happy, but let me beg of you not to forget, or perhaps I shall come to you, for Edward is my first and only love, and he always gave me the best of advice. But I am happy to think I can make my peace with God; but let me request of you both to put your trust in God, and never fear, as I die happy, though its [sic] cruel to come to such untimely end. Oh! I am innocent, dearest parents. Pray for your only child, and dear child.

I am, dearest Father and Mother, your only child in death. Farewell forever.

Eliza Fenning.[44]

Eliza also wrote two sympathetic letters of a religious nature to a fellow inmate, William Oldfield, who was housed in the condemned cell reserved for males; he later thanked Eliza for reversing his atheistic convictions.[45] All her actions were capable of sustaining two interpretations: posthumously, she

---

43 Watkins, 201-202.
44 Watkins, 203.
45 Watkins, 203-204; 210-211.

Introduction.

was accused of being licentious and forming an inappropriate liaison whilst in Newgate.

It would seem that the following letter was written to Thomas William Wansbrough,[46] a young medic living in Chelsea who played a vital role in the appeals for clemency which followed Eliza's conviction. He had made a number of experiments proving that arsenic would not blacken knives or have any effect on dough, detailing the results of these experiments at length in a paper which he sent to the Secretary of State, Lord Sidmouth. Despite making numerous requests for the return of his notes, both in writing and in person at Lord Sidmouth's office, he was unable to retrieve them.[47]

13 June.

Dear Friend,

Impressed with a just sense of your kindness towards me, I feel myself in want of words to express my gratitude for the same; but they ever will bear record in heaven in your favour, in the part you have taken in proving the injustice of the aspersions that was said of me; but, believe me, I shall for the future be very circumspect in every action, and keep myself as private as possible. I return you thanks, and hope you will not be offended at my making an objection to receive the Holy Sacrament, but I think I am not in a proper state of mind to receive it: situated as I am, with those that are in the same room, there is little time for the reflections that are proper for so sacred an occasion; but I trust that a merciful God, that knows the most secret thoughts of all hearts, will grant me grace, and renew me with a new heart, that my past and present sufferings may prove an acceptable sacrifice for my past faults, and that they may be so imprinted in my breast, that they may prove a sufficient monitor, to deter me from violating the laws of God, should I be so happy as to be once more restored to society again. For the particulars of your misfortunes I am sorry to hear, but hope they will

---

46 Thomas William Wansbrough was a Fellow of the Royal College of Surgeons and a member of the Royal Humane Society. During his career, he published many articles in *The Lancet* on subjects ranging from the treatment of rheumatism with acupuncture, spasmodic cholera, laceration of the brain and the treatment of gout. He developed a metal shield for his female patients suffering from sore nipples. He was twenty-eight years old at the time of his involvement with the case of Eliza Fenning and died in 1859, aged seventy-two. An ardent Methodist, he wrote a pamphlet entitled *An Authentic Narrative of the Conduct of Elizabeth Fenning from the Time that the Warrant Arrived for her Death till her Execution*, published by Ogles, Duncan and Cohran, 295 Holborn and 37 Paternoster Row, 1815 (price: one shilling). In 1830, Wansbrough was involved in the social reformer Thomas Wakley's campaign to ensure that all coroners were equipped with some medical knowledge. He sent an open letter in the form of a handbill endorsing Wakley's bid to become Coroner for West Middlesex, which covered most of London – in this Wakley succeeded in 1839. Wakley was co-founder and editor of *The Lancet*. Adopting some of Watkins's emphatic lettering in *The Important Results*, Wansbrough cited the Eliza Fenning case in his letter as, he wrote, 'it bears importantly on the question … Ought not a Coroner to possess CONSIDERABLE MEDICAL KNOWLEDGE?'

47 Watkins, 69.

end to your satisfaction; and I hope you will, with myself, pray to the Lord to forgive our enemies. For what you have done I shall always feel myself under the greatest obligation, as I am thoroughly convinced that you have acted from the sole motives of humanity.

Suffer me to remain

Yours, with due respect,
Eliza Fenning.
Please to write soon.[48]

IV.

To many who read about the trial of Eliza Fenning in the newspapers in the weeks that followed, the verdict and sentence seemed particularly harsh and, moreover, the case for the prosecution left many questions unanswered. The disquiet and scepticism was felt by many in the general public, but also by men of influence.

Soon after her incarceration in Newgate, letters and articles concerning her case started to appear in the press. On 14 May 1815, *The Examiner* reproduced a letter from a correspondent who claimed to have had contact with the prisoner:

> It has been observed by many gentlemen that, if they had been on the jury of Eliza Fenning, they could not have found her guilty because there was no proof that she was the actual person that put the poison into the pan, knowing it to be poison.
>
> I visited the unfortunate young woman a few days ago: she still declares her innocence, she still says she did not know there was arsenic in the house, nor never saw any there; she burst into a flood of tears, and said she wished she might drop down dead if she knew what arsenic was. Here her father became deeply affected on hearing his daughter declare her innocence in so solemn a manner. He said he had fought for his king and his country, and now he was deprived of his only child for a crime of which he believed her to be totally innocent. The mother of this unfortunate young woman was so affected that it was thought she could not live.[49]

Below the letter, the editor of the newspaper added his own thoughts:

> The observations of our correspondent prove nothing, but still many persons are of the opinion that the guilt of this young woman has not been sufficiently shewn.

---

48 Watkins, 204-205.
49 Fairburn, 16.

Introduction.

The arsenic, it appeared, was kept in an open drawer with waste paper to which every one might resort – this was a very negligent practice, to say the least of it.

The following letter (from a correspondent identifying himself only as 'M') was sent to the editor of the *Morning Chronicle* and published on 18 May 1815:

> I trust you will give the following lines a corner in your valuable paper. Having been present at the trial of Eliza Fenning at the Old Bailey Sessions, where she stood indicted for attempting to poison the family of Mr Turner, Chancery Lane, I witnessed a very extraordinary circumstance, which I think ought to be made public, previous to the Recorder's making his report of those under sentence of death at Newgate.
>
> After the Recorder (in his usual clear and comprehensive manner) had summed up the evidence, the jury consulted five or ten minutes, when they returned a verdict of Guilty with the observation from the foreman (addressing himself to the Recorder):
>
> 'My Lord, we should have returned the verdict sooner, had it not been that one of our brother jurymen is deaf, and we have been obliged to explain to him.'
>
> Now, Mr Editor, an English jury ought to consist of twelve persons in the full possession of all their faculties; and had this person been so, he perhaps might have dissented from the rest and the girl been acquitted.[50]

Another letter, dated 15 May 1815 and apparently originally published in the *British Press*, a daily newspaper, on 20 May, was later quoted in John Fairburn's pamphlet, *Affecting Case of Eliza Fenning*. It bears a strong resemblance in style and content to the writing of William Hone in the pamphlet attributed to John Watkins,[51] and the historicity of the designated author, F. M. Barran, has

---

50 *Morning Chronicle*, 18 May 1815.
51 A note here on the authorship of *The Important Results of an Elaborate Investigation into the Mysterious Case of Elizabeth Fenning*, an 1815 pamphlet (and an extensive one, at book-length, presenting the transcript of the trial of Eliza Fenning, and supplemented by a detailed analysis of the proceedings, investigations into the inconsistencies in the evidence given at the trial, and interviews with hostile witnesses by campaigners for justice) which was published under the name of John Watkins. The truth behind the authorship of this text is neatly summarised by Ben Wilson, 102: 'The book was attributed to Dr John Watkins, a legal expert, but this was only a device to give it an air of authority. Watkins collaborated with Hone, advising him and providing some letters he had written to the Regent. In the Hone papers in the British Library, there is a note in his own autograph stating bluntly: "I wrote the work entitled *An Elaborate Investigation into the Case of E. F.* – on the title page John Watkins LL.D appears as the author – He had interested himself to save her, and lent me his name." *The Examiner*, when it came to review it, was clear that it was "a pamphlet by Mr Hone."' See also Appendix IX, where the autograph note and a letter from Watkins to Hone confirming their division of responsibilities are reproduced in transcript. In this book, references to *The Important Results* are typically given under the name of 'Watkins', but clarifications are provided wherever a distinction needs to be made between the actions of Hone and the actions of Watkins.

Fenning.

been difficult to prove:

> Sir – permit me, through the medium of your esteemed paper, to lay before the public the information which I have acquired in the extraordinary case of Eliza Fenning – I say extraordinary, for I have never read or heard of a case equally wicked in one light, and foolish in the other – wicked in the extreme, for contriving to take away the lives of those who had never offended her – insane, by taking such a quantity of the bane as subjected herself to as great a degree of affliction as any one of the family.
>
> Far from being wickedly cunning does she appear to me, as it is evident she left the pan in which the dumplings were made unwashed till the next day, nor did she attempt to put the remainder of the dumplings out of the way, the doing of which the perpetrator of such a crime would not have omitted.
>
> The unfortunate young woman in question is in the twenty-first year of her age, is a diminutive person, not such a one as my Lord or my Lady would have either for a housemaid or cook; a place of all work was, therefore, the situation of this little female previous to going into Mr Turner's family, which made her feel perfectly contented with her late situation.
>
> Mr Smyth, of the Colonade [sic], No. 8, Brunswick Square, gave the prisoner an excellent character;[52] he swore that he had met the prisoner two evenings previous to the melancholy catastrophe; she declared that she was very comfortable in her situation, and that she was never happier in her life. There are two other persons who can prove similar expressions made use of by the prisoner, two days before the accident, when she happened to be out on business for her employers.
>
> Now, sir, after such proof of her being satisfied is it likely that she could have conceived such a diabolical plan of murder, and suicide? I have been informed, sir, and I believe the information to have been founded on fact, that a professional man [Thomas Wansbrough] has had arsenic mixed in dumplings for experiment, and that they rose as is customary, were neither black nor heavy, nor did they particularly colour the knives.
>
> Now, sir, it was a pity, as two surgeons attended the family, that they did not both attend the trial. For Surgeon Marshall says he had no doubt of the arsenic having a particular effect on the knives. Now, as Surgeon Ogilvy attended the family at five o'clock [times differ in other accounts] and Mr Marshall did not arrive till nine, I repeat it is a pity Mr Ogilvy had not been called as a witness.
>
> I am informed, and I believe correctly so, that a professional gentleman in the law, from the unsatisfactory statement of this case in the papers, waited on Mr Ogilvy, who informed him that on his arrival at Mr Turner's he found the prisoner in as distressed a state as any of the family. She had been informed by the officers

---

52 The reference is to Mr John Smith.

Introduction.

one evening that she was to die next morning, which deeply affected her. I must here express my opinion that alarming prisoners, and repeatedly, as she has been, shows but very little feeling in the doers, to say the least of it.

However, she asked for paper to write to her disconsolate parents; in doing so she professes her innocence in the most solemn and affecting manner. She requests to be buried by her little brother, who met his death by an accident.[53] She expresses a confident hope of meeting her father and mother hereafter in heaven and in this world she bids them an everlasting adieu.

The Paymaster-General of his Majesty's land forces, under whom the prisoner's father had served as serjeant [sic] of the band, in the 15th regiment of foot, at the taking of Martinique, Guadaloupe and St Lucia, on seeing the letter above alluded to, declared he would not believe that it had been written by a guilty hand.

A number of respectable people have signed a petition praying for the royal clemency, among whom I believe there are at two Noble Lords – Mr Turner, however, contrary to the expectation of the prisoner and many of her friends, refused to set his name thereto.

The petition, her letter from prison, together with her father's discharge, I flatter myself is, by this time, before his Royal Highness the Prince Regent, and the prayers of everyone who believes her innocent, as I do, I trust will accompany them. I visited her deeply afflicted parents yesterday: the bleeding tear rolled quick over their aged cheeks; their souls seemed heavily oppressed with poignant grief; my heart was rent for misfortunes which it was not in my power to alleviate.

F. M. Barran.
Pleasant Retreat,
Blackfriars Road,
May 15, 1815.[54]

Although it was said that Eliza was unusually literate for a girl of her station in life, her letters from Newgate exhibit a degree of sophistication in their grammar and phrasing that suggests that they were probably written under the guidance of her spiritual advisors. The first of the following letters was sent to the Right Honourable Lord Sidmouth, his Majesty's Secretary of State for the Home Department:[55]

---

53 In one of Eliza's letters to her parents (already cited), she asks to be buried beside with her *two* brothers.
54 Fairburn, 17-19.
55 Henry Addington, 1st Viscount Sidmouth (1757-1844): Prime Minister, 1801-1804. Home Secretary, 1812-1822. His father was Anthony Addington, William Pitt's physician; he and Pitt's son, William Pitt the Younger, both served terms in high office, as Prime Minister and Chancellor of the Exchequer.

Fenning.

Newgate 27th June, 1815

My Lord,

With deference I most humbly beg leave to address your Lordship; at the same time, am entirely at a loss how I dare venture such a presumption; but your Lordship's well-known goodness and mercy, which has repeatedly been extended to many miserable creatures under calamities like myself, encourages me, with all submission, to state my real situation to your Lordship.

I most humbly beg leave to inform your Lordship that I am under the awful sentence of death, on suspicion of poisoning Mr Turner's family, which heinous crime I never was guilty of, I most solemnly declare to a just God, whom I must meet, and my blessed Redeemer, at the great and grand tribunal, when the secrets of all hearts will be known. Innocence induces me to solicit a fuller examination. I am the only child of ten, and to be taken off for such an ignominious crime strikes me and my dear parents with horror.

I, therefore, most humbly beg leave to solicit your Lordship's merciful interference in my behalf to spare my life, and my parents, with me, will be ever bound to pray for you.

I remain,
With due submission,
Your poor, but innocent servant,
Eliza Fenning.[56]

Eliza also wrote to Lord Eldon, High Chancellor of Great Britain,[57] on 12 June 1815:

My Lord,

When the life of an innocent person is at stake it needs no apology for intruding upon your Lordship's invaluable time: I therefore, with all humility, submit my case to your Lordship's humane consideration, which cannot be doubted.

I protest, before God and man, that I am not guilty of the crime charged to me, although I feel the great difficulty of proving my innocence.

Mrs Turner swore that I carried a pie to the baker's about 12 o'clock; that she went into the kitchen after my return, and gave instruction to make the dough, which she found placed before the fire to rise, half an hour after such order; and further, that she saw the dough two or three times between half past twelve and three o'clock, until it was divided into dumplings; that it did not rise as usual, but

---

56 Fairburn, 24.
57 John Scott, 1st Earl of Eldon (1751-1838): Lord Chancellor between 1801 and 1806, and then again between 1807 and 1827. Roger Fulford (48) says of him that 'he was in the amplest meaning of the word a conservative, a doughty supporter of everything established by time and tradition'.

Introduction.

kept a singular shape to the last; while, in another part of her evidence, she swore the dough was divided into dumplings 20 minutes before 12 o'clock.

Other instances might be mentioned to prove many mistakes, especially on the part of Mrs Turner. The particular and unusual orders Mrs Turner gave not to leave the kitchen, and her assertion that she was sure no one was there, are circumstances your Lordship may think worthy of notice.

Thomas King (one of the apprentices, who was not examined at the trial) was in the front kitchen while I was in the back room cleaning the knives; I thought it was my mistress; but as I was going into the kitchen I met him and asked what he was doing. To which he made no reply, but went upstairs. Now, God forbid that I should impeach any person; I only relate this circumstance as I am informed that arsenic, merely sprinkled over the dough, would infuse itself through the whole; and it appeared that the arsenic was put by Mr Turner in a place open to anybody.

It was stated by Mr Turner, and Gadsden, the apprentice, that the arsenic was missed a fortnight before the occurrence; but surely, if it had been me, the person who was most likely to be accused, I should not have made any dumplings of the over-night, thereby inducing the apprentice to eat again; neither should I have omitted cleaning the utensils; and, least of all, to have eat of them myself, whereby I was affected as much as any of the family, as could have been corroborated by Surgeon Ogilvy; but although he attended the family five or six hours before Mr Marshall, and might have stated other favourable circumstances, yet he was not examined on the trial.

However eager I feel to live, and, above all, to avoid unworthy ignominy, I know not how to prove my innocence, most humbly craving your Lordship's humane attention, which I doubt not will cause investigation to be made in my unfortunate case.

I am, My Lord,

Your Lordship's unfortunate servant,

Eliza Fenning.

Newgate, 12 June 1815.[58]

She had earlier written the following letter to Mr Turner [it is unclear whether the recipient was Orlibar or Robert Turner.]

Honoured Sir,

With due submission I most earnestly entreat of you to sign my petition, to save my life which is forfeited for what I am not guilty of.

---

58   Watkins, 74.

Fenning.

Honoured sir, I do here most solemnly declare I never meant to injure you or any of your family; picture to yourself the distressed mind of my dear parents, to see their only child suffer such an ignominious death; but innocent I am.

May the blessed God give my ever dear parents strength to bear the dreadful affliction to see their only child suffer; but may you never feel the pangs of a broken heart, which your unfortunate servant endures.

Prayers for you and your family.

Eliza Fenning.

P.S. If your goodness will comply with my request, I shall ever be bound to pray for you.

This letter, sent by Eliza to the editor of *The Examiner*, was published on Sunday 23 July 1815:

July 18, Felons' side, Newgate.

Sir,

With the greatest submission, I most humbly beg leave to return my grateful thanks and acknowledgements for your humane charitableness that has been extended towards me, an unfortunate victim, in endeavouring to restore a lost and only child to her distressed and afflicted parents; and I trust and hope all those who help the afflicted in mind, body, or estate, will bear reward in heaven. Believe me, cruel and pitiable is my distressing case; to be even confined in this abode of wretchedness, much more to be continually warned of my approaching destiny.

Dear sir, I do solemnly declare with firmness and perseverance my innocence to God and man. I am innocent of the crime that is laid to my charge; but how can I convince the world when brought in guilty at the bar of man? Yet there will be a grand and great day when all must stand before the tribunal bar of God, then where will the guilty criminals stand or fly to secure themselves from the vengeance of the Almighty just God, who knows the secrets of all hearts, and will reward all according to the work done in the body.

What a pleasing consolation within my distressed mind to think I am clear of such a heinous and dreadful crime, and never hurted man or mortal, in thought, word, or deed. My dear parents and myself will feel in duty bound to pray for your kind interference in my behalf in your paper, as you have done.

I remain your humble servant and much injured,

Eliza Fenning.[59]

---

59   Fairburn, 20-21.

Introduction.

On 20 July, the dreaded Report – listing those to be executed – was shown to Eliza, and she learned that she was to be hanged on Wednesday 26 July.[60] The next day she wrote the following heart-broken letter to her parents:

Felons' Side, Newgate,

July 21, 1815.

Dear and affectionate Parents,

With heart-rending sighs and tears, I for the last time, and ever last time, write these solemn lines to you, hoping and trusting the Almighty to give you strength and fortitude to bear the distressing, awful, and dreadful scene, that is about to take place. Believe me, cruel and pitiable is my unfortunate and affecting situation; but God's will be done: and with humble resignation I must bear my untimely fate: but what pleasing consolation within my tortured breast, to suffer innocent! Dear parents, I do solemnly declare, was I never to enter the heavenly mansion of heavenly rest, I am murdered! Yes, dear father and mother, believe I am your only child, that speaks the sentiments of a breaking heart. Don't let me distress your breaking heart, I wish to comfort you, dearest of parents: be happy: pray take comfort: let me entreat of you to be reconciled, and I will be happy in heaven, and with my dear sisters and brothers, and will meet you by and by: pray read the blessed Bible, and turn your hearts, and live a religious and holy life, and then we shall be where sorrow and troubles will be no more. I grieve more to think I had an opportunity sooner, and did not make use of it; yet there's time, though short, to pray to my heavenly Father, to forgive me all my sins and offences in my life past: it's only the passage of death that I have [to] go through, which, I hope and trust, will soon be over. Oh my blest and beloved parents, think what are my present and distressed feelings, to part from you who gave me my being, and nourished me at that breast, and was my sole comfort, and nursed me in my helpless and infant years, and was always my directors, to keep me in [the] sacred path of virtue, which I have strictly kept, and will be one sin less to answer for, as a spotless frame will be acceptable in the eyes of God. I mention this, as I let you all [know] I have not done amiss. Oh dear parents, what an affecting scene, to part from you, which must endured by the laws of justice! but justice has not been shown at [the] bar. Man judges man: God will judge us all, who knows the secrets of hearts, and those who swore my life will never enter with me into rest. God bless you both, and may you live happy! Adieu from your injured and unhappy child.

Keep these few lines in remembrance of me, as that is all [the] comfort I can afford, with my imperfect prayers. Adieu, dear parents, God bless you both!

---

60   According to Wansbrough (3), the Report was issued on 19 July.

Fenning.

Eliza Fenning,
Aged 21 Years.[61]

V.

In the days before Eliza's execution there was a flurry of activity amongst her supporters and several urgent meetings were convened by persons anxious to present the authorities with a case deserving of a reprieve.[62] On the evening of Monday 24 July, two days before the execution, the Quaker banker, Mr Corbyn Lloyd, visited Sir John Silvester and requested a respite of Eliza's sentence of death to allow for further investigations to establish whether she or someone else had added arsenic to the dumplings. The plea fell on deaf ears, for Silvester was convinced that Eliza was guilty – or was determined to see her hang even if she was innocent. He merely suggested that he, Corbyn Lloyd, and his campaigning friends were only fighting for the girl's life – and giving her false hopes of a reprieve – because she was a pretty woman.

That same evening a meeting had taken place at the home of Mr J. M. Richardson, a bookseller at 23 Cornhill, at which a gentleman called Mr Blathwaite said that he had heard that someone in the Turner household had been showing signs of insanity and had publicly threatened to poison the family and himself. Richardson wrote to Lord Sidmouth, the Secretary of State, and to Sir John Silvester with this alarming information, but it was decided that there were no grounds for any change in either the verdict or the sentence of death.

The following afternoon, Tuesday 25 July, Richardson wrote to Basil Montagu,[63] a distinguished lawyer, entreating him to try to persuade Silvester to intervene on behalf of 'the unhappy girl'.[64]

The reply to his letter was not sent until 10 August 1815, two weeks after Eliza's execution:

> Sir,
>
> I am to apologise for my apparent inattention to your letter respecting Elizabeth Fenning by stating that the instant I received it I waited upon the Recorder and

---

61 Fairburn, 31-32. Versions of this letter were also published by Watkins and Wansbrough.
62 In 1810, a 14 year old servant girl, Elizabeth Hinchcliff, was charged with attempted poisoning of her mistress and two others with arsenic. She was found guilty and sentenced to death, but the jury recommended mercy on account of her youth and the fact that her parents were 'honest people'. The following year she was reprieved and, in 1812, she was transported to one of Australia's penal colonies. It must have been hoped that a similar concession would be made for Eliza Fenning. (Old Bailey Online t18100919-37).
63 Basil Montagu (1770-1851): see Appendix XII.
64 Watkins, 82.

Introduction.

informed him of the communication you had kindly made to me; and, as I was wholly ignorant of the merits of the case, I requested the Recorder to inform me, 'whether any alteration could be formed in the opinion respecting the propriety of her execution, if satisfactory evidence were adduced that there was an insane person in the Turners' house, who had declared that he would poison the family', as it appeared by your letter that such evidence could be produced. The Recorder assured me that the production of such evidence would be wholly useless. I therefore retired. I, at the time, had not read the trial of this unfortunate young woman; and she was executed early the next morning.

I am very sensible of your kind exertions, and I trust you will forgive my apparent neglect.

I am, Sir, your faithful servant,
B. Montagu,
Lincoln's Inn.[65]

'Mr Richardson's letter to Montagu,' Hone (as Watkins) writes, 'and Mr Montagu's application to the Recorder on Tuesday [25 July], were in consequence of information received only the night before,' following a meeting held at the house of Mr Newman, (the chief gaoler of Newgate) and in the presence of the Reverend Horace Cotton (the Ordinary),[66] the Reverend Dr Perkins (Chaplain to H.R.H. the Prince Regent), Mr Under-Sheriff Leigh, and several other gentlemen. Mr Gibson, who worked for Corbyn & Co., chemists and druggists in Holborn, made a statement about the disturbing behaviour of Robert Turner. It was agreed that the proper course of action was to contact the Under-Secretary of State (Lord Sidmouth was out of town) with this startling revelation.

Accordingly, between three and four o'clock in the afternoon, Mr Sharp, Mr Ogle, Mr Blathwaite, Mr Aberdour and Mr Gibson met the Under-Secretary, John Beckett, at the Secretary of State's office and Gibson repeated the allegation he had made against Robert Turner. Beckett suggested that Gibson should go to the Recorder's house, in Bloomsbury Square, that evening at eight o'clock.

---

65 Watkins, 82-83.
66 Rev. Horace Salusbury Cotton, (1774-1846): Newgate Ordinary; Anglican chaplain, active in extracting confessions from convicted prisoners and providing evidence of contrition. With this agenda, he supplied Eliza with books entitled *Thoughts on Death* and *The Punishment of the Wicked in the Next World*. The Ordinaries wrote accounts of those executed – the *Newgate Calendar* – in part to illustrate the wickedness and weak character of offenders, but also as cautionary tales to deter others from taking a similar path. Cotton exhibited a messianic enthusiasm for haranguing the condemned with the certainty of eternal damnation for those who did not confess. He was eventually censured for overdoing the hell-fire rhetoric in his pre-execution sermons held in the chapel at Newgate. It is clear from her letters that Eliza Fenning distrusted him, as he was a friend of the Turners and pestered her to confess. See Appendix VII.

Fenning.

Mr Gibson and Mr Sharp duly arrived at the Recorder's house as arranged, and Mr Gibson gave the Recorder and Mr Beckett the following information:

> About the month of September or October last [1814], to the best of my recollection, Mr Turner, junior [ie, Robert], called at our house, and appearing in a wild and deranged state, I invited him into a back room, or counting house, where I detained him, whilst Mr Crockford, another gentleman at Messrs. Corbyn's house, went to his father's. In this interval, Mr Turner, junior, used the most violent and incoherent expressions – such as, 'My dear Gibson, do, for God's sake, get me secured and confined, for, if I am at liberty, I shall do some mischief; I shall destroy myself and my wife; I must and shall do it, unless all means of destruction are removed out of my way; therefore do, my good friend, have me put under some restraint; something from above tells me I must do it, and unless I am prevented, I certainly shall do it.'[67]

Mr Gibson assured the Recorder and Mr Beckett that Robert Turner clearly exhibited the symptoms of a deranged mind. He further stated that Mr Crockford could confirm the fact of Robert Turner's mental derangement at other times. Gibson concluded by saying that, in the interval between Eliza's apprehension and her trial, he went to see Mr Orlibar Turner and strongly urged him not to proceed in his prosecution of Eliza Fenning and, furthermore, 'to consider the state of his son's mind', adding that some mutual friends of the Turner family and himself were also concerned that, under the circumstances, Robert Turner remained at large.

In the course of the conversation with Silvester and Beckett, Mr Gibson stated that the arsenic had been purchased some time previous to Robert Turner's disturbing tirade in the shop. 'On leaving the Recorder's house, Mr Gibson, with the same laudable and honourable anxiety that he had shown during the whole of that day, expressed his sincere hopes that the knowledge of these circumstances would lead to an extension of mercy to the poor girl – at least a respite until some further enquiry should be instituted.'

That same evening, Tuesday 25 July, in a last minute attempt to save Eliza's life, Thomas Wansbrough called at the Turners' home in Chancery Lane to explain the results of his experiments with arsenic, proving its negative effect on both yeast dough and metal. He pleaded for a respite of Eliza's sentence so that his results, which he was convinced would exonerate her, could be considered. To convince Orlibar Turner of his findings, he produced a dumpling which he had made in his own kitchen: when at the dough stage, he had left it by the

---

67   Watkins, 84.

Introduction.

fire to rise and, when his maid was not looking, he had sprinkled some arsenic on the mixture. Unaware of her master's actions, the maid then cooked the dumpling in the usual manner and there was nothing unusual in its appearance. This demonstrated that his maid was entirely innocent and had not adulterated the dough in any way – so it was possible that that same had happened in the Turners' kitchen that day. Someone else could easily have sprinkled arsenic on the dough without Eliza's knowledge. All he asked, said Wansbrough, was that Orlibar Turner would sign a petition requesting the respite of the death sentence to allow for further investigations. Turner seemed on the point of signing; and when his son, Robert, joined the two men in the drawing room, he, too, was prepared to sign.

However, at this crucial point, John Marshall arrived. Thomas Wansbrough repeated his explanation of his experiments. Not surprisingly, Marshall's reaction was dismissive and he left within minutes, obdurate in his views and still totally convinced of Eliza's guilt. Orlibar and Robert Turner, however, seemed more open to the notion that she may have been innocent and both were still prepared to sign a petition for mercy.

Like some ghastly malevolent spirit, the Recorder, John Silvester, suddenly entered the room, casting doubt on Wansbrough's conclusions. The doctor then repeated the results of his experiments he had made and explained that they proved that arsenic would not prevent dough from rising or blacken knives.[68] Totally unconvinced, the Recorder left, escorted to the door by Robert Turner. If only chroniclers of this case could have been privy to the exchange between these two men as they parted company at the door of the house in Chancery Lane – but the content may be surmised, for, on Robert's return to the drawing room, he told his father: 'The Recorder says you must not sign any petition – if you do, it will throw suspicion on the rest of your family'.[69]

One can only conclude that someone from the Turner household had been swiftly dispatched to alert both John Marshall and Sir John Silvester to the meeting with Dr Thomas Wansbrough, with one objective – to prevent the signing of the petition. The result of this intervention was to the detriment of Eliza Fenning. Leaving aside the question of whether it was *illegal* for not only the chief medical witness but also the judge at Eliza's trial to intervene in this

---

68   In 1828, the University of London appointed John Gordon Smith as its first Professor of Medical Jurisprudence. In one of his lectures, he referred to the case of Eliza Fenning and conducted an experiment to prove that arsenic would not blacken knives. He had left a knife in a solution of arsenic for ten hours and another immersed in a pickled walnut solution. For dramatic effect, he held aloft the untarnished knife from the arsenic container and the blackened one from the pickled walnut solution. He died in the Fleet debtors' prison in 1831, aged forty-one.

69   Watkins, 78.

way, we can still be satisfied that the collusion between Silvester, John Marshall and the Turners was certainly *unethical*.

The full extent of the efforts of a number of professional people on Eliza's behalf became common knowledge from press reports after her execution. On 5 November 1815, for example, *The Examiner* published a letter of protest that had been written by Mr Corbyn Lloyd after Silvester had suggested that he and others who had campaigned for a reprieve were swayed by the fact that Eliza was physically attractive:

> Without having personally witnessed the unfortunate Elizabeth Fenning's prettiness, as Mr Recorder unquestionably did when she was personally on her trial before him, it cannot be expected that those who are sincerely earnest in the exercise of their judgement upon her case should think, with the Recorder, that nothing but a woman's prettiness could be a motive for humanity towards her; and it is not from anything favourable in Elizabeth Fenning's person that these gentlemen, who, like Mr Corbyn Lloyd, never saw her, have interested themselves in her case.[70]

Sadly, the efforts of the many reporters, pamphleteers and petitioners who had tirelessly campaigned for a reprieve for Eliza Fenning came to nothing. The date for her execution was set for Wednesday 26 July 1815, and it was to be held in public outside Newgate. Two other convicts, William Oldfield and Abraham Adams, were to be hanged at the same time.[71]

VI.

In the meantime, Eliza received a number of compassionate letters from supporters conscious that the day of her execution drew near; these were mostly couched in religious and repetitive terminology.

The newspapers continued to publish articles and letters from the public commentating on the case. One such letter – attributed only to 'C. A.' – was included in Fairburn's *Affecting Case*:

> There is in the nature of the crime of which she has been convicted a degree of

---

70 *The Examiner*, 5 November 1815. Thomas Wansbrough had not seen Eliza Fenning before he conducted his experiments with arsenic, but later regularly visited her in Newgate and offered unwavering support, even as far as the scaffold. A deeply religious man, his initial motive for visiting her after she was under sentence of death was, in his mind, for the sake of her soul. If she was guilty, he hoped to persuade her to confess and die repentant.

71 Twenty-four year old William Oldfield was convicted of the rape of a nine year old girl. Abraham Adams, fifty-one, had been convicted of sodomy.

Introduction.

improbability, arising from its very enormity, which is only to be surmounted by the most ample and unanswerable evidence of guilt, and I have looked in vain for such evidence in the proof which has been adduced.

It is a maxim consecrated by the tenets of our religion and adopted in the practice of our laws that the guilty should escape rather than that the innocent should suffer and, in this case, where the scales of justice hang in equal poise, may we not yet hope that his Royal Highness the Prince Regent may extend over this young and wretched female the protecting sceptre of his mercy, without sacrificing the cause of justice or compromising the interests and safety of his people. ...

But what is the proof that is to justify the public immolation of this victim? The most desperate malignity of the most practised offender would not incite him to commit these many murders without a motive. Yet no evidence has been adduced of any motive that should excite this young woman to rush at once into such complicated guilt.

Without a motive, then, we are to believe that she has formed and attempted to execute the desperate offence of poisoning a whole family, and herself with them, for she had administered the poison not only to an individual against whom she nourished an unmitigable spirit of revenge, but to an entire family – not only to the family, but to other individuals and to herself.

It has, indeed, been said she participated in the poison that, by an artifice, she might escape suspicion ... It seems to me incredible that this person should have taken a mortal poison to escape the suspicion of administering it to others. She knew that arsenic would produce death, but she could scarcely believe herself competent to balance nicely the quantity, greater or smaller, which was requisite to produce a mortal effect.

The writer suggests that all members of the household could have had access to the arsenic in the office drawer and, as it was stored so negligently, it might also have been mixed in food accidentally. He – presumably, he – continues:

There seems to me to have been no positive proof that the crime imputed to her was ever committed. There is certainly no positive proof that she committed that offence. It is not improbable that it should have been committed by others. Every circumstance from which her guilt is inferred is susceptible of an easy and rational explanation and, on the other hand, the very nature of the offence renders its commission by such a person, and under such circumstances, highly improbable.

I trust the high importance of this subject may excuse my laying these crude and hasty suggestions before the public.[72]

---

72   Fairburn, 21-23.

Fenning.

On the Sunday before her execution, she received the sacrament and heard the condemned sermon. According to John Fairburn, she was 'overcome by the intensity of her feelings, which brought on violent hysterics that continued the greater part of the day'.[73]

From the condemned cell, she wrote to a number of chapel ministers[74] declaring her innocence and asking them to pray for her. Fairburn takes up the story:

> On Monday [24 July] she wrote a letter to her late master and mistress, Mr and Mrs Turner, requesting they would favour her with an interview in the prison. This they complied with, and visited her in her cell.[75]

An additional specification of the letter was that Thomas King, one of the Turners' apprentices, should attend with them. The Turners probably hoped that Eliza was about to confess her guilt and that, by doing so, she might relieve their guilty consciences. But she was having none of it.

> She then protested to them, in the most solemn manner, that she had not administered the arsenic, and expressed a hope that ere long Providence would point its finger at the real criminal, and relieve her character from the foul aspersion with which it had been undeservedly blackened.[76]

Eliza herself described the meeting in the following way:

---

73 Fairburn, 37. Watkins (88-89) quotes the following account, from the *Morning Advertiser*, 25 July 1815: 'On Sunday last, being the day appointed for the condemned sermon, an immense concourse of spectators assembled at the doors of Newgate, anxious to be present at the awful ceremony. At ten o'clock, the avenues leading to the chapel were thrown open, and in a few minutes the chapel and galleries were crowded to a degree almost unprecedented …' Cotton, making vindictive remarks about Eliza being persuaded by the Devil to seek revenge, caused her to faint. 'At the conclusion of the service, the whole of the prisoners went to the altar and received the Sacrament, Elizabeth Fenning continuing to protest that she was innocent.' In his journal, the Methodist preacher Charles Wesley (brother of John) records that, in July 1738, he visited Newgate Prison to preach to criminals destined to die on the gallows the following day. Whilst commenting that the Ordinary preached 'most miserably', he proceeds to congratulate himself on his own ability to so inspire the wretched condemned that they began to feel 'impatient to be with Christ'.

74 Rev. Mr Grieg, Minister of the Scots Chapel; Rev. Mr Griffith Williams, Minister of Gate Street Chapel; the Rev. Mr Joseph Ivimey, Minister of the Baptist Congregation at Eagle Street and the Minister of Queen Street Chapel.

75 Fairburn, 37. By contrast, John Marshall stated that 'a friend of the prisoner [undoubtedly Thomas Wansbrough] waited upon Mr Turner on the Saturday evening … with a request from Eliza Fenning that the family would visit her on the Monday morning'. (Marshall, J., 36.)

76 Fairburn, 37.

Introduction.

When Mr Turner came to me, he said, in the presence of Mr Wansbury [Wansbrough], he would do everything in his power to spare my life, but when going I refused my hand. I firmly and most solemnly declare to God and man, I am innocent of the crime, and how was it possible I could do it [offer her hand] to a person who swore my life away? But may the Almighty God forgive them; believe me they are almost the death of my dear parents.[77]

'Of her approaching fate,' we are told, 'she spoke with firmness, and took leave of her visitors in the most affecting manner. She was afterwards visited by her father and some of her friends, to whom she expressed her perfect resignation.'[78]

But other accounts of the visit of the Turners and King ran differently. In the version published in John Marshall's pamphlet, *Five Cases of Recovery* (which was not favourable to Eliza's cause), Eliza – no longer the beatified presence depicted by Fairburn – began to insult her visitors as soon as they had arrived, and 'arrogantly told her mistress that she had sent for her because she could give a better account how the arsenic got into the dumplings than she herself could. Mrs R. Turner was surprised and shocked at the impudence of her conduct, and said she had hoped to have witnessed a very different deportment in her truly awful situation. Mr King then asked her what she could mean by endeavouring to injure his character, in accusing him of such a dreadful crime? She answered by addressing Mrs R. Turner and Mr King: "It laid between you, ma'am, and you, sir."'[79] For Marshall, outbursts of this sort – if indeed they actually occurred – were inconsistent with Eliza's previous defences, and the last resort of the guilty criminal facing death. For those in Eliza's camp who chose to give any credence to them, they suggested a dark, exculpatory secret or a hidden truth, although, like Marshall, they could hardly say whether the confrontation had really occurred in the way described.

On the Tuesday afternoon, about four o'clock, she was visited by her mother, 'to whom, in taking a last leave, she said, "Now, my dear mother, I embrace you for the last time; and, with this embrace, receive the only consolation I can give you, and that is a solemn and a sincere declaration of my innocence of the horrid crime for which I am to suffer."'[80]

Later, Eliza sent some ear-rings to her mother with the following note:

---

77 Fenning, 9.
78 Fairburn, 37.
79 Marshall, J., 36-37.
80 Fairburn, 37.

Fenning.

Wear my ear-rings, dear mother, for my sake. Don't part with them, dearest mother. I die innocent of the crime, indeed.[81]

VII.

Dawn arrived, and John Fairburn surveyed the scene outside the prison:

> The morning was wet, gloomy and disagreeable; but the unfavourable state of the weather did not prevent the accumulation of an immense crowd at an early hour. Public curiosity was strongly excited, and perhaps to a greater degree than on any similar event since the execution of Haggerty, Holloway, etc.[82] For, in the case of Eliza Fenning, many had taken up an opinion that her guilt was not clearly established.
>
> A great portion of the public have taken an uncommon interest in the fate of this young female ever since her conviction, and the feeling which generally prevailed was that she would on the scaffold make an open and decided disavowal of any participation in the crime imputed to her.[83]

In his pamphlet, *An Authentic Narrative*, Thomas Wansbrough describes the scene in the condemned cell that morning.[84] He arrived at six o'clock – at which time, Eliza was 'seated on the bench against the partition of her cell, with

---

81   Wansbrough, 18-19.
82   John Holloway and Owen Haggerty were executed on Monday 23 February 1807 for the murder of John Cole Steele. Elizabeth Godfrey was executed alongside them, having been convicted of the murder of Richard Prince. One newspaper stated that 'the crowd that attended the melancholy spectacle was as great as perhaps was ever seen on any similar occasion. It is with deep regret we add that many fell victims to their curiosity, for the pressure was so great that – the crowd in front giving way – about twenty persons were trampled to death on the spot, and a much greater number were carried to St Bartholomew's Hospital in so lamentable a state that few of them are expected to recover' (*Kentish Gazette*, 24 February 1807). V. A. C. Gatrell estimates that 45,000 people attended the execution of Holloway, Haggerty and Godfrey (Gatrell, 355).
83   Fairburn, 35.
84   He had called at the prison at eleven o'clock the previous evening, but Eliza was in a profound sleep (Wansbrough, 18). Watkins's account states that Eliza 'slept sound until four o'clock in the morning, when she arose and washed herself; and, in particular, she washed her feet very carefully. She gave each of the women who attended her a lock of her hair, "to keep," she said, "in remembrance of her."' (Watkins, 90.) This observation could only have derived from the women who were assigned to watch over Eliza in the condemned cell. Nobody else would have been in the cell to witness the time she awoke or the manner in which she washed herself. Wansbrough, who did not arrive until six o'clock in the morning, did not witness the four o'clock washing episode and does not mention it. However, the notoriety and public uproar about Eliza's conviction would have ensured that the women freely gossiped about her last hours on earth. John Watkins must have heard about the more intimate details of the scene in the condemned cell when he interviewed witnesses during the investigations he conducted prior to the publication of *The Important Results*. In V. A. C. Gatrell's *The Hanging Tree*, 356, he says 'there were stories circulated about her last hours' – no doubt a cautious understatement of the prurient truth.

Introduction.

her elbow on the table, and her head reclining on her hand' and 'exceedingly dejected, insomuch that she could not speak'. He prayed with her until seven o'clock and 'a little before seven o'clock, she said she was bewildered, and that it all appeared like a dream to her. ... I left her at seven o'clock, to be attired in the dress she intended to wear at her execution, which was a white muslin gown and cap; emblematical, as she expressed it, of her innocence.'[85]

He returned to the cell half an hour later, by which time the Reverend Mr Thomas Vasey (replacing the Reverend Mr Sutcliffe, who had not turned up) and the Reverend Horace Cotton were attending her. At eight o'clock, Eliza knelt for a last prayer with Thomas Wansbrough, removing her gown so that it would not become soiled by the dirty floor of the cell.[86]

The pamphlet attributed to John Watkins describes the terrible progress of the formal ceremony:

> During prayer, the officer tapped at the door: she approached him smiling, and enquired if he was ready. As she departed, she lifted up the sash of the window, and looking through upon the prisoners, who remained locked in their cells, but who had mounted up to their different windows to see her go out to die, she kissed her hand to them, and said cheerfully, 'Good bye! good bye! to all of you'.
>
> She leaned on Mr —'s arm, and for a moment he perceived that the weakness of human nature prevailed – she staggered, but recovered instantly, and passed on to where the criminals are bound. ...[87]

She was pinioned – 'her arms, by the elbows, to the body, and ... her hands together in front' – and William Hone, writing as Watkins, indicated that he

---

85 Wansbrough, 19. Watkins (93) also mentions 'a worked muslin cap, bound with white satin riband ... a white riband round her waist, and pale lilac boots laced in front. Her appearance was very interesting.'
   Modern writers on Eliza Fenning routinely describe her outfit as her wedding dress, and say that she was meant to have been married on the day of her execution. From her 11 April letter to him, it seems that, for her part, Eliza had, before her conviction, considered herself engaged to be married to Edward. However, the description of her on the scaffold wearing her wedding dress on the day she had planned to marry was probably a journalistic embellishment intended to add an extraordinary poignancy to the tragic scene. Neither the account attributed to John Watkins nor that of Thomas Wansbrough mentions a wedding dress. According to John Fairburn's account, the execution was delayed for an hour as the hangman, John Langley, was running late, having only reached London at eight o'clock that morning after hanging Elizabeth Wollerton in Ipswich the previous day (Fairburn, 38). In addition, *The Kentish Weekly Post*, 28 July 1815, informed its readers that 'the suspense created by this circumstance excited a belief that a reprieve had been received for some one or all of the criminals'. In the same article, Eliza is described as 'the unfortunate woman [who], although short in stature, was a very pretty figure. Her face was expressive, and had none of the characteristics of a woman capable of committing the foul deed of which she had been, after a patient and impartial trial, pronounced guilty'.
86 Wansbrough, 21.
87 Watkins, 91. The anonymised man is presumably Thomas Wansbrough.

Fenning.

saw her withstand it: 'No tear started from her eye; her lip did not quiver for an instant; not a feature changed; not a muscle of her countenance moved'.[88]

Then they were approaching the scaffold, and still Eliza was insisting to the anxious Ordinary that an irremediable miscarriage of justice was about to take place. 'I die innocent,' she said. She even prayed – 'I *hope* He may, I *wish* He may' – for a heavenly revelation, a sign of the wrong that had been done to her, and would be done to her.[89]

Watkins – or rather Hone – again:

> She seemed in earnest and solemn devotion as she passed on to the further end of the scaffold. Her step was rather quick, but not hurried … She stood still – with her face towards Ludgate Hill; the Ordinary stood opposite her, with a book; the hangman, standing behind her, took a white cotton night-cap from his pocket, and attempted to draw it over her face, but it was too small, as were two others, which he also tried. He then tied a white muslin handkerchief over her face: but not considering this to be sufficient covering, he produced a pocket handkerchief which had evidently been used. She disliked this, and desired it might not be put on. She cried, 'Pray do not put it on – pray do not – pray do not let them put it on'. … 'Pray,' said she, 'Mr Cotton, do not let him put it on – pray let him take it off – pray do, Mr Cotton'.
>
> Mr Cotton replied, 'My dear, it must be on – he must put it on'. She was very dissatisfied with it, and felt much uneasiness; but it was, nevertheless, tied across her eyes by the hangman. He then placed the cord round her neck, and ascending a pair of steps, threw the other end of it over the beam, and made it fast with several knots.[90]

Oldfield and Adams followed Eliza – seeing nothing, hearing the mob – onto the drop, and Oldfield 'inclined his head to listen to her last accents. She expressed her firm assurance of happiness hereafter – denied that she was guilty – and resolutely persisted in her innocence.' Hone captured the final act: 'The platform fell: she raised her arms, and dropped them immediately. Her last words were, "I am innocent!" She died without a struggle.'[91]

---

88 Watkins, 91. Hone – the true author of the pamphlet attributed to Watkins – later stated that, although unwittingly present at the execution, he 'saw nothing, but … heard all'. See Appendix IX.

89 Watkins, 92. Thomas Wansbrough, who was standing beside the scaffold, did not include an account of this conversation between Eliza and Cotton in his description of the scene in *An Authentic Narrative*.

90 Watkins, 93.

91 Watkins, 95. According to the Fairburn account, the last words spoken by Eliza were: 'I know my situation and may I never enter the kingdom of Heaven, to which I feel confident I am going, if I am not innocent'. (Fairburn, 36.)

It is suggested that Eliza endured a drop of about twelve to eighteen inches – a brutal and sadistic short drop, but not an uncommon one at the time. James Berry, who acted as a principal executioner from 1884

Introduction.

The execution of Eliza Fenning provided a tragic yet spectacular piece of theatre – a tiny figure in white, calmly waiting with her arms pinioned and a noose around her neck, declaring her innocence before a vast crowd of 45,000 people who had come to watch her die. Mercifully, she did not suffer long. Hangings were often grotesquely bungled, resulting in death by slow strangulation rather than a quick dislocation of the neck – but not in Eliza's case.

A contemporary newspaper account described the scene differently, under the headline, 'Execution of Elizabeth Fenning, William Oldfield, and Adams':

> Wednesday being the day appointed for the execution of the above mentioned unfortunate delinquents, the public curiosity was strongly excited. ... In the case of Fenning (for attempting to poison the family of her master, a law stationer in Chancery Lane), many had taken up an opinion that her guilt was not clearly established, for she had uniformly protested her innocence. ... About eight o'clock in the morning, the Sheriffs proceeded from Justice Hall along the subterraneous passage to the press yard. Fenning was dressed in white, with laced boots, and a genteelly-worked cap. Oldfield went up to her in the press yard, and enjoined her to prayer, and assured her they should all be happy.
>
> The Sheriffs preceded the cavalcade to the steps of the scaffold, to which the unfortunate girl was first introduced. Just as the door was opened, the Rev. Mr Cotton stopped her for a moment to ask her if, in her last moments, she had anything to communicate. She paused for a moment, and said: 'Before the just and Almighty God, and by the faith of the Holy Sacrament I have taken, I am innocent of the offence with which I am charged'. This she spoke with much firmness of emphasis and followed it up by saying what all around her understood to be, 'My innocence will be manifested in the course of the day'. The last part of this sentence was spoken, however, so inaudibly that it was not rightly understood and the Rev. Mr Cotton, being anxious to hear it again, put a question to get from her her positive words; to which she answered, 'I hope God will forgive me, and make manifest the transaction in the course of the day'.
>
> She then mounted the platform with the same uniform firmness she had maintained throughout. A handkerchief was tied round her face, and she prayed fervently, but, to the last moment, declared her innocence. Oldfield came up next, with a firm step, and addressed a few words in prayer to the unhappy girl.
>
> About half-past eight o'clock, the fatal signal was given. One emotion only was perceptible in Fenning. After hanging the usual hour, the bodies were cut down and given over to their friends for interment.[92]

---

to 1892, helped to devise a Table of Drops, adjusting the length of the rope based on the weight and stature of the prisoner in order to ensure a quick and more merciful death by vertebral dislocation – as opposed to slow strangulation. This method was later perfected by Albert Pierrepoint, executioner from 1932 to 1956.

92 *Bristol Mirror*, 29 July 1815.

Fenning.

Of course, the public's sense of their own emotional investment in the case was not assuaged by the simple fact that the execution had taken place, and that Eliza was dead. They continued to express sentiments ranging from pity to outrage, and their behaviour ran from prurience, at one end, to altruism at the other.

> During the remainder of the day numerous groupes [sic] of people assembled at the Old Bailey and also, in the evening, opposite the house of Mr Turner (the prosecutor) in Chancery Lane, conversing on the subject, with whom pity for her sufferings and a firm belief of her innocence seemed to be the prevailing sentiment. At the last-mentioned place, the tumult became so great it was found necessary to send for the assistance of the police to disperse the multitude, and preserve the peace.
>
> It is remarkable that no part of the body of this unfortunate female, from the crown of her head to the sole of her foot, changed colour in the least after her execution until the evening of the following Friday, with the exception of a small mark under her chin, made by the rope. She lay in her coffin seemingly as in a sweet sleep, with a smile on her countenance.[93]

Eliza's father had to pay 14s 6d for the 'executioner's fees' before he could redeem his daughter's dead body for burial.[94] This, in addition to the cost of the funeral, had clearly caused considerable financial hardship for the Fennings; Fairburn's readers were informed that

> early in the day, the friends and relatives of Eliza Fenning assembled at the house of Mr Millar, picture-cleaner and repairer, No. 14, Eagle Street, Red Lion Square (where the body lay), who had been maligned in some of the public prints as having made a show of the body of the girl for interested purposes. We have, however, the solemn assurance of this man and his wife that they with reluctance

---

[93] Fairburn, 38. Later in his life, William Hone recalled the execution of Eliza Fenning in this way: 'I got into an immense crowd that carried me along with them against my will; at length I found myself under the gallows where Eliza Fenning was to be hanged. I had the greatest horror of witnessing an execution, and of this in particular; a young girl of whose guilt I had grave doubts. But I could not help myself; I was closely wedged in; she was brought out. I saw nothing, but I heard all.' (Hackwood, 99-100.)

[94] If unclaimed, the bodies of convicts executed in the city were sent to the Royal College of Surgeons for dissection and anatomisation, to be used for research and tutorial demonstrations. However, William Hone, writing as John Watkins, noted that, had her family not paid for Eliza's body 'the public sympathised so generally in the fate of the deceased that an eminent surgeon, whose anatomical theatre is largely supplied with subjects for his pupils' dissection, in order to avoid an outrage upon popular feeling, gave especial orders to the persons who usually supply him with bodies, that the corpse of Elizabeth Fenning, however desirable to possess, should on no account be brought to him'. (Watkins, 98.) There was a lucrative trade in providing corpses for anatomists and unseemly scenes were sometimes enacted at hangings, with relatives and friends fighting for possession of the corpse against those intent on seizing it and selling it for dissection.

Introduction.

> admitted many of the numerous applicants to see the corpse, and such of them as chose to leave a donation for the relief of the distressed and unhappy parents, were permitted; the donations were faithfully paid into the hands of the father. Those persons, in the trying hour of affliction, had opened their doors for the reception of the father and mother of this unfortunate female after they had disposed of every article of their furniture and were compelled, in consequence, to quit their usual lodging.[95]

Five days after her death, their daughter was buried in the churchyard of St George the Martyr, behind the London Foundling Hospital, in Bloomsbury,[96] and, such was the feeling of injustice done to her, her funeral cortège was followed by a huge crowd, estimated at least ten thousand.

> The funeral began to move from the house of her father, in Eagle Street, about half-past three o'clock, preceded by about a dozen peace officers, and these were followed by nearly thirty more; next came the undertaker, immediately followed by the body of the deceased. The pall was supported by six young females, attired in pure white: then followed eight persons, male and female, as chief mourners, led by the parents of the unfortunate girl.[97] These were followed by several hundreds of friends, two and two, and the whole was closed by a posse of peace officers. Many thousands accompanied the procession, and the windows, and even the tops of the houses, as it passed were thronged with spectators.[98]

Years later, in 1867, it was written that 'the people of London wept for her, and the great generous heart of London is seldom in the wrong in such a case'.[99]

The *Caledonian Mercury* of Saturday 5 August kept its eye on the behaviour of the crowd:

> The body of this young woman, whose fate has excited such interest, was, on Monday evening at four o'clock, consigned to its 'last home', in the burial

---

95 Fairburn, 39.
96 In 1777, at St George the Martyr, a grave digger, John Holmes, and his assistant, Robert Williams, were found guilty of digging up the corpse of Mrs Jane Salisbury to sell to anatomists at the city's teaching hospitals. Both men served six months imprisonment but escaped the sentence of being whipped along the half-mile journey from Kingsgate Street to Dyott Street, in the St Giles area of the city.
97 In Fairburn's account, 'the coffin was neatly covered with sky blue cloth, with white nails. On the coffin plate was inscribed, "Eliza Fenning, died July 26, 1815, aged 22 years"'. (Fairburn, 39.)
98 *Norfolk Chronicle*, 5 August 1815. In John Fairburn's pamphlet, he states that 'the funeral procession took its departure from the house in the following order: the undertaker, with a white hat-band; the body, in a grey coffin, carried by six men in black, covered with a rich pall, which was borne by six young women dressed in white, followed by eight mourners in mourning scarfs [*sic*] and cloaks, the first and most interesting of which were the father and mother'. (Fairburn, 40.)
99 Thornbury, W., 'Eliza Fenning. (The Danger of Condemning to Death on Circumstantial Evidence Alone.)' in *All the Year Round* (ed. Charles Dickens), 13 July 1867. See Appendix X.

ground of St George the Martyr, Bloomsbury. An intention had existed that the melancholy ceremony should not take place till five o'clock; the clergyman who was to perform the service, however, having given notice that he should be at the ground at four o'clock to receive the corpse and would not wait beyond that period, it became necessary that the procession should commence its movement from Eagle Street, Red Lion Square, where the body had lain, at half past three. Notwithstanding this alteration of the time, however, the multitude which assembled, from a feeling of curiosity to witness the scene, was immense.

As early as two o'clock the crowd began to assemble in Eagle Street and in all the avenues leading to the burial ground. Every window was thronged and in many places the tops of houses were covered with spectators. Every precaution had prudently been taken by the police magistrates to preserve the peace and nearly a hundred constables were in attendance to prevent confusion. At half past three, the coffin was brought forth, carried by six men in black. It was covered with a rich pall which was borne by six young girls in white dresses and was followed by eight mourners in mourning scarves and cloaks: the father and mother being, of course, the chief mourners. Several constables went before to clear the way and a posse also followed to prevent the encroachments of the mob which pressed in thousands behind.

The whole proceeded in a steady and solemn pace and the most perfect order prevailed, till the arrival of the procession at the gate of the burial ground, when, although the constables endeavoured to keep back the crowd, a vast number forced their entrance and thus a temporary confusion was excited. This soon subsided, however, and the body having been lowered into the grave, the Rev. Mr Force, curate of St George's, Bloomsbury, read the service of the dead with becoming solemnity. We lament to state, however, that towards the conclusion, a man, dressed in livery, made use of an expression relative to the deceased, which excited the indignation of the crowd.[100]

According to Fairburn's account, the outraged spectators were angered not only by the use of the offensive word, but also because the man was without a hat, considered as 'a violation of all decency'. They waited until the distraught parents had left the graveside before following the man, shouting, 'Shame! Shame!' and spitting in his face; he was 'shuffled and hissed off the ground over the wall' and 'the men shook him and pulled him by the ears'.[101] The *Caledonian Mercury* went on:

He was knocked down and the churchyard became a scene of great disorder. Some gentlemen at length interfered, quelled the riot, and having obtained the name of

100 *Caledonian Mercury*, 5 August 1815.
101 Fairburn, 41.

Introduction.

the offender's master, declared their intention to complain of his misconduct.

The unhappy mother of the young woman was dreadfully affected throughout the whole of the ceremony, and was in fits three times,[102] and indeed the whole of the persons connected with the procession exhibited the strongest marks of sympathy. The parties afterwards returned to Eagle Street, in the same order as they had come, but although they were followed by an immense concourse, no mischief or accident occurred.[103]

The press remained divided in its opinions on the case – some were staunchly pro-Eliza Fenning and others were extremely critical of the arguments which had been made in her favour. A lengthy article published in *The Observer* on 30 July 1815 was the most notorious and revealing example of the campaign against her: detrimental and aggressively hostile to Eliza, it dug into Eliza's history, and was flatly dismissed by Watkins as a 'fabricated statement'.[104] The casual character assassination is given here without further editorial comment:

> It appears that her father and mother are both from Ireland, and that they are both Roman Catholics: the former is a servant to Mr Hutchins, a potatoe-seller [sic] in Red Lion Passage; the other is, as far as we have been able to learn, an industrious woman and the mother of eleven [incorrect; ten] children, of whom Eliza was the last living.
>
> Eliza, at a proper age, was sent to the Gate Street (Lincoln's Inn Fields) Charity School for education, which is made the protection of the dissenters. Here it was endeavoured to instruct her in the Christian religion, and whatever instructions she received in that way was derived from this source. Notwithstanding every effort to correct a wayward and vicious disposition which at this early period manifested itself, however, it became necessary, at twelve years of age, for the preservation of the morals of the other children, who were her school-fellows, to expel her; and in the books of the charity is this memorandum, written on that occasion:
>
> 'Eliza Fenning, aged twelve years, turned out of the school for lying and lewd talk.'
>
> From this period she did but little to redeem her lost character. *Truth* was a practice with which she seemed to be at war, and there was not a place in which

---

102 Fairburn (41) states that, towards the end of the ceremony, Eliza's mother 'fell on the ground in strong hysterics'.
103 *Caledonian Mercury*, 5 August 1815.
104 Watkins, 194. According to Hone, writing as Watkins, it was even claimed in one newspaper that the infant Eliza attempted to murder her mother by setting fire to the bed in which she was sleeping. Hone utterly refutes this story, stating that Eliza, aged about a year and a half, simply accidentally knocked over a rush lamp beside her mother's bed, causing a small fire. See Watkins, 2.

Fenning.

she was employed (for she went out to service almost immediately afterwards) that she did not leave behind her the character of a confirmed liar.

In the service of Mr Hardy, a grocer in Portugal Street, Lincoln's Inn Fields, she gave particular manifestations of her vicious disposition. She there denied her mother, and applied to her language which none but the most abandoned could use when speaking of a parent. She was also in the constant practice of inventing falsehood; and by her general demeanour impressed her master with an opinion, to use his own words, 'that she was capable of any act, however malevolent', and so strongly did this impression weigh on his mind that he was not happy till she was out of the house.

Mr Hardy had also a suspicion that there was something deleterious mixed in a pot of porter which she brought from the public-house for the use of the family but which was not, from the idea that was entertained of it at the moment, used. Of any attempt to poison here, however, although strongly reported, there is no positive proof.[105]

In every place in which she lived afterwards, she unhappily obtained for herself the character of being most spiteful and malicious. She did not live long in each place, and went to Mr Hardy for three characters [references]; and there are numerous instances of a treacherous mind recited which we cannot afford space to detail.

While with Mr Hardy she imbibed an affection for a young man which seemed greatly to have unsettled her mind, and perhaps to that may be attributed many of her subsequent follies.

Her last place was that of Mr Turner's, where her conduct, as appeared on her trial, soon exposed her to the reprehension of her mistress, and she received warning to quit. It was after that warning, which she seemed to have taken much to heart, that she committed the crime imputed to her.

In Mr Turner's service she had shown a very amorous inclination which, while even under sentence of death, was more strongly manifested.

Of her trial we can say no more that it was most impartial and in our estimation, from the evidence which was produced, the verdict could not have been otherwise than it was pronounced. If, however, the shadow of a ground existed for concluding her innocent, the steps which were taken to examine her case subsequently would have discovered it. Twice were the facts studiously and minutely investigated by the Privy Council. Every circumstance which could be urged in her favour was deliberately weighed. Enquiries were made and witnesses examined innumerable.

At nine o'clock on the night previous to her execution, another enquiry took place; and again were all the facts scrupulously re-examined; and the result of

---

105   See Appendix VI.

Introduction.

the whole was a conviction upon the minds of men of high rank, of well-known humanity and strict impartiality, that there was no just cause for delaying the dreadful sentence of the law. With these facts before us, it naturally occurs to us to ask upon what fair argument persons who have merely the ipse dixit of the criminal herself can support her innocence? There can be none; and if there were, her conduct in the prison would tend to weaken, if not to overturn them.

For how does it appear she conducted herself there? From the day of her trial she behaved in a manner so flippant and so unbecoming that she frequently called down the animadversion of the Rev. Mr Cotton, by whom she was attended; a gentleman of whom it is but justice to say, no man could fulfil the arduous functions of his office with a more exemplary spirit or a more pious zeal.

Her first act of impurity was that of writing a letter to Oldfield,[106] who suffered with her, and who, it will be recollected, was convicted of a rape – the last man of all others with whom a virtuous mind would have communication.

This was followed by *billet-douxs* [sic] written to other prisoners, and among others was a letter written to a prisoner in custody on a charge of forgery [possibly Edward Harland], couched in the most voluptuous language and enclosing a lock of her hair. To this man, who had been admitted to assist her in preparing a petition, she was heard to say, 'If she did not die otherwise she would in love of him'. He felt a passion equally strong for her, short as had been their acquaintance.

A few days before her execution, she accused various persons of having committed the crime charged to her account; and lastly, desired that a young man, named King [Thomas King, the second of Mr Turner's apprentices], who had lived in Mr Turner's house, might be brought before her and confronted with her, observing that she was sure he would, by his confession, convince those who were witnesses to the scene that he alone was guilty.

This wish was complied with, and King, who is constitutionally very timid, was introduced into the cell in the presence of the Rev. Mr Cotton, Dr Moore, Mr Newman and several other gentlemen. The test which the prisoner required of his innocence was that he should go upon his knees and, placing his hand upon an open Bible, solemnly declare that he was not in the kitchen the day on which the dumplings were made.[107]

The boy expressed his willingness to do all this, notwithstanding the prisoner addressed him in the most vehement and passionate manner; upon which, finding that she had failed in producing the intimidation she expected in his mind, she

---

106 See for example Letter 26, Appendix VII.
107 Eliza had said that, on the morning she made the dumplings, she left the kitchen while she attended to a delivery of coal. Both Charlotte Turner and Sarah Peer denied there was a delivery that day; however, when the coal merchant's order book was eventually checked, it appeared that coal *was* delivered to the Turner household that day. See Appendix III.

Fenning.

said she would not be satisfied even if he did swear it. Mr Cotton, however, having brought the lad to the test, insisted upon his going through the form, which he did, in the most solemn manner, declaring he neither was in the kitchen, or knew anything of the mixing of the poison.

Upon hearing this, she clapped her hand on the Bible and said, in the most passionate way, 'I am glad of it, you have sworn a lie'. Upon being reprimanded by Mr Cotton for expressing joy at conduct in a boy which would destroy his soul, she equivocated and said, 'She did not mean that; but she was glad she could contradict him'.

All the women who attended her declared their perfect conviction that she was guilty, as did every turnkey about the prison, and they all said they never saw a woman of a more malevolent disposition. She was heard to say, more than once, that she wished she could get leave to tear the heart out of her prosecutors; and to the woman who sat up with her for some nights before her execution, she admitted that there were two things which if they were to cut her in pieces she would not divulge. What these were could not be discovered, although it may be inferred that she had made some mental reservation to avoid telling her guilt.

It appears also, from the observation of several respectable individuals who made a point to attend her throughout her confinement, that her manners partook rather of a ranting and theatrical turn than of the serious conduct of a person who was really innocent. As inducements for not divulging her guilt, even in the last instant, when [sic – were] the hope of reprieve, which we know she entertained; and the exhortation of her father to persevere in the declaration of her innocence for the sake of his character.

She exhibited throughout an uncommon strength of mind and a degree of talent, which was displayed in her letters, far above her situation in life.[108]

Eliza's alleged immorality was juxtaposed with the conduct of the gossipy, volatile, lawless crowd – in the view of *The Observer*, they became analogies for one another.

On the morning of the execution, several persons who had been witness to the awful scene, and who had been informed of the solemn asseveration of the culprit, proceeded to the house of Mr Turner, in Chancery Lane, and conducted themselves in the most unbecoming manner. This conduct was repeated on several successive occasions. Straw was brought for the purpose of setting fire to the house and we fear, but for the interference of the civil power, much real mischief would have been done.[109] During these scenes persons were busily employed in

---

108   *The Observer*, 30 July 1815.
109   Hone, writing as Watkins, anonymously quoted a source which contradicted *The Observer's* account: 'As to *straw* having been brought to set fire to Mr Turner's house, after every enquiry I have found this to be

Introduction.

the circulation of reports and anecdotes wholly groundless but which had the effect of forming [sic – fanning?] the flame of public discontent, and the most dreadful threats were uttered by the crowd.

Among other stories told, it was said that Mr Turner [Robert Turner] himself had been the mixer of the poison, a circumstance which is utterly disproved by the facts that transpired on the trial. It was then said that he had shot himself in despair; and if not him, that his apprentice, who had given evidence against the culprit, had committed suicide but that his death was concealed. To these are added other reports, all equally incorrect.[110]

Such were the transactions passing in Chancery Lane; but, in Eagle Street, Red Lion Square, in which the father of the deceased lived, and whither the body had been conveyed, the scene was different. There an immense crowd was attracted by curiosity to see the body which, to use an Irish expression, was waking in all due form, being placed in the kitchen of the house, and dressed out in ribbons, flowers, etc. All persons who presented themselves were admitted. As fast as one set came out, another went in, and although no money was actually demanded for this exhibition, we learn that the pecuniary contributions towards defraying the expenses of the wake and funeral exceeded £40.

The most respectable persons were present on these occasions; and the statements which were made, as well as the compassion excited by the melancholy spectacle, naturally produced new converts to the opinions of the innocence of the deceased, and the most serious alarms were entertained that some ill consequences would ensue. To correct as much as possible the effects thus produced, it was deemed proper that steps should be taken to counteract the assertions of the advocates of the deceased. For this purpose, Samuel Davis, one of the principal turnkeys of Newgate, made an affidavit before the Lord Mayor on Friday, a copy of which was circulated in the immediate neighbourhood of the riotous assemblages.[111]

Davis's counter-narrative, signed both by him and the Lord Mayor of London, read thus:

Samuel Davis, one of the principal turnkeys of his Majesty's Gaol of Newgate, maketh oath and saith that at an interview which lately took place between the

---

false. A little boy threw into the area half a handful of the straw rubbish with which Chancery Lane abounds, from its vicinity to the greatest coach stand in London.' (Watkins, 32 [appendix numbering].)

110 It could be wondered whether the frequent, violent epileptic episodes afflicting both Robert Turner and Roger Gadsden described by John Marshall in *Five Cases of Recovery*, 10-17, were, in fact, panic attacks brought on by fear or guilt, and whether Marshall used the term as a 'catch-all' definition. He states that after suffering numerous epileptic seizures for three weeks following the poisoning incident, Gadsden had to return to his parents' home in Cheltenham. Although he went back to work at Chancery Lane after a few weeks, he continued to suffer from frequent fits.

111 *The Observer*, 30 July 1815.

Fenning.

late convict Elizabeth Fenning, who was executed on Wednesday last, and her father (at which interview this deponent and the Rev. Mr Cotton, Chaplain of the said prison, were both present) and on several other interviews between them prior to her execution, her said father urgently entreated her in the following words, or words to the like effect: (that is to say) 'Oh! my dear child, when you come out on the gallows, tell everybody that you are innocent, and then I can walk the street upright as a man; but if you say you are guilty, I shall never be able to hold up my head among the public any more.'

Sworn at the Mansion House, in the City of London, the 28th of July, 1815.[112]

The *Observer* looked uncritically at this affidavit:

This had some trifling weight with the minds of those who would take the trouble to think, but the crowd continued flocking to Eagle Street and to Chancery Lane on Friday night, till ten o'clock, at which time the police officers very properly insisted upon old Fenning's house being closed; after which the populace dispersed.

Yesterday [Saturday 29 July], however, the multitude again assembled although, we have the pleasure to state, they were not so violent in their conduct as on the preceding days.[113]

VIII.

The justice (or otherwise) of Eliza Fenning's fate continued to divide opinion in the press, even after her execution. An example of press comment favourable to her case was a report in *The Examiner*, dated 12 November 1815, in which the validity of some of the Recorder's comments at her trial was contested: he had included the following opinion in his summing-up:

Gentlemen, if poison had been given even to a dog, one would suppose that common humanity would have prompted us to assist it in its agonies; here is the case of a master and a mistress being both poisoned, and no assistance was offered.

'What were the conclusions,' wondered the newspaper, 'which the Recorder evidently meant that the jury should draw from these statements?'

---

112 *The Observer*, 30 July 1815. Samuel Davis later retracted this affidavit, which he said was ordered by the Turner family. After the funeral of his daughter, William Fenning also swore an affidavit denying the slur contained in Davis's statement. See Appendix IV.
113 *The Observer*, 30 July 1815.

Introduction.

Why, in the first place, that as the dough made by Fenning was heavy and would not rise, there must have been arsenic in it (though it is clearly proved that arsenic will not prevent the dough rising but that the want of skill in the making it will) – and, in the second, that as the family above stairs were poisoned and very ill, and Fenning did not offer her aid, it was a mark that she either wanted common humanity; or she had her reasons for not assisting the sufferers. The Recorder, it is true, does not make use of Fenning's name in the above passage; but if he did not allude to her, to whom did he allude?

He, of course, then did not know that arsenic would *not* prevent the dough from rising; and he did not know that the girl had partaken of the poisoned food, was herself extremely ill, and could not afford that aid, the not rendering of which, even to a dog in agony, was a clear proof of the absence of common humanity. …

That the Recorder might reasonably know nothing of the effects of arsenic upon dough may be readily supposed; but why in his ignorance did he venture on conveying such a notion to the jury when the life of a fellow creature was at stake?

That he could not have known of the illness of Fenning when he spoke of no assistance being offered, and must have imagined she was able though unwilling to give it, must be concluded; but his strong allusion to the girl's apparent misconduct must have had a decided influence on the minds of the jury, and the Recorder's misconception of the fact must be allowed to be deplorable in the extreme. Had he altogether omitted these two points in his charge, it appears more than probable that the jury would not have returned a verdict of guilty; and that he *ought* not to have suppressed them both is now quite clear, we dare say, even to himself.

These things, dreadful as they may have been in their consequences, may be attributed to error; but what is to be said for the after behaviour of the Recorder to Mr Corbyn Lloyd when that gentleman waited upon him? That the Recorder might be 'surprised' at what he termed the presumption of an individual's differing in opinion with jurymen and judges is very likely; but persons of good information know well that the fallibility of judges and juries is on record in many afflicting instances.

The Recorder must have known that the difference in opinion was not confined to an individual. And how dare any man, official or unofficial, presume to tell a gentleman that his interference could only have arisen because the object of it was a pretty woman?[114]

Propagating the other side of the argument, and propping up his own testimony to the court, the surgeon John Marshall issued a pamphlet, extracts of

---

114   *The Examiner*, 12 November 1815.

which were quoted in *The Times*, that was adamant in its conviction that Eliza was guilty as charged. He cited instances where, in his opinion, her actions indicated guilt: one being that she did not assist other members of the household when they were taken ill; another that she refused his suggestion that she take milk and water for her pain and vomiting. (This was quite understandable when it is remembered that she felt sure it was the milk in the sauce that had made everyone so ill.) He even suggested that she had eaten some of the dumplings in order to 'destroy herself to evade justice'.[115]

He also referred to a book – a copy of Henry Fielding's novel, Amelia, found in her box – that contained advice on procuring abortion; yet the policeman, Thiselton, had searched her box after her arrest and found nothing incriminating. Marshall stated, as fact rather than hearsay, that Eliza made spiteful and revengeful remarks about her mistress, and pronounced that 'these facts serve to illustrate how greatly Mr Turner and his family have been exposed to unmerited rancour by the artful and revengeful conduct of the wretch who has inflicted on them so much suffering and anxiety'.[116]

IX.

In November 1815, four months after Eliza's death, a ground-breaking and incisive publication attributed to Dr John Watkins was published by the radical campaigner, William Hone,[117] entitled *The Important Results of an Elaborate Investigation into the Mysterious Case of Elizabeth Fenning*.[118] In it, Watkins – really William Hone, who had merely borrowed Watkins's name for the purpose – detailed the results of his investigations, which included, among its assorted parts, accounts of interviews with hostile witnesses. In addition, a thorough analysis of the transcript of the trial emphasised the many inconsistencies in the testimony given at the trial: Orlibar Turner, for instance, had said that he had not seen Eliza eat any of the dumplings – but then, he wouldn't, as she and the other servants ate in the kitchen, the room in the house which the master would

115 Marshall, J., 34.
116 Marshall, J., 38.
117 William Hone (1780-1842): radical journalist, bookseller and friend of William Hazlitt and Charles Lamb; and editor of *Critical Review*, a publication that shared political principles with those expounded by *The Examiner*. He also campaigned vigorously on Eliza's behalf in his newspaper, *Traveller*. A fearless political agitator, he was tried and acquitted three times for blasphemy against the Church of England and producing satirical works, some with cartoons by George Cruikshank, lampooning the Prince Regent. The trials took place at the Guildhall on 18, 19 and 20 December 1817. He conducted his own defence and the verdicts were greeted with great jubilation.
118 Published from his office at 55 Fleet Street, London.

Introduction.

have no call to visit. Why, 'Watkins' asked, had the first apothecary, Mr Henry Ogilvy, who was called to attend the family as soon as they had fallen ill, not been questioned and allowed to testify in court? The only medical evidence heard had been from John Marshall, who had arrived nearly six hours after the dumplings had been eaten and, from the start, was clearly convinced that Eliza was guilty.

'Watkins' also referred to evidence given at the trial at the Old Bailey that was not recorded by the court's shorthand writer.[119] The presence of Eliza's father, William, and his offer to give evidence as to the Turners' hostility towards his daughter, was not included in the official transcript. Sir John Silvester's summing-up was, 'Watkins' thought, highly prejudicial. 'Watkins' also pointed out that both John Marshall and Orlibar Turner were acquainted with the clerk of the Hatton Garden police court, Mr Shearman, who had been appointed as solicitor to the prosecuting barrister. Even more disturbing was the fact that Orlibar Turner and Sir John Silvester had been acquainted for several years – not surprisingly, since Turner was a reputable law stationer in business in the heart of the judicial centre of the City of London. 'Watkins' also turned his attention to the toxicological evidence in the case. He estimated that the residue which John Marshall said he had extracted from the pieces of dough stuck to the pan would have contained – by Marshall's own reasoning – at least fifty grains of arsenic; there was, perhaps, enough dough stuck in the base of the average dumpling pan (after serving) to form one-eighth of a dumpling: therefore, the four and a half dumplings eaten that day contained something like 1800 grains of arsenic. If a total intake of five grains of arsenic – or even less in some cases – was considered to constitute a fatal dose, how was it that nobody died?

Then there was the chemical evidence. First, 'Watkins' stated, a knife used to cut a dumpling that contained arsenic would not blacken; and, second, Marshall's assertion that the dough's failure to rise showed that it contained arsenic was a faulty one – the presence of arsenic, 'Watkins' averred, does *not* prohibit the action of yeast.[120]

Having dealt with the anomalies and assumptions in the physical evidence, 'Watkins' turned his attention to the shockingly speculative defamation of the character of Eliza Fenning. Vicious rumours about her were widespread after

---

119 See Watkins, 51ff.
120 Watkins, 68-69: 'Arsenic mixed with dough containing yeast will not prevent the mixture from rising, although the quantity of arsenic exceed two-thirds of the mass. It is generally known that yeast contains a large quantity of carbonic acid gas in a concentrated state: the effect of heat extricates the bubbles of gas, and in the act of extrication distends the dough, until all further attraction for caloric, or heat, ceases, by the total absence of gas. In this state, if the mass be confined at its sides, its surface will become elevated, and present the appearance of what is termed rising.' See Appendix V.

Fenning.

Orlibar Turner made public a letter from Mr Shuter, a solicitor,[121] who maintained that, when she worked for him, she had tried to poison him and, moreover, had tried to cut the throat of another previous employer. When questioned, the solicitor admitted that Eliza had not tried to poison him but that 'he thought Mr Turner had done what was proper in hanging the girl – as nobody would be safe if these Irish wretches were suffered to get into respectable families'.[122] This sentiment was included in a letter Shuter sent to Orlibar Turner, which the latter forwarded to Silvester. In addition, the woman whose throat Eliza was supposed to have cut admitted to 'Watkins' that she had never even met the girl.

Of course, when Watkins's – really Hone's – radical analysis was published, it was received with outrage by those who had been determined to see Eliza Fenning hang. *The British Critic*, to choose just one example, was unequivocal in its condemnation:

> Of all the wretched attempts which have ever been made to shake the confidence of the people in the administration of public justice, this is the most audacious.[123]

X.

In 1829, some fourteen years after the execution of Eliza Fenning, there was published a Penny Dreadful of uncertain authorship and entitled *Circumstantial Evidence: The Extraordinary Case of Eliza Fenning*.

> The Trial and Execution of Eliza Fenning in 1815, for an attempt to poison the family of Mr Turner, the law stationer, will be in the recollection of most of our readers. The event excited great attention and interest at the time on account of the conviction having taken place on circumstantial evidence only and the powerful asseverations of innocence on the part of the unhappy woman up to the very moment of her death.
>
> At that time a large portion of the public thought her wrongfully condemned, and some of the newspapers espoused her cause very warmly; but, after a patient and impartial trial and a subsequent investigation before the Privy Council, the evidence was considered too strong to leave a doubt of her guilt; and she was executed.
>
> Years passed away without there appearing any reason to doubt the justice of

---

121 Watkins, 146-147.
122 Watkins, 146. Prejudicial and virulent remarks against Roman Catholics were freely expressed and largely without censure at this time. The *Newgate Calendar* accounts written by the Ordinary were often detrimental in tone to criminals of that faith. At the time of the Eliza Fenning case, the Monument to the Great Fire of London still had an inscription on it which attributed the outbreak of the fire to 'Popish frenzy'.
123 *The British Critic*, December 1815, 631.

Introduction.

the verdict; but fresh interest has been lately given to the subject by a report that has been circulated charging another with the dreadful deed; and it is, therefore, thought that a reprint of the trial will be acceptable as the first of a series of extraordinary Convictions on Circumstantial Evidence, intended to be given in the Universal Pamphleteer.[124]

After giving details of the evidence presented at the trial, the text continues:

Within the last few weeks, a paragraph has appeared in many of the newspapers stating that the son of Mr Turner [that is, Robert Turner, the son of Orlibar Turner][125] had died lately in a hospital after confessing that he had mixed the poison in the food prepared by Eliza Fenning, and was consequently guilty of the offence for which she suffered. Upon this statement, the Examiner newspaper of June 14, 1829 remarks:

'We saw the paragraph alluded to but know not whether its statement be correct. We think it very likely, because this we do know – that a son of the prosecutor, Turner, did on one occasion betray symptoms of insanity in the shop of Messrs Corbyn, Holborn, where he went to purchase arsenic, and was refused by a gentleman of the establishment.

'This was not long previous to the affair of the alleged attempt to poison by Eliza Fenning; and when the unfortunate girl was so strangely found guilty by the jury, the gentleman alluded to thought it his duty to submit Mr Turner's situation and conduct to the consideration of the Recorder Silvester. That man, however, had made up his mind, and nothing could move him.

'We took considerable pains at the time to obtain all the testimony adduced, and our firm conviction was that there was not sufficient evidence to convict. Arsenic was kept in the house, and some of it certainly found its way into the flour that Eliza Fenning had made into a pudding. Of this she partook, as well as Mrs Turner and the children,[126] and was extremely ill in consequence. She had occasionally quarrelled with her mistress upon common matters, but there appeared no cause for anything like a feeling of revenge such as so deadly an

---

124 *Circumstantial Evidence*, 2.
125 Robert Gregson Turner had married Charlotte Churchman on 24 May 1814 at St Matthew's church, in Ipswich. In 1820, both Orlibar and Robert Turner were listed in the Ipswich Poll Book. In 1825, Orlibar Turner was declared bankrupt. In 1826, Orlibar and Robert were still on the list. The report of Robert's death in an Ipswich workhouse in 1829, when he was thirty-eight years old, was later denied. No record of his death has been found. In 1834, Orlibar Turner – but not Robert – was back in London, living in Cursitor Street, and listed as an 'innholder'.
126 Clearly this was an error in the reporting: Robert and Charlotte had no children in March 1815. Charlotte was nearly seven months pregnant at the time of the poisoning; John Marshall stated in his pamphlet that she went full term, so it may be assumed that she gave birth while Eliza was in Newgate (Marshall, J., 14). Although the precise date of the birth is not known, the child was baptised on 18 August 1815 and named Sophia Gregson Turner.

Fenning.

attempt as that to poison a whole family would indicate.'[127]

On Wednesday 27 May 1829, the *Bury and Norwich Post* published the following announcement:

> A correspondent in the *Morning Journal* of Monday [25 May 1829], under the signature of John Grant, says, 'I am assured that a son of Orlibar Turner (of Chancery Lane) has recently died miserable in Ipswich workhouse, confessing that he put arsenic into some yeast dumplings to poison his family, and for which crime Eliza Fenning was hanged innocently.'
>
> It may be remembered that it was proved on the trial that the poor girl was very ill from having partaken of the dumplings (which was considered by many as a strong proof of her innocence) and persisted to the last that she had not committed the crime for which she was about to suffer. The then Recorder (Sir. J. Sylvester [sic]) thought differently, and a numerously signed petition in her favour, expressing doubts of her guilt, and recommending her to mercy, was ineffectual.[128]

This statement was repeated elsewhere, but on Tuesday 30 June 1829 the following denial was printed in the *Essex Herald*:

> A paragraph appeared a few weeks back in a respectable daily paper (the *Morning Journal*) which we are now assured was not only not founded in fact, but it is altogether untrue. It stated 'that a person had died in Ipswich workhouse, acknowledging that he had put the arsenic in the yeast dumplings, for which crime another had suffered at the Old Bailey some few years since.'
>
> The party here alluded to is still alive, and living respectably; consequently our contemporary must have been imposed upon, and we are led, in quoting from that journal, and commenting thereon in our paper of the 25th ult. into a similar error, which we hasten to correct by repeating, on the very best authority, that the paragraph in question is totally false.[129]

XI.

Despite the fact that forty-two years had passed since Eliza Fenning was hanged, memories of her were awakened by the trial of Madeleine Smith in

---

127 *Circumstantial Evidence*, 7.
128 *Bury and Norwich Post*, 27 May 1829. This news followed, on page two of the newspaper, the revelation that 'there is now in the possession of Mr Ely, cabinetmaker of this town, a *white blackbird*, which has attracted the notice of great numbers of the curious'.
129 *Essex Herald*, 30 June 1829. In fact the clarification was a belated reprint, having been originally published in the *Dispatch*.

Introduction.

1857 [NBT 1] – indeed, William Roughead describes that year as 'Eliza's apogee', forty-two years after her death.[130] Her case was referred to in an article entitled 'Circumstantial Evidence' in *The Times*, 21 July 1857, which told of a supposed confession:

> Dr Fletcher, minister of Finsbury Chapel, London, narrates the following in regard to the case of Eliza Fenning, referred to by the Dean of Faculty in his defence of Miss Madeleine Smith:
>
> 'A considerable number of years ago I was sent to visit on a Sabbath-day Eliza Fenning in prison, who was sentenced to be executed on the following Monday [sic – she was hanged on a Wednesday] in the front of Newgate, and who was found afterwards – alas! though too late – innocent of the crime. She was executed for a deed she never committed. In company with the Ordinary of Newgate, I conversed and prayed with her. She was dressed in white, an emblem of her innocence. In the same garments she suffered death as a criminal on the following day. I had no opportunity of judging as to her innocence. The expression of her countenance will never be erased from my remembrance. It is literally stereotyped upon my heart. From what was communicated to me some years after the fatal and melancholy event I can now explain the expression of her countenance. It was the demonstration of injured innocence!
>
> When the event of her execution was almost forgotten, a baker, dying in a workhouse in the vicinity of London, said to the matron of the ward, or some other individual, to the following effect:
>
> "My mind is heavily burdened. I cannot die until I make the following communication: Eliza Fenning died innocent of the crime for which she suffered.

---

130 Roughead, 112. Madeleine Smith was charged with poisoning her lover, Emile L'Angelier, with arsenic. Her trial in Edinburgh, in August 1857, caused a sensation. The jury returned a verdict of Not Proven and she was released. She married an artist, George Wardle, and had two children. She eventually moved to New York, changed her name to Lena Wardle Sheehy, and died in 1928, aged ninety-three.
The Dean of Faculty, John Inglis, defending Madeleine Smith, referred to Eliza Fenning's case in the following terms: 'Do you know the story of Eliza Fenning? She was a servant girl in the city of London, and she was tried on the charge of poisoning her master and family by putting arsenic into dumplings. When the charge was first made against her, she met it with a calm but indignant denial; she maintained the same demeanour and self-possession throughout a long trial; and she received sentence of death without moving a muscle. According to the statement of an intelligent bystander, when brought upon the scaffold, she seemed serene as an angel, and she died as she had borne herself throughout the previous stages of the sad tragedy. It was an execution which attracted much attention at the time. Opinion was much divided as to the propriety of the verdict, and the angry disputants wrangled even over the poor girl's grave. But time brought the truth to light; the perpetrator of the murder confessed it on his deathbed – too late to avoid the enacting of a most bloody tragedy. That case, gentlemen, is now matter of history. It happened at a time beyond the recollection of most of those whom I now address; but it remains on record – a flaming beacon to warn us against the sunken rocks of presumptuous arrogance and opinionative self-reliance, imbedded and hid in the cold and proud heart; it teaches us, by terrible example, to avoid confounding suspicion which proof, and to reject conjectures and hypotheses when they are tendered to us as demonstrations.'

Fenning.

I am the murderer of her mistress. I put the poison into the morsel which effected her death."[131]

On the trial the jury concluded it must have been the cook who had administered the poison, as they had not the slightest clue to suspect the baker. Yesterday, in the vestry of my own chapel, one of my elders stated to me that the baker was a relative of the deceased.[132] There is no doubt that he accomplished his murderous purpose to gratify some long-cherished passion of revenge from an offence given him, real or imaginary, by the fated victim of his malevolence.'[133]

Confession was likewise the subject of the following letter, which appeared in *The Times* on 5 August 1857:

Sir,

In the late trial at Edinburgh allusion was made by the Dean of Faculty to the case of Eliza Fenning. He mentioned it as illustrating the danger of trusting to circumstantial evidence and assumed that the verdict had since proved to be a wrongful one. ...

My late uncle, Mr William Brodie Gurney, shorthand writer to the Houses of Parliament, was well known to a wide circle of friends, and to many of our leading public men, as a man of strictest integrity. His accuracy all who were familiar with him can testify was perfectly unimpeachable. To dress up a story for effect, or to take a side and support it by doubtful statements, was as foreign to his character as robbery or murder.

I happened to be spending an evening with him a year or two before his death, and he produced a little book of anecdotes and conversations in which things worth remembering had been jotted down for his own use, or for those who might come after him. ...

Having the book in his hand, he said, 'Oh! Here is something that will interest you about Eliza Fenning. You have heard, I dare say, that a person of that name was executed for poisoning (or attempting to poison, I forget which) the family with whom she lived as a servant, and that a good deal of popular feeling was excited on the subject, many persons being persuaded that she was wrongfully convicted, because she maintained her innocence in prison, and on her way to the scaffold.'

He then read the underwritten statement. I dare say Eliza Fenning will live in history as one unrighteously doomed to death, notwithstanding; and that writers who are very capriciously tender of human life will still argue from her case to

---

131 Charlotte Turner did not die from the poison.
132 It is not clear whether the writer is referring to the 'deceased' as Eliza Fenning or her supposed victim, Charlotte Turner, since he seemed to think that Charlotte Turner had died.
133 *The Times*, 21 July 1857.

Introduction.

their conclusion, that poisoners should not be convicted unless someone swears in the witness box that he saw the poison bought, mixed, and given by the accused party; but, at any rate, it is desirable that the candid and reasonable portion of the public, and especially men of influence and authority like the Dean of Faculty, should know how the case really stands – namely, that Eliza Fenning did confess her guilt in prison to a minister of the Gospel, who visited her as a friend; though afterwards, when persons came about her who doubted her guilt and gave her to understand that a reprieve might be hoped for, she changed her tone, and, like Palmer and Patch[134] and many others whose guilt no one doubts, went out of the world unconfessed.

The extract which follows is copied verbatim from my uncle's notebook, and has been supplied to me by his son, Mr Joseph Gurney, the present shorthand writer to the Houses of Parliament:

Doubts having been on several occasions expressed of the guilt of Eliza Fenning, I feel it my duty to record the facts with reference to her case which came within my knowledge.

Feeling as strongly as anyone can do the objection to the infliction of death by a human tribunal, I still feel that there is a justice due to prosecutors, who are bound conscientiously to speak the truth, and to jurymen, who are sworn to find a verdict according to the evidence, which in many instances has been disregarded.

Having heard from a friend that the master and mistress of Eliza Fenning were esteemed highly respectable and conscientious, I was glad to find that the doubts entertained referred rather to the question whether the evidence, which was circumstantial, established her guilt. The jury and the judges thought it did, and I believe those who were present at the trial pretty generally concurred. In a few days, however, I heard that her strong asseverations of innocence had created a doubt, and that many who visited her felt a strong interest in her case, believing her to be innocent, and a petition to the King was sent in. The grounds of it were examined by the Secretary of State, the attention of the learned judge was called to the case, and, on his report that he felt no hesitation as to the propriety of the verdict, the law was directed to take its course, which it did. Still some people retained their doubts.

Shortly after her execution I heard that the Rev. James Upton, a Baptist minister, preaching in Church Street, Blackfriars Road, had visited her while under sentence of death, having been requested to do so in consequence of her having, when young, attended at his chapel, whether with her family or in the Sunday school I am not aware. I knew him to be a very excellent man – a man of great kindness of heart; I felt satisfied that he would not form a more unfavourable opinion than

---

134 William Palmer (1824-1856), the Rugeley poisoner [NBT 15]. Richard Patch (1770-1806), executed for the murder of his master.

circumstances called for and I took an opportunity of seeing him. He informed me that, on his entering the cell, Eliza Fenning, with great earnestness and tears, exclaimed that she was innocent of the crime imputed to her – that it was a cruel charge, and so on. That he replied, 'Eliza, I have not come here to talk to you about that. I do not mean to ask you whether you were guilty of that crime or not, but I come to you as a minister of Jesus Christ, hearing that you are probably very shortly about to appear before your Judge, to remind you that you are a sinner and that unless those sins which you are conscious you have committed are repented of and pardoned, you can have no good hope for eternity. I come to set before you Jesus as a Saviour able and willing to save.' He said, 'I was somewhat affected, considering the situation of this poor girl about to suffer, and I talked to her earnestly, entreating her to seek mercy, and avoiding altogether the subject of her conviction. Before I had done she was quite melted down, and then it all came out.' I said, 'Do you mean that she confessed the crime?' 'Oh, yes,' said he, 'there was no reserve then. She confessed that it was all true, and I besought on her behalf the forgiveness of all her sins, and of that among the rest, and I hoped at the time that she had joined in that prayer, but I understand that after this she still persisted in assuring those who visited her of her innocence.'

I have felt it important to secure a wide circulation for this decisive refutation of a very current story, while the recent trial [of Madeleine Smith] is fresh in men's minds. ... The facts are important with reference to the criminal jurisprudence of the country. But, having got upon the subject of reprieves and confessions, I should like, if you will allow me, to go on and speak of the fearful mischief often done within the walls of prisons by those who profess themselves the friends of doomed criminals. The questionings which go on there, the repeated solicitations to confess, the importance attached to persevering denials of guilt, must necessarily have a blinding effect on those who are thus beset.

Numbers, I believe, will not confess just because so much is made of confession. 'They want me to confess that they may feel secure in hanging me,' is the natural feeling at such times. 'The verdict does not satisfy them unless I admit its justice. I won't do that. If I deny my guilt stoutly I shall perhaps be believed at last, and escape.'

Thus, during the awful interval which is the murderer's brief preparation time for eternity, he is balancing probabilities of escape, demeaning himself so as to make a favourable impression on bystanders, heaping up lies which, by possibility, he thinks may gain him long time for repentance hereafter – doing anything, in fact, but realising his position and opening his ears to the godly counsel of those who desire to save his soul alive. If a criminal wishes to confess there is no hindrance in his way. The penitent, without compulsion, will unlock the secrets of his heart to his spiritual adviser at any rate, and to the world at large I do not know that he is bound to proclaim his guilt.

Importunity, on the other hand, will not wring out of the dogged malefactor what

Introduction.

he is determined to conceal; and if he is to be softened at all and brought to a better mind it must be, not by repeating questions to which he has given one answer already, not by turning his thoughts back again to life and suggesting the hope that oft-repeated asseverations will stay the uplifted hand of justice, but by going to work as good Mr Upton did, speaking compassionately, as a sinner to a fellow-sinner, of our common guilt and the common redemption, appealing to the conscience, stating plainly that all transgressions secret and open must be repented of, and pointing to the Lamb of God whose blood cleanseth from all sin, while to the impenitent and unbelieving, the hardened and self-justifying, it is declared plainly that there remaineth only judgement without mercy. 'It all came out,' says the narrator, when he thus addressed the poor girl, whom he had known in happier days. Alas! she had other advisers afterwards – persons who meant kindly, but who did her fearful wrong. The confession was retracted. Hope was strong, doubtless, in that young bosom, and the efforts making on her behalf were sure to be reported to her.

Between her cell and the scaffold the Ordinary 'stopped her for a moment', says the *Annual Register*, 'to ask her if in her last moments she had anything to communicate?' (She had better, surely, have been let alone; her tongue was not tied; she could speak then, as before, all she wished to speak; who shall say that she might not hope, even then, that another lie might save her? It did make her a heroine, and a supposed martyr with the populace.)

'She paused a moment and said, "Before the just and Almighty God, and by the faith of the Holy Sacrament I have taken, I am innocent of the offence with which I am charged."'

By her own confession at another time she was a murderess; dying thus with a lie upon her lips, she was no penitent. My fear is that the time of probation was lost, the faithful admonition forgotten, the course of repentance arrested, and the soul retained in the bondage of sin, because she was buoyed up with false hopes and her fatal gifts of youth and beauty, coupled with protestations of innocence, made a party in her favour who hoped up to the last hour to extort a reprieve from Government.

I am, Sir, your obedient servant,
J. H. Gurney, Rector of St Mary's, Gloucester Place, Marylebone.[135]

On 13 July 1867, the case decorated the pages of Charles Dickens's weekly journal, *All the Year Round*. The article was entitled 'Elizabeth Fenning (The Danger of Condemning to Death on Circumstantial Evidence Alone)', and was written by journalist Walter Thornbury, under the proprietor's watchful editorial eye. In a letter to Thornbury dated 5 October 1867, Dickens expressed his

---

135 *The Times*, 5 August 1857.

opinion that the culprit was one of the apprentices; but his ire was reserved for the Baptist minister, James Upton, who had claimed that Eliza had confessed to the crime whilst in Newgate. He wrote:

> I was never more convinced of anything in my life than of the girl's innocence, and I want words in which to express my indignation at the muddle-headed story of that parsonic blunderer whose audacity and conceit distorted some words that fell from her in the last days of her baiting.

In an earlier letter to Thornbury (this one dated 22 December 1866), Dickens pointedly observed that 'the argument that the Government of the day hanged her' – that is, that they made a consciously self-interested decision to proceed with the execution in order to insulate themselves from any further embarrassment associated with the increasingly compelling agitation against the justice of the verdict – 'is stark imbecility'. No special measures were required in those unforgiving times, and hangings were an expeditious, thoughtless means of dealing with situations which might otherwise have become executive dilemmas. 'The Government of the day,' Dickens went on, 'would have hanged anyone.'

XII.

The trial of Eliza Fenning lasted for only one day, but the John Watkins / William Hone document included a copious – and frequently repetitious – analysis of the anomalies in the proceedings: they concluded that these were wilfully and artfully biased in favour of the prosecutors, and that any evidence to Eliza's advantage was either dismissed or glossed over. Their insightful and often outraged analysis of the case was unremitting, as were their exhaustive investigations with witnesses and scandalmongers amongst the Turners' neighbours and associates in the weeks following the execution. It was in the course of these enquiries that they uncovered convincing evidence of the collusion between the Turners and members of the Establishment with whom they were on cordial terms – the judge, Sir John 'Black Jack' Silvester; the magistrates' clerk, Mr Shearman; John Marshall; the Reverend Horace Cotton; and others – to ensure that Eliza Fenning was blamed for the attempted poisonings and hanged.

The first questions that were put to Charlotte Turner set out to establish not only a presumptive motive but also to insinuate that Eliza Fenning's behaviour was morally unacceptable. But why weren't the apprentices questioned on what happened when Eliza entered their room? Eliza insisted that one of the

Introduction.

apprentices, Thomas King, could have verified her statement that she only went into the boys' room to fetch a light for her candle, and that Roger Gadsden had 'taken liberty' with her. In addition, it was supposedly the recollection of someone whom John Watkins described as 'a person present' at the committal proceedings at Hatton Garden that Charlotte Turner did *not* testify at that time to finding Eliza in the boys' room, but instead swore that she had discovered Eliza 'in her own room, undressed, as if she had, on hearing her come up, run from the boys' room in that state'.[136] If true, then Charlotte's story had changed by the time the case reached the Old Bailey, where she stated that she had seen Eliza, already partially disrobed, entering the boys' bedroom. The brief and limited accounts of the Hatton Garden hearings make it impossible to be sure about the true content of Charlotte's deposition, and the original was never made public and was almost certainly destroyed. The clerk to the magistrates, Mr Shearman, was a friend of the Turners, and in a position to spot the damaging evolution of Charlotte's tale. If it was considered that embarrassment would be the likely result of closer popular scrutiny of the discrepancies in Charlotte's evidence, the documentary proof could be quietly disposed of.

Either way, we get the sense that Eliza was being closely watched by Charlotte Turner. Why? Why was she so concerned at what might have been going on in the boys' room – so piqued that she decided to climb the stairs to the attic, where the boys slept in one room and Eliza in the other, to investigate? Was she suspicious that her husband, Robert Gregson Turner, might be attracted to the pretty young maid – a common enough concern for newly-married and pregnant wives?

Charlotte Turner stated that Eliza was 'extremely sullen' after she had been reprimanded, yet only the maid, Sarah Peer, mentioned it when questioned, adding, for good measure, that Eliza had told her that she no longer liked Mr and Mrs Turner. Eliza may well have felt aggrieved that she had been unjustly accused of misbehaviour, but, if she did develop a grudge against the family, surely she would have exacted her revenge at the time? If she had been aggressively resentful of her mistress's treatment, then she had every opportunity to adulterate a variety of foodstuffs – or she could simply have quit her job and found employment elsewhere. She was an intelligent young woman, a hard worker and experienced in domestic service. An acquaintance, Mr John Smith, signed an affidavit affirming that he had met Eliza in Holborn shortly before the poisoning incident and that she had then told him how happy she was working for the Turners, but his attempts to introduce this evidence into court

---

136   Watkins, 118.

were apparently curtailed at the whim of the judge.

So many factors in this case were never fully addressed. Why did Charlotte Turner keep going back to the kitchen on the day of the poisonings to check on the condition of the dough – was she fully aware of her husband's mental state and, if she had an inkling that he might try to poison his family as he had once threatened, was she being especially vigilant about what was going on in the kitchen? As for the evidence relating to those persons who were in the kitchen that day, she admitted that Eliza had left the room to take the pie for the servants' meal to be baked at about 12.00 pm. While she was gone, any person in the house could have, without her knowledge, adulterated the flour or, later, when Eliza left the kitchen on another errand, perhaps to take delivery of the coals, sprinkled arsenic over the prepared dough which had been left to rise in a pan by the fire.

The testimony of both Charlotte Turner and Sarah Peer was revealed as false when the receipt for the coals delivered that day was later provided by the coal merchant: this was information that Orlibar Turner was alleged to have known before the trial, and kept to himself.[137] It was of vital importance to establish whether the coals *were* delivered that day for, if they were, this would account for Eliza being absent from the kitchen whilst taking delivery of them. It was emphasised by tradesmen that Eliza was unusually (and even tiresomely) meticulous about deliveries and insisted on checking that the details on the orders corresponded with the goods delivered to the Turner household. It was remarked that, unlike many other servants, she didn't 'cook the books' and indulge in pilfering small amounts for herself or her family, even though they were living on or near the breadline.

Charlotte Turner stated in court that there was nobody other than Eliza in the kitchen during the time the dough was made. Yet she says that she herself went upstairs and was absent for about half an hour. How could she possibly be certain that no one else, besides Eliza, was in the kitchen, which was on the ground floor? In the interval between twelve and three, Charlotte said that she went into the kitchen two or three times to check on the making of the dumplings; so it follows that she must also have absent as many times. What could be the motive for Charlotte Turner's frequent examination of the dough? She remarked on the fact that it was not rising, and she noticed its singular shape and position; why did she keep peering into the dough pan and commenting upon the contents? Did she suspect that there might be something sinister in the dough? Or did Orlibar Turner advise her to be vigilant in the kitchen?

---

137   See Appendix III.

Introduction.

Watkins and Hone pointed out that it was reprehensible that the judge should have allowed Sarah Peer to be present in the courtroom, listening to Charlotte Turner's testimony. It was not surprising, therefore, that the girl repeated her mistress's evidence.

Furthermore, according to Watkins and Hone, heaviness in dough can be caused by a very simple mistake in its preparation, known as scalding the yeast. This occurs when the water used in the mixing of the dough is too warm; this will affect the fermenting power of the yeast, and the dough will not rise. This may have happened on the day of the poisonings, as Eliza used the same flour and yeast as she had done the night before; on that occasion, the dumplings had turned out perfectly white and light. The ingredients may not have been to blame, but the *method* of mixing the dough may have resulted in the heaviness of the dumplings the second time around. However, whether caused by the scalding of the yeast or not, the heaviness could not have been, as experiments have proved, occasioned by arsenic.

Orlibar Turner's evidence that Roger Gadsden 'was very ill in a similar way' to himself in 'not more than a quarter of an hour' after the onset of his own symptoms is not consistent with Gadsden's own evidence. He was not so bad as to prevent his being sent to Lambeth to fetch Margaret Turner, and he did not vomit until he had left the house. Where was the apprentice, Thomas King, who hadn't eaten any of the dumplings – and why wasn't he sent instead of Gadsden?

Why wasn't Thomas King examined at the trial? The excuse given was that he suffered with his nerves. It was a telling and unacceptable omission. Where was he on the afternoon of the poisoning? Roger Gadsden testified that Thomas King had also, many times, seen Eliza go to the drawer where the poison was kept. Why couldn't Thomas King speak for himself? The judge should have insisted on his appearing in court to be questioned. Indeed, Eliza begged for him to be brought into court to testify, convinced that he could prove her innocence – but the judge rejected her plea; later, he tired rapidly of the evidence of the witnesses to Eliza's good character and refused to allow Eliza's father, William Fenning, permission to speak in his daughter's defence.

Watkins and Hone questioned how much time elapsed between the making of the dough and Orlibar Turner's 'taking custody' of the pan in which it was mixed. During that period – when Eliza was sometimes out of the room – someone else could easily have sprinkled arsenic around the pan. This possibility was not eliminated by the evidence produced at court. On the other hand, if Eliza had been guilty of poisoning the dough, surely she would have made sure that the bowl in which she had made the mixture was thoroughly washed out, removing

Fenning.

any trace of arsenic?

It was Sarah Peer who had taken the dumplings upstairs to the dinner table at three o'clock that day – at which point Charlotte had commented on their unsatisfactory appearance. Returning to the kitchen, surely Sarah, out of spite, would have delighted in repeating Charlotte's remarks to Eliza as a parting shot before leaving the house for the rest of the day. According to John Marshall, when Eliza then took the steak and potatoes upstairs and collected the leftover dumplings, 'Mrs R. Turner observed to her that "the dumplings were by no means what she expected" – the cook made no reply, but blushed, and appeared in great agitation'.[138]

Marshall was of the opinion that Eliza's reaction was indicative of guilt. On the contrary, it was much more likely that she was acutely embarrassed by Charlotte's reprimand, especially as she had boasted about how well she could make the dumplings. When she returned to the kitchen, she ate a piece of dumpling to check – even though, as she subsequently said, 'milk is a thing that does not agree on my stomach'.[139]

Eliza's gentle naïveté comes through in other ways, too. She had noticed that Charlotte Turner did not become violently ill immediately after eating the dumplings as, contrary to her testimony in court, she was well enough to remain at table and finish the meal of steak and potatoes.[140] However, when Roger Gadsden came into the kitchen at about 3.20 pm and spotted a dumpling and a half on a plate, Eliza – no doubt bearing in mind her mistress's comment about the dumplings – tried to stop him from eating it, saying, 'It is cold and heavy. It will do you no good.' Others might have been tempted to let the cheeky lad go ahead and eat the unpleasant dumplings by way of repaying him for taking a 'liberty' with her. However, Eliza seems to have had a more forgiving nature than many young women might possess in similar circumstances.

Eliza's warning to Gadsden was presented in court as the product of a guilty conscience, but as she had been told that there was something wrong with the dumplings she was merely warning Gadsden.[141] Certainly Orlibar Turner professed to suspect that there was arsenic in the dumplings and repeatedly questioned Eliza in the days that followed, even though she was confined to

---

138   Marshall, J., 33.
139   Fenning, 8.
140   If there had been a large dose of an irritant poison such as arsenic – as Marshall inferred – those who ate the dumplings would have been immediately and violently sick.
141   John Fairburn (23) quotes from the letter of C. A. to *The Day* newspaper (edition of 25 July 1815; letter dated 24 July 1815): '… the same observation which she [Eliza] made to the boy had been previously suggested to herself by one of the family'. The author of the letter stated this as if it were a fact, but there is no proof of it in the transcript of the trial, at least.

Introduction.

her sick-bed until Thursday, 23 March. Faced with an accusation of poisoning against her, she suggested other possible sources of the trouble – the flour, the yeast, the milk.

Watkins and Hone also pointed out that Robert Turner swore that he ate none of the sauce – 'not a portion of it whatever'. He knew, of course, that his wife had made the sauce. It would hardly have behoved him to confess to wolfing it down. The dumplings became a way of steering attention away from the family towards Eliza, the outsider.

Referring to the two apprentices, Roger Gadsden and Thomas King, John Watkins had this to say:

> The mind is never so prone to mischief as when unemployed; and the vacations between the terms afford a law-stationer's office many long days and even weeks of leisure. To the apprentice, whose daily industry is interrupted by frequent and tedious hours of idleness, a paper of arsenic is neither an agreeable nor a useful object for contemplation; and the master deserves something more than a mere reproach who could expose half-employed and thoughtless youth to the temptation of untying a paper of deadly poison and examining, playing, and making experiments with its contents. To the mischievous it presented facilities which are too dreadfully obvious from the circumstances which gave rise to the trial.[142]

And let us stay with Watkins (and his overworked compositor) as he continues to deconstruct the case for the prosecution:

> Thiselton, the officer who took the prisoner into custody, swears that she told him she saw a *'red'* settlement in the yeast. Did he not swear before the magistrate that she told him it was 'WHITE'? Thiselton's conversation, however, with the prisoner, even as stated by himself, tends to exculpate her from all *appearance* of guilt. Her answers seem simple and natural, and have the semblance of ingenuousness. But was it necessary to the strength of the prosecutor's case that *this* man should have been put up into the witnesses' box? That a *thief-taker* should have been transformed into *an evidence*? …[143]
>
> Mr Edmonds's yeast is celebrated amongst bakers for its superior quality to that of other brewers' yeast. How this superiority is acquired is a secret. Probably some other ingredient being chemically combined with yeast contributes to its improvement. Bakers seem to think its better quality is owing to its scientific management. Mr Edmonds's yeast, as well as other yeast, deposits a *red*

---

142 Watkins, 43.
143 Watkins, 43.

sediment....[144]

Mr Marshall deposes that there was, in the remains of the dough sticking round the dish in which the Turners' dumplings were made, half a teaspoonful of arsenic. If the arsenic was mixed with the flour at the time of making the dough, it was doubtless spread and incorporated throughout the whole mass in uniform proportion. Everyone in the habit of going into the kitchen knows how much dough is left in the dish after making dumplings; if collected, it would scarcely exceed the size of a walnut, or one eighth of a dumpling. If, therefore, there was in that quantity half a teaspoonful of arsenic, which it has been ascertained would weigh *at least fifty* grains, there would have been, in the four dumplings and a half actually eaten, a quantity of arsenic weighing 1800 grains.

Now, as five grains of arsenic would destroy any human being who swallowed it, the quantity in Mrs Turner's quarter of a dumpling was equal to the death of ten persons; that in her husband's dumpling and a half would have killed 120; and if Mr O. Turner and Elizabeth Fenning's proportions of dumplings were alike, each of theirs held a portion equal to the death of 110 persons; so that the quantity of arsenic in the four dumplings and a half would have destroyed 360 people![145]

The large portion of arsenic, therefore, in the small quantity of dough remaining in the dish after the making of the dumplings is only to be accounted for by supposing that a portion of *arsenic* was sprinkled or strewed upon the surface of the dough whilst in the pan or dish before the fire; in which case, upon making the dough into dumplings, although the greater quantity would be incorporated, yet a considerable portion would fall off into the dish. But, after all, was it not possible for any person to have put arsenic into the dish after the boiling of the dumplings, previous to the finding of the dish by Mr Turner?

Mr Marshall says he 'examined the dish the next morning; he washed it with a tea-kettle of warm water. He first stirred it and let it subside; he decanted it off; he found *half a teaspoonful of white powder*. He washed it the second time. He decidedly *found* it to be *arsenic*,' but he has not stated how he *knew* it to be so.

---

144   Watkins, 44.
145   Some of the sums here are wrong. Charlotte Turner testified that she 'did not eat a quarter of a dumpling'. A quarter of a dumpling, according to the ratios described, would contain 100 grains of arsenic, or twenty fatal doses, rather than ten. Since her actual consumption was less than a quarter of a dumpling, we can suppose that there were, perhaps, less than twenty fatal doses in Charlotte's eaten portion, but whether it was one fatal dose, or less than one, or nineteen, we cannot know. The concentration of arsenic in Robert's portion is correctly calculated. Hone, writing as Watkins, has subtracted the doses in Robert's portion (600 grains) and Charlotte's portion (100 grains – which is the right figure for a quarter of a dumpling, which makes his mistake in the earlier part of the calculation all the more difficult to understand) from the total (1800 grains) in the four and a half dumplings which were consumed that day. This leaves 1100 grains, which he splits evenly between Orlibar Turner and Eliza Fenning: 550 grains each, or 110 fatal doses each, or one and three-eighths of a dumpling each. Of the remaining dumpling and a half, a one-eighth portion (or thereabouts) was eaten by Gadsden (implying a dose of fifty grains, ten times as great as a fatal dose; despite this, Gadsden made it to Lambeth and back).

Introduction.

Did Mr Marshall, by mere *inspection*, find it to be so? or did he *find* it to be so upon the authority of any other person? Did he *test* it? and when? What *tests* did he use?[146] What *became* of the arsenic? Why did he not produce it in court? Did he think it ought not to have been produced in court? Or was it because he had parted with it out of his possession, and could not identify it? Was the *dish* the only vessel, except the flour-tub and yeast-basin, that Mr Marshall examined? Did it not occur to him to examine the pot in which the dumplings were *boiled*? What became of the water they were boiled in? Was there any more arsenic held in solution in the water, after a quarter of an hour's boiling of the dumplings, than would have escaped from them? Did Mr Marshall inquire where the water was got from that the dumplings were mixed with, and did he inspect the vessel it was fetched in? Did he examine the *milk-can, that hung in the kitchen*? and the salt vessel, from which the salt was taken for the dumplings? Did he examine the SAUCE?

Mr Marshall does not say one word about arsenic *in the dumplings*; all that he deposed to was the presence of arsenic in the remainder of the dough in the dish the dumplings had been made in. What experiments did he use to discover that there was *poison* in the *dumplings*? Was any of the remaining dumpling and a half given to a cat or dog or other animal? Were the contents discharged from the stomachs of any of the family given to an animal, examined or analysed? …[147]

IT IS NOT TRUE *that arsenic will produce the effect of* BLACKNESS *upon a knife; it will not*, it CANNOT produce it. And yet, upon Mr Marshall's swearing ALONE, the PRESUMPTION appears to have rested of ARSENIC having been in the DUMPLINGS with which the family were poisoned.[148]

XIII.

Invariably, by its nature, deliberate malevolent administration of poison with intent to kill is covert in essence and any evidence suggested can only be circumstantial; and so it was with the Eliza Fenning case. No one had seen her take the packet of arsenic from the drawer in the office or sprinkle it into the dumpling mixture. Unless we accept that Eliza had an irrational wish to take revenge on Mrs Turner by poisoning the whole family following her reprimand for inappropriate behaviour, what motive for the crime is left?

And why, for instance, wasn't the apprentice, Thomas King, called to give evidence? Why did Eliza insist on confronting him in her cell at Newgate,

---

146 Some of these objections were discussed by Marshall in his *Five Cases of Recovery*, to which we have already referred.
147 Watkins, 45-46.
148 Watkins, 47.

Fenning.

adamant that he could exonerate her? He was a nervous young man, scrupulously protected from interrogation, and the most notable character in the case to avoid examination in court. What would he have said under pressure? Would he have self-incriminated; would he, perhaps, have incriminated Robert Turner? Eliza said that while she was cleaning knives in a back room she heard someone in the main kitchen and assumed it was Charlotte Turner nosing about once more; but, when she went in, she met Thomas King. When she asked him what he was doing, he made no reply and scuttled out. Where did he go from there? His absence and his subsequent avoidance of the dumplings could be interpreted as fortuitous – suspicious, even. The maid, Sarah, was also absent from the house that afternoon, nor did she eat any of the dumplings. Did either of them have the motive to poison the family, knowing that Eliza, the cook, would get the blame? They certainly had every opportunity. Did one of them sprinkle some white arsenic over the dough – did they do so, perhaps, on Robert Turner's orders – when Eliza was out of the kitchen? It was a clumsy, random poisoning, not aimed at any one person in particular, as there was no guarantee which member of the family would eat enough arsenic to kill them. Likewise, if Marshall's estimations were to be believed, there was such a massive amount of arsenic in the dough and the pan that it was clear that the perpetrator was ignorant of the properties of arsenic and its catastrophic effects. If the culprit was Thomas King, is that the reason for his disappearance that afternoon? Did he realise too late that what may have been intended as a harmless prank to get Eliza into trouble had become a very serious situation indeed – a case of attempted murder.

    A rather farcical suggestion was made by those determined to incriminate Eliza – Orlibar Turner and John Marshall in particular – that she had eaten food containing arsenic in an attempt to divert suspicion from herself. Why on earth would Eliza risk her life by eating a dumpling if she knew it contained arsenic which could kill her or, at the very least, make her extremely ill? Marshall testified that when he attempted to treat Eliza (who, he admitted, was seriously ill at the time, and who was still unwell after being sent to the Infirmary at Clerkenwell Prison), she had declared that she 'wanted to die'. But perhaps this remark is not surprising, if restored to its context: she was in agony, and she must have realised that – even if she was not held to be legally responsible for the poisoning – the stigma of her association with the incident would remain with her, and it was unlikely that any other family in the vicinity would employ her. She never denied that it was she alone who had mixed the dough for the dumplings.

    Why didn't her detractors ever consider that abstaining from eating food containing arsenic, as in the case of both Thomas King and Sarah Peer, was

Introduction.

equally suspicious? Could Sarah have been the culprit? She admitted in court that she and Eliza had their differences: Eliza described Sarah as 'sly and artful' and insinuated that she had put something in the milk that was used to make the sauce. Little wonder that Eliza refused to drink the milk that John Marshall prescribed when she was convinced it was the milk that was contaminated. Was Sarah perhaps jealous of Eliza's looks and intelligence and, moreover, envious of the fact that she was engaged to be married to, by all accounts, a caring and hard-working young man.

John Marshall was making a wild guess when he estimated that the residue in the dough pan contained half a teaspoonfull of arsenic. He had no way of ascertaining the precise amount of arsenic present. It was only after 1836, when the Marsh test was introduced – further refined in the Reinsch test, six years later – that the presence and quantity of arsenic could be accurately detected in food, body tissue and fluids. John Watkins, as we have seen, pointed out that Marshall estimated the presence of 1800 grains of arsenic in the four and a half dumplings consumed that day. It was generally accepted that five grains of arsenic constituted a fatal dose, though a smaller dose would sometimes kill; if Marshall's estimate was correct, the Turners must have consumed enough arsenic to kill the whole household many times over. So why didn't it kill any of them outright?

Products containing arsenic were, at the time, readily available for domestic use and widely used to kill rodents and other pests. Arsenic was also freely available for medicinal purposes – women used it to improve their complexions and men as a tonic to restore strength and vigour.[149] But how would Eliza Fenning have known the correct dosage to use to ensure a bad attack of vomiting and diarrhoea, but not death?

It would seem that whoever put the arsenic in the dumplings that day didn't intend to kill the Turners – just to make them ill. Someone intent on killing them outright would have mixed a massive dose of arsenic to ensure death. John Marshall should have realised that the vast quantity of arsenic he assumed to be present in the dumplings would have, once ingested, resulted in a quick but agonising death. He was either an incompetent medic or absolutely determined to incriminate Eliza.

Did it not occur to Marshall, Orlibar Turner and those who sat in judgement on Eliza during her trial, to ask themselves this question – would an intelligent

---

149 James Maybrick [NBT 17] was a dedicated arsenic eater: was Robert Turner similarly familiar with arsenic as a tonic? The publicity surrounding the prosecution and conviction of Mrs Maybrick reawakened memories of Eliza Fenning's case, and the Home Office retained mentions of it in the newspapers in TNA: PRO HO 144/263/A56680.

girl like Eliza, if she had poisoned the Turner family, leave the 'poisoned' remains of the dumplings in the pan overnight? The principal concern of such a poisoner would be to remove all trace of the incriminating food as quickly and thoroughly as possible, not to leave it around for the likes of Orlibar Turner and John Marshall to rake over and use as evidence against her.

Except for the evidence presented by Mr Gibson, there is no proof that Robert Turner had become so mentally unbalanced that he had threatened to kill the whole family, though it seems unlikely that Gibson would have fabricated such a story. The elite group of powerful men who had it within their capacity to influence the outcome of the case – that is, the Recorder, the Home Secretary, and others – were given this information on the eve of Eliza's execution, but, appallingly, they declined to question Mr Gibson further, or to interview either Robert Turner or members of his family regarding the allegations. If Eliza had been afforded a committed defence counsel and Robert Turner had been questioned in court more stringently, he might, under pressure, have displayed signs of the mental instability that Mr Gibson evidently saw in his shop the previous September, when Robert had tried to buy a quantity of arsenic and begged to be restrained in case he poisoned himself and the whole family.

Was Eliza a scapegoat, taking the blame for poisonings perpetrated by Robert Turner? The following scenario might be worth considering: Orlibar Turner knew that the packet of arsenic was missing. The date that he and Gadsden gave for their realisation that the arsenic was missing – 7 March – seems arbitrary and uncorroborated; there was no reasonable explanation why Orlibar and Gadsden should know (or profess to know) this precise, specific information. But this was the evidence they gave, and, at the time, it served a purpose: the arsenic may well have been missing for several months; by giving the date of 7 March, however, they were saying that it was 'taken' while Eliza was living in the house. When Mr Gibson informed Orlibar Turner about his son's threatening tirade, did this do much more than confirm or consolidate Orlibar's existing suspicions and anxieties? Was he simply hoping that Robert would never carry out his threat? Suspecting that Robert had taken possession of the packet of arsenic, did Orlibar Turner decline to confront him for fear of a violent reaction? Did he choose instead to keep quiet but to remain vigilant, instructing Charlotte to watch with especial care all the food preparation in the kitchen? When the family members became ill with violent symptoms, did he suspect that Robert had carried out his threat to poison his family and himself?

One cannot help wondering why the Turners waited so long to send for John Marshall – he arrived at 8.45 pm – after falling ill shortly after three o'clock that afternoon? Why, after being attended to by Henry Ogilvy, did they think

Introduction.

it necessary to send for Marshall more than five hours later? Marshall lived out of the area. Did the Turner family decide to call him that evening because, being unfamiliar with the neighbourhood, he may not have been aware of any rumours relating to Robert Turner's odd behaviour, or his ranting about poison only a few months before? His threats were made in public so would have been discussed throughout the area as a particularly alarming piece of gossip.

Why did John Marshall harbour such intense hostility towards Eliza, an animus evident in his pamphlet pronouncing his conviction of her guilt? Was there some connection between the Turners and John Marshall that would ensure Marshall's co-operation in pointing the finger at Eliza, and thereby exonerating Robert? A Masonic or business link, perhaps? It was noted by John Watkins in his analytical document that both Orlibar Turner and John Marshall were acquainted with Mr Shearman, the magistrates' clerk, who wrote down the original depositions (which were subsequently destroyed) and went on to act as the solicitor for the prosecuting barristers.[150]

Whether or not the Fenning family and their friends were aware that Mr Gibson had voiced his concerns about the disturbed behaviour of Robert Turner, it seems evident that at least some of the citizens who had gathered in huge numbers at Eliza's execution were convinced that Turner was the poisoner. They surrounded his house, baying for blood, and were only prevented from burning the house to the ground, and possibly attacking him as well, by the police officers who were on crowd control duty that day.[151] The most crucial omission in this case seems to have been the failure to confront Robert Turner with Mr Gibson's evidence and question him, and his father, in more detail.

It is possible, of course, that Charlotte, newly married and pregnant, envied Eliza's looks and intelligence and suspected that Robert might be attracted to her. Eliza's father, William Fenning, had tried to testify in court that the Turner family were hostile to his daughter, but the Recorder had refused to hear his testimony. Yet Charlotte Turner, of course, could have given Eliza notice to leave at any time – servants like her were two-a-penny, and there were no 'unfair dismissal' tribunals or redundancy payments to worry about.

By the same token, why would Eliza risk everything by indulging in such a spiteful and dangerous act of poisoning? If she had been given the sack following the supposedly flirtatious goings-on in the boys' bedroom, she could have found another job easily enough – she may not even have needed to work after her marriage (which was due to take place, it was said, on the day she was hanged)

---

150   See chapter 'Judges and Barristers' in Stephen Knight's book, *The Brotherhood*, regarding the traditional links between Freemasonry and the judiciary.
151   *The Observer*, 30 July 1815.

as her fiancé, Edward, was described as 'much affected and industrious' – in other words, a decent young man. And why would she choose to poison the dumplings when she freely admitted that she was the person who made them? She had every opportunity to pollute any number of foods that passed through the kitchen without associating herself quite so explicitly with their preparation.

Some press reports referred to Eliza's behaviour as 'lewd' and 'salacious' both prior to, and during, her incarceration in Newgate Prison. It was even suggested that a book advocating abortion was found amongst her belongings, although William Thiselton, the policeman who arrested her, testified at Hatton Garden that he had found nothing suspicious. He may, of course, have chosen not to mention such a book out of decency. She may well have been a bit of a flirt – she was, after all, young and pretty – but in the anguished letter she wrote to her parents shortly before her execution she seems to be desperate to assure them – without being explicit – that she had not lost her virginity; to have done so was clearly considered by her to be a sin, a notion instilled in her by her parents and her religious upbringing. There was plenty of defamatory material in the public domain: the cover image of one publication – *Circumstantial Evidence: The Extraordinary Case of Eliza Fenning*, the text of which was actually favourable towards her case – nonetheless depicted her adopting a flirtatious and frolicking pose, mop in hand and standing adjacent to a steaming bucket of water on which was written 'R.C.' The allusion is a difficult one to unravel, but to some readers it would no doubt have implied that Eliza was a Roman Catholic, and Catholics were stereotypically held to be mischievous and criminal by antagonistic Anglicans.[152] No wonder Eliza was desperate to convince her parents that she was a 'good girl'.

The disparaging comments made by the bigoted Mr Hardy, who was interviewed by Watkins after Eliza's execution, revealed underlying anxieties about the meaning and function of murder-by-servant. By declaring that he disapproved of servants being able to read, Hardy hinted at the fear then prevalent among the upper classes that servants would question the status quo,

---

152 Another interpretation – equally unkind – is available. Within a few years at the very most (and, quite possibly, by the time of the Eliza Fenning affair), 'dolly-mop' would become a pejorative term used for young maids who, whenever they had any free time, would entertain gentleman they met in parks and streets of the city in return for trinkets or small amounts of money. The earliest citation in the *Oxford English Dictionary* dates from 1834, in Captain Marryat's *Peter Simple*, but earlier references – 1823 being the earliest found at this time – are available in newspapers, and there was even a racehorse going by that name by 1831. As the *Circumstantial Evidence* pamphlet was pro-Eliza, it seems odd that its anonymous creator would choose to depict her in such a derogatory way – if indeed that was their intention at all. Eliza's presentation as a cleaner with a mop, rather than a cook with pots and pans, further separates her depiction in this image from the true details of her life.

Introduction.

the authority of the master, and the entitlement of the privileged to a life of ease by an accident of birth.[153] Mr Hardy clearly wasn't very bright and felt threatened by and ill at ease in the company of a servant girl whose intelligence was superior to his own. Mr Shuter's letter, enthusiastically ventilated by Orlibar Turner, was founded on similarly reactionary feelings towards the empowerment of the working classes in general, and women in particular.

We have no way of assessing the veracity of a second purported death-bed confession, mentioned in a letter written by a Dr Fletcher and published in *The Times* on 21 July 1857. This time, the alleged culprit was a baker who, it was said, was related to the deceased; apparently, as he lay dying in a London workhouse, he had confessed to the poisoning. The idea of a last minute confession to the crimes ascribed to Eliza Fenning took on a life of its own. A further variant of this story and that of Robert Turner's alleged admission was published by the *Dundee Courier*, excited by the Maybrick case, in 1889:

> On a bed, in a mean dwelling at Chelmsford, in Essex, lay a man in the throes of death, his strong frame convulsed in agony. To those surrounding that bed and watching his fearful exit from the world, he disclosed that he was the nephew of a Mr Turner, of Chancery Lane; that, many years since, irritated with his uncle and aunt, with whom he resided, for not supplying him with money, he availed himself of the absence for a few minutes of the servant maid from the kitchen, stepped into it, and deposited a quantity of powdered arsenic on some dough he found mixed in a pan. Eliza Fenning, he added, was wholly ignorant of these facts.[154]

Likewise, we cannot know whether Reverend Upton's account of his meeting with Eliza in Newgate Prison, as given in a letter from Reverend Gurney to *The Times* in August 1857, was the truth, a knowing fabrication, or the result of wishful thinking. One must also wonder why this revelation was not made

---

153 In June 1816, the newspapers reported on a slave insurrection in Barbados in which many plantations were set alight and many hundreds of slaves slaughtered in the battle for control. The cause of the insurgence was blamed on the fact that some of the ringleaders, who were able to read and write, had 'availed themselves of [the Slave Registry Bill], and the public anxiety it occasioned, to instil into the minds of the slaves generally a belief that they were already freed by the king and parliament' (*Evening Mail*, 5 June 1816). This sort of catastrophic conflict between master and servant – at home and in the colonies – was seen as a potent threat to law and order and, of course, to entitlement.

154 *Dundee Courier*, 15 August 1889. In this case, it is perhaps easier to dismiss the story of the apparent confession. No mention of a nephew of Mr Turner – *either* Mr Turner – is made in the contemporary sources. Richard Abbot, the son-in-law of Orlibar Turner and the brother-in-law of Robert Turner, was potentially the *father* of a nephew of Robert Turner – but since he had married Robert's sister Mary as recently as February 1813, it is impossible to imagine that any son of Richard and Mary could have been old enough to commit the offence.

Fenning.

public in 1815, instead of forty-two years later. Could it be that the Reverend Upton's overzealous determination to prise out evidence of contrition – or, the ultimate goal, a confession – from a terrified and desperate girl who was facing public humiliation and a truly horrible death might have been considered to have placed her under extreme duress, rendering the outcome of the enterprise invalid? Already distraught and primed since childhood in fearful and fervent religious dogma, she was now called to task by the Reverend gentleman who had taught her at Sunday school and who was, therefore, to her, a figure of authority.

Eliza may have seemed ripe for last-minute redemption, but did she actually confess to the attempted murders? How could that be? Upton says that he didn't actually mention the crime, relying merely on more general religious sentiments to provoke and inspire the subject of his ministry. It is possible that, in the awful tension of the highly emotive encounter, Eliza said what she knew he wanted to hear, only to retract the 'confession' as soon as he had gone away to intimidate someone else with his talk of hell-fire and brimstone. But none of this is subject to proof.

Upton suggested that Eliza, encouraged by her friends and advocates to believe she might get an eleventh-hour reprieve, had kept up the pretence of innocence. Yet surely, with her arms and legs pinioned and the hangman's noose already around her neck and his filthy handkerchief covering her face – she had to wait thus shackled while John Langley turned his attention to the other two convicts awaiting execution – she would have conceded that a reprieve was *not* going to arrive and, as a girl with religious convictions, she would surely have confessed to the poisonings in that last moment before certain death. Unless, of course, even at this moment, she found it impossible to admit guilt, not only to all the people who had tried so desperately hard to save her from the gallows, but also to her distraught and traumatised parents, and to the young man she had hoped to marry.

The judgemental snobbery of the men in power in the Regency era ensured that the scales of justice were definitely weighted against Eliza Fenning. Although she was a pretty young woman – so much so that her detractors accused her champions of being swayed by her prettiness – some press reports referred to her, in derogatory terms, as a Roman Catholic, presumably because her mother was Irish. The implication of some of these comments seemed to have been designed to somehow couple that faith with criminality in the minds of the public who lapped up every spurious, and often inaccurate, detail surrounding the case.

Introduction.

XIV.

One of Eliza's supporters was Leigh Hunt,[155] who had recently served a two-year prison sentence in Horsemonger Lane Gaol for libelling the Prince Regent in an article in *The Examiner*; his brother, John, co-founder of *The Examiner*, was sent to Coldbath Fields, in Clerkenwell. Leigh Hunt's comment on the case of Eliza Fenning was unequivocal:

> In the conviction of that ill-fated girl, circumstance did little, fact less, and situation everything.[156]

Eliza was only a servant, but she was in possession of skills and abilities that may have caused her to be perceived as somehow 'above her station', 'giving herself airs and graces' and 'too big for her boots'.[157] She even owned several books given to her by a previous employer and, it was noted, she could actually read them! This combination of youth, looks and intelligence sat uncomfortably with the people who employed servants to work long hours, often for inadequate pay, and, above all, to refrain from questioning the judgement or authority of their superiors. For these reasons, Eliza is a riddle even now, the victim of her social status and of fears about her growing agency as much as she was the victim of the dubious evidence against her; the Battle of Waterloo (and the defeat and abdication of Napoleon Bonaparte) occurred in the period between her conviction and her execution, and it would become increasingly difficult for the state to justify withholding political and civic rights from people whom they would also ask to endanger themselves on the battlefield. Popular sentiment was beginning to challenge the casual assumptions of class and privilege, and a British repetition of the bloody scenes of the French Revolution was feared.

But there may be a simpler explanation behind this puzzling case. Surprisingly, it was never suggested that the sickness suffered by the Turner household that day was caused by food poisoning, a common cause of vomiting and diarrhoea in the pre-refrigeration days of the early nineteenth century. And, of course, as John Watkins noted, the Turners' Chancery Lane home was close to a busy horse-drawn coach terminus: the streets would have been strewn with dung-soaked straw, the breeding ground for infections and sicknesses.

In addition, the primitive sanitary facilities and lack of personal hygiene

---

155 James Henry Leigh Hunt (1784–1859): critic, essayist, poet. Whilst incarcerated in a well-appointed room in Horsemonger Lane Gaol, he was visited by many of his literary friends – Percy Bysshe Shelley, Charles Lamb, John Keats, William Hazlitt, Lord Byron and Jeremy Bentham.
156 *The Examiner*, 13 August 1815.
157 Hone, writing as Watkins, 138, said that Mr Hardy referred to her as 'hoity-toity'.

Fenning.

– there were, after all, two teenaged boys living there – may well have been to blame. There would have been a number of other opportunities for contamination. The milk that Sarah Peer fetched after two o'clock that afternoon may well have been contaminated by the time it reached Chancery Lane, and Eliza herself seemed to think it might have been the cause of the sickness.[158] Likewise, the yeast from the brewer or the flour from the bakery may have been kept close to arsenic put down in a storeroom to get rid of rats and mice.[159] Furthermore, if Charlotte Turner had ingested arsenic whilst in an advanced stage of pregnancy, would she have been well enough to make her statement at the police office in Hatton Garden six days later – and, soon after, to give birth without complications? In fact, it was Eliza herself who seems to have suffered longer than anyone else in the household.

A little down the road from Chancery Lane, the River Fleet had been culverted, but it remained choked with debris and waste, and it accordingly wended its malodorous way, slugglishly and unhealthily, through the City to the Thames, which was little better. Germ theory was still some way off, but, viewed retrospectively, all the conditions were in place *chez* Mr and Mrs Turner for what may well have been a severe case of food poisoning. That the illness that struck the household was attributed to felonious activity was, perhaps, a natural and animistic explanation for something that could not, at the time, be understood differently. But perhaps the family are not quite off the hook, even so: one suspects that the inadequacy of the science available to them was much less of a concern than the urgent fear that Robert had indeed carried out his threat to poison his loved ones. Of course, they immediately closed ranks.

The fate of Eliza Fenning provides us with one of the most interesting and disturbing cases of the early nineteenth century. Although Charles Dickens was only three years old when Eliza Fenning was hanged, as an adult he was familiar with the case, taking Eliza's side. He was not against capital punishment *per se*, but against *public* executions specifically. Having visited Newgate and witnessed hangings, including that of Courvoisier in 1840, he was so appalled at the behaviour of the mobs who attended them that he campaigned vigorously in letters to *The Times* against public executions – a practice that finally ended in 1868, two years before his death. The following statement was issued in *The*

---

158 *Coxiella burnetii* in milk causes Q fever – symptoms include the sudden onset of high fever, severe headache, nausea, vomiting, diarrhoea, abdominal pain, chest pain, chills and sweats.

159 On 17 April 1847, seventeen year old Catherine Foster was hanged at Bury St Edmunds for murdering her husband with a poisoned dumpling. Whereas Eliza Fenning went to the gallows proclaiming her innocence, Catherine Foster made a full confession. On 29 March 1961, *The Times* reported the death of a Mrs Alice Jones; arsenic was found in some dumplings she had eaten and traces of the poison were also found in the flour used to make them.

Introduction.

Times on 27 May 1868:

> London yesterday witnessed the last of those hideous spectacles familiar enough to the hard eyes of our predecessors, but more and more repulsive to the taste of these days.[160]

In 1819, more than three years after Eliza's execution, Fowell Buxton, the Member of Parliament for Weymouth and Melton Regis, critiqued the deterrent effect of capital punishment, invoking the dithering spectre of Horace Cotton in the process:

> It has been asserted that executions produce a great effect, but that the effect cannot be calculated precisely. I meet this by direct contradiction, contending that the effect is small, and may be calculated; it may be calculated by anyone who will expose his feelings to the pain of witnessing a public execution. There he will see how little solemnity, and how little seriousness, accompany this awful exercise of power. Sir, it is notorious, that executions very rarely take place without being the occasion on which new crimes are committed. At the very last, a pickpocket was apprehended. On being asked by the chaplain of Newgate how he could venture on such a deed at such a time, he very frankly replied that executions were the best harvest that he and his associates had, for 'when the eyes of the spectators are fixed above, their pockets below are unprotected'.[161]

We can never know whether Eliza was the tragic victim of a lax and prejudicial legal system, a revengeful little minx or, in modern parlance, a bit of a drama queen. However, many would agree with the Dean of Faculty in the case of Madeleine Smith, who believed that 'it is better that a hundred murderers should escape than that one innocent person should perish by "circumstantial evidence"'.

---

160   *The Times,* 27 May 1868.
161   House of Commons debate, 2 March 1819 (vol. 39, cc. 777-845). The most recent execution at Newgate was that of John Corderoy and John Fellowes on 16 February 1819. Both had been convicted of burglary. The identity of the pickpocket – if indeed he ever existed – is lost to history. Many pickpockets were children, and Hone, in the pamphlet attributed to John Watkins, had already preserved one newspaper's response to the declared attitude of Sir John Silvester to youthful offenders: 'It was reported the other day in the newspapers that the Recorder of London, referring to the wretched state of the children that prowl about the streets of the metropolis, stated that, to check their increasing profligacy, it was resolved to hang them, however tender their years, when any of the almost innumerable crimes rendered capital by our laws should for the future be brought home to them. Hanging, then, is the best expedient which a Judge of England, in the year 1815, can devise for amending the morals of boys and girls of ten, twelve, and fourteen years of age! What will be thought of this hereafter?' (Watkins, 45-46 [appendix numbering].)

Fenning.

XV.

Eliza Fenning is invariably described as a 'girl', but a physically mature female of twenty-one years was considered a woman in 1815, not a child. The image of her as a girl infantilised her, further fuelling chivalrous feelings in male campaigners that may not have been afforded to an old, illiterate and ill-favoured 'drab'.[162]

In his essay in *Critical Survey*, Tim Marshall suggests a reason why Eliza Fenning has become such an iconic figure, a martyr to the rigours and unfairness of the Regency class system. This is partly on account of her prettiness and purity (probably exaggerated), and partly to the enduring image of her bravely ascending the scaffold wearing a white 'wedding dress', steadfastly declaring to the very end that she was innocent of the crime for which she was to hang. This symbol of tragic innocence was guaranteed to spark a rush of noble indignation to ignite a campaign in her defence.

The martyrdom of Eliza Fenning was mainly due to the canny marketing hype of William Hone. Ben Wilson, in his biography of Hone, reminds us that he was dependent on selling his articles and pamphlets and was in very poor financial straits when, with John Watkins, he was investigating and writing *The Important Results*. In fact, he was destitute, and unable to provide for his large family. To expand his readership, he had to drum up a frenzy of outrage at the injustice of Eliza's conviction and set out to embellish and exaggerate not only her innocence but also her literacy – Hone admitted that he edited Eliza's Newgate letters and corrected spelling errors before publication to further elevate Eliza in the eyes of his readers – and her religious convictions to provoke such an interest in her and her plight that the public would buy his pamphlet.[163]

Tim Marshall also proposes that, as Eliza was buried intact (rather than being dissected and therefore rendered disposable like so many others who died in similar circumstances), her image remains unfragmented and unsullied, the victim of men of privilege and power. It has the quality of a fairy tale, a legend, folklore morphing into an unrealistic paragon of virtue, unusually honest in her dealings with tradesmen, so much so that her meticulous checking of orders had begun to annoy them. She appeared to embody the 'poor but honest syndrome'.

---

162 John Philpot Curran, Irish advocate, was inclined to 'declaim glowingly' when commenting on Eliza Fenning (Thornbury). In 1858, Charles Phillips described Eliza as 'so young, so fair, so innocent, cut down in early morn, with all life's brightness only at its dawn' (Hackwood, 99).

163 Wilson, 123: '*The Important Results of An Investigation into the Mysterious Case of Elizabeth Fenning* stands at the very beginning of a long tradition of criminal journalism which combined assiduous research with poignant melodrama.'

Introduction.

Yet she was probably neither a shrinking violet nor a flirtatious hussy – just an ordinary, feisty, fun-loving young woman who, according to friends and detractors alike, desired nothing more than to gossip with friends, to sing and dance, and to enjoy an evening at a playhouse where bawdiness was *de rigueur*.[164] Linda Stratmann summarises the effect of all of this:

> Cited by the defence in later murder trials and appeals, romanticised by Charles Dickens, immortalised in song and on stage, resurrected in parliamentary debates on the death penalty, Eliza's memory was to weigh heavily on the minds of wavering jurors who were all too willing, when faced with an alleged poisoner in the dock, to give the accused the benefit of the smallest doubt.[165]

Eliza Fenning could never have imagined that, more than two hundred years later, her trial and execution would still be the subject of debate. The controversy surrounding her case has even ensured her an entry in the *Oxford National Dictionary of Biography* – though this is little recompense, I suggest, for the wrong that was done to her.

---

164 See for example Watkins, 130: 'Mr Perkins [a bootmaker of Red Lion Street] states, that he, with an extraordinary degree of trouble, inquired into the poor girl's conduct; and from the inquiries he made, in every direction, he had every reason to think her an industrious, good servant, fond of the amusement of dancing and going to the playhouse: but, from every information he obtained, he by no means thought her an immoral girl – unless dancing and the playhouse were immoral.'
165 Stratmann, 4.

Fenning.

BIBLIOGRAPHY.

The British Critic (December 1815).
Circumstantial Evidence: The Extraordinary Case of Eliza Fenning (London, 1829).
Fairburn, J., *Affecting Case of Eliza Fenning, Who Suffered the Sentence of the Law, July 26 , 1815* (London, 1815).
Fenning, E., *Eliza Fenning's Own Narrative* (London, 1815).
Fulford, R., *The Trial of Queen Caroline* (London: B. T. Batsford, 1967).
Gatrell, V. A. C., *The Hanging Tree: Execution and the English People, 1770-1868* (Oxford: Oxford University Press, 1994).
Hackwood, F. W., *William Hone: His Life and Times* (London: T. Fisher Unwin, 1912).
Hale, L., *Hanged in Error* (Harmondsworth: Penguin, 1961).
Knight, S., *The Brotherhood* (London: Grafton, 1985).
Marshall, J., *Five Cases of Recovery from the Effects of Arsenic* (London, 1815).
Marshall, T., 'Not Forgotten: Eliza Fenning, Frankenstein and Victorian Chivalry' in *Critical Survey*, Vol. 13, No. 2 (Oxford: Oxford University Press, 2001).
May, A. N., *The Bar and the Old Bailey, 1750-1850* (Chapel Hill, North Carolina; London: University of North Carolina Press, 2003).
Polson, A., *Law and Lawyers, or Sketches and Illustrations of Legal History and Biography* (London: Longman, 1840).
Roughead, W., 'Miss Fenning's Misfortune?' in *Malice Domestic* (Edinburgh: W. Green and Son, 1928).
Stratmann, L., *The Secret Poisoner* (New Haven, Connecticut: Yale University Press, 2016).
Thornbury, W., 'Eliza Fenning. (The Danger of Condemning to Death on Circumstantial Evidence Alone.)' in *All the Year Round* (ed. Charles Dickens), 13 July 1867.
Vian, A. & Gilliland, J. (revised), 'Fenning, Elizabeth (1793–1815), convicted attempted murderer' in *Oxford Dictionary of National Biography*.
Wansbrough, T., *An Authentic Narrative of the Conduct of Elizabeth Fenning from the Time that the Warrant Arrived for her Death till her Execution* (London, 1815).
Watkins, J., *The Important Results of an Elaborate Investigation into the Mysterious Case of Elizabeth Fenning* (London, 1815).
Wilson, B., *The Laughter of Triumph: William Hone and the Fight for the Free Press* (London: Faber and Faber, 2005).

Archival Sources.

British Library, Add MS 40120 & 41071 (Hone Papers).
Harvard Law School Library, MSS HLS MS 4130 (Montagu, Basil, 1770-1851. Miscellaneous papers respecting the trial, conviction and execution of Elizabeth Fenning, 1815). iiif.lib.harvard.edu/manifests/view/drs:454771233$1i
TNA: PRO HO 144/263/A56680.

Introduction.

ACKNOWLEDGEMENTS.

Trial of Eliza Fenning owes much to the diligent and persistent investigations of Dr John Watkins, William Hone, Dr Thomas Wansbrough and others who, outraged at the mendacity and collusion of witnesses at the Old Bailey trial, tirelessly sought justice for Eliza Fenning, a young woman whom the Establishment considered dispensable. A main source of information is therefore *The Important Results of an Elaborate Investigation into the Mysterious Case of Elizabeth Fenning*, a document edited by Watkins and published by Hone in November 1815, a few months after Eliza's execution.

This volume is a work of collaboration made possible by the generous exchange of research material and the invaluable expertise of the Notable British Trials editing team: Mark Ripper (M. W. Oldridge), editor of *Trial of Israel Lipski* [NBT 84], Adam Wood, editor of *Trial of Percy Lefroy Mapleton* [NBT 86], and David Green, author of *The Havant Boy Ripper*.

Additional thanks are due to David J. A. Cairns and Linda Stratmann.

The editor and publishers would like to thank the following for permission to quote from copyright material: V. A. C. Gatrell for *The Hanging Tree: Execution and the English People, 1770-1868*, reproduced by permission of Oxford Publishing Limited through PLSclear; Tim Marshall for 'Not Forgotten: Eliza Fenning, Frankenstein, and Victorian Chivalry' in *Critical Survey* 13(2), 2001, reproduced by permission of Berghahn Books.

Leading Dates in the Case of Eliza Fenning.

1793

    10 June — Eliza Fenning born in Dominica, tenth child of William Fenning and Mary Swayne.

1815

    30 January — Eliza is employed as a cook at the home of Robert Gregson Turner and his wife, Charlotte, at 68 Chancery Lane.

    18 March — Eliza orders some yeast from a brewer.

    20 March — The maid, Sarah Peer, takes delivery of the yeast from Joseph Penson, the brewery worker. Charlotte Turner gives Eliza permission to make yeast dumplings the following day.

    21 March — Robert, Charlotte and Orlibar Turner (father of Robert) are all affected with vomiting after eating dumplings prepared by Eliza. Roger Gadsden, one of the Turners' apprentices, is similarly affected, and Eliza experiences similar symptoms after tasting the dumplings, about which the family had complained before the onset of their symptoms. John Marshall, a friend of the Turner family and a doctor, attends to treat the patients.

    22 March — Marshall, with the assistance of a chemist named Joseph Hume and at the instigation of Orlibar Turner, detects arsenic in the leftover dumplings.

    23 March — Marshall accuses Eliza of poisoning the inmates of the house, and she is arrested on a magistrates' warrant. She is subsequently charged with the offence at the Hatton Garden Police Office and removed in custody to the infirmary ward at Clerkenwell Prison.

    27 March — Second hearing at Hatton Garden. Depositions are given by the Turners, Marshall, Peer, Gadsden and William Thiselton (who effected Eliza's arrest).

    30 March — Third and final hearing at Hatton Garden. Eliza is committed to trial at the Central Criminal Court and removed to Newgate Prison.

    11 April — Trial of Eliza Fenning at the Central Criminal Court, Old Bailey, before the Recorder of the City of London, Sir John Silvester. Verdict: guilty. Sentence: death.

    20 July — Date of execution fixed for 26 July 1815.

    24 July — Robert Turner, Charlotte Turner and Thomas King (one of the Turners' apprentices) visit Eliza in Newgate at her request. She continues to deny the offence for which she has been condemned.

Fenning.

24 July *(cont.)*	A Mr Gibson states that Robert Turner has previously attempted to buy arsenic and has made deranged threats to poison his family and himself. Sir John Silvester is advised of the new information, but declines to recommend a respite of Eliza's sentence.
25 July	Thomas Wansbrough, a supporter of the case for Eliza's innocence, attempts to persuade the Turners to sign a petition for a respite of her sentence. Marshall and Silvester both arrive at the house in Chancery Lane while this attempt is being made. Marshall does not sign; Silvester does not sign; the Turners, although initially appearing tempted to do so, do not sign.
26 July	Execution of Eliza Fenning outside Newgate Prison.
31 July	Funeral of Eliza Fenning. She is buried in the churchyard of St George the Martyr, Bloomsbury.

Eliza Fenning
Author's collection

CIRCUMSTANTIAL EVIDENCE.

THE EXTRAORDINARY CASE
OF
ELIZA FENNING,
WHO WAS EXECUTED IN 1815,
For Attempting to Poison the Family of Orlibar Turner, by Mixing Arsenic in Yeast Dumplings.

WITH

A STATEMENT OF FACTS,
SINCE DEVELOPED, TENDING TO PROVE
HER INNOCENCE OF THE CRIME.

LONDON:
PUBLISHED BY COWIE AND STRANGE, PATERNOSTER ROW;
PURKESS, WARDOUR STREET, SOHO;
AND SOLD BY ALL VENDERS OF PAMPHLETS.
[*Price* ONE PENNY.]

Sir John Silvester
Author's collection

John Gurney,
Barrister for the Prosecution

Author's collection

Peter Alley,
Barrister for the Defence

Author's collection

Scene of Eliza Fenning execution outside Newgate

THE
IMPORTANT RESULTS
OF AN
ELABORATE INVESTIGATION
INTO THE
𝔐𝔶𝔰𝔱𝔢𝔯𝔦𝔬𝔲𝔰 𝔈𝔞𝔰𝔢
OF
ELIZABETH FENNING:
BEING A
DETAIL OF EXTRAORDINARY FACTS
DISCOVERED SINCE HER EXECUTION,
INCLUDING
THE OFFICIAL REPORT
OF HER
𝔖𝔦𝔫𝔤𝔲𝔩𝔞𝔯 𝔗𝔯𝔦𝔞𝔩,
NOW FIRST PUBLISHED,
AND COPIOUS NOTES THEREON.

ALSO,
NUMEROUS AUTHENTIC DOCUMENTS; AN ARGUMENT ON
HER CASE; A MEMORIAL TO H. R. H. THE PRINCE
REGENT; & STRICTURES ON A LATE PAMPHLET
OF THE PROSECUTORS' APOTHECARY;

By JOHN WATKINS, LL.D.

WITH
THIRTY ORIGINAL LETTERS, WRITTEN BY THE UNFORTU-
NATE GIRL WHILE IN PRISON; AN APPENDIX, AND
AN APPROPRIATE DEDICATION.

" If imputation and strong circumstances,
" Which lead directly to the door of truth,
" Will give you satisfaction, you may have it."
SHAKSPEARE.

London:
PRINTED FOR WILLIAM HONE, 55, FLEET STREET.

1815.
PRICE SIX SHILLINGS AND SIXPENCE.

Henry Addington

Basil Montagu

William Hone

John Scott

LA PIE VOLEUSE.

THE NARRATIVE OF

THE MAGPIE,

OR, THE MAID OF PALAISEAU.

BEING THE HISTORY OF

THE MAID AND THE MAGPIE.

FOUNDED UPON THE CIRCUMSTANCE

OF AN UNFORTUNATE FEMALE

HAVING BEEN UNJUSTLY SENTENCED TO DEATH,

ON STRONG

PRESUMPTIVE EVIDENCE.

WITH A PREFACE, AND CURIOUS ANECDOTES.

The romantic Drama of the MAID AND THE MAGPIE has excited the deepest and most extraordinary interest, and is received with UNANIMOUS AND REPEATED SHOUTS OF APPLAUSE, at the Theatres of Covent Garden, Drury Lane, and Lyceum, London.

THE KING
versus
ELIZA FENNING

Proceedings on the Trial

of this Indictment at Justice Hall, Old Bailey,

before the Honourable Sir John Silvester, Recorder of the City of London,

Tuesday 11 April 1815.

ELIZA FENNING was indicted for that she, on the twenty-first day of March, feloniously and unlawfully and with malice aforethought did administer to and cause to be administered to Orlibar Turner, Robert Gregson Turner and Charlotte Turner (his wife) certain deadly poison (to wit, arsenic) with intent the said persons to kill and murder.

Second count, that she did cause to be taken by the same persons arsenic with intent to kill and murder them.

Third and fourth counts, as in the first and second counts, only charging the offence to be committed against Robert Gregson Turner only, and another count against Charlotte Turner only.

Mr Gurney was counsel for the prosecution.

Mr Shearman, clerk to the magistrates, at the Police Office, Hatton Garden, where the prisoner was examined
and who took the depositions upon her examination,
was the attorney for the prosecution.

Mr Alley was counsel for the prisoner.

Fenning.

List of the Jury.

William Bent of Parliament Street, coal merchant (foreman).
Jacob Jeans of Bridge Street, hatter.
William Bell of Bridge Street, mercer.
William Barnett of Bridge Street, sadler.
Francis Mackley of Bridge Court, gentleman.
Thomas Close of Manchester Buildings, coal merchant.
William Worsley of Charles Street, vintner.
William Crawford of Charles Street, cutler.
John Wilkinson of Charles Street, pawnbroker.
James Wood of Charles Street, huckster.
Thomas Gullan of Manchester Buildings, gentleman.
Edward Beesley of Charles Street, bottle dealer.[166]

---

166 This juror was noted to be 'deaf and obliged to have part of the evidence related to him by his brother jurymen, which he could not hear'.

The Trial.

Evidence for the Prosecution.

Mrs CHARLOTTE TURNER, sworn and examined by Mr GURNEY.[167]   **Charlotte Turner**
You are the wife of Mr Robert Gregson Turner? — I am.
He is a law stationer in Chancery Lane? — He is, sir.
I believe, Madam, your husband's father, Mr Orlibar, is a partner? He lives at Lambeth? — He does.
At what time did the prisoner come into your service? — About seven weeks before the accident, as cook.
After she came into your service, had you occasion to reprove her? — I had, about three weeks after she came.
What was the occasion that you reproved her? — I observed her one night go into the young men's room partly undressed. I said it was very indecent of her to go into the young men's room thus undressed.
What age were the young men? — I suppose seventeen or eighteen years old.
Sir JOHN SILVESTER: How many of them were there? — Two. I reproved her severely the next morning for her conduct; the excuse was that she was going to fetch a candle. I threatened to discharge her and gave her warning to quit, but she showed contrition. I forgave her for it, and retained her. That passed over.
Mr GURNEY: What was her deportment after that, for the remaining month? — I observed that she failed in the respect that she before paid me, and appeared extremely sullen.
Did she, after this, say anything to you upon the subject of yeast dumplings? — She did. A fortnight before the transaction, she requested me to let her make some yeast dumplings, professing herself to be a capital hand. That request was very frequently repeated.
On Monday 20 March, was anything said to you upon the subject of yeast? — She came up into the dining room and said the brewer had brought some yeast.
Had you given any order to the brewer to bring any yeast? — Oh, no! I told her I did not wish to trouble the man. That was not the way I had them made – I generally had the dough from the baker's; that saved the cook a great deal of trouble, and was always considered best – but, having this yeast, I said it was of no consequence. As the man had brought a little, the next day she might make some, I told her. On Tuesday morning, the

---

167   Charlotte Turner, born Charlotte Churchman [date unknown]; married 24 May 1814 to Robert Gregson Turner at St Matthew's, Ipswich, Suffolk; died [date unknown].

Fenning.

Charlotte Turner

twenty-first, I, as usual, went into the kitchen. I told her she might make some, but, before she made the dumplings, to make a beef steak pie for dinner for the young men. As she would have to leave the kitchen to get the steaks, I did not wish her to leave the kitchen after the dumplings were made. I told her I should wish the dough to be mixed with milk and water. She said she would do them as I desired her; this was about 11.30 am. She carried the pie to the baker's before the kneading of the dough commenced. I told her I wished her not to knead the dough, that she might carry the pie to the baker's.

At about what time did she carry the pie to the baker's? — I suppose near 12.00 pm.

How soon after 12.00 pm did you go into the kitchen again, after she had been to the baker's? — I gave her directions about making the dough. I said, I suppose there was no occasion for me stopping. She said, Oh no, she knew very well how to do it; and then I went upstairs.

How soon after that did you go into the kitchen again? — Not more than half an hour. I then found the dough made; it was set before the fire to rise.

What other servant had you? — We have one more, a housemaid. Her name is Sarah Peer.

Where was she at the time the dough was made? — I had given Sarah Peer orders to go into the bedroom to repair a counterpane.

Then during the time that the dough was made, was any person in the kitchen but the prisoner? — I am certain there could be nobody.

This was about 12.30 pm? — I suppose it might be 12.30 pm. We dine at 3.00 pm, the young men at 2.00 pm.

In the interval between 12.30 pm and 3.00 pm, were you again in the kitchen? — I was in the kitchen two or three times, until the dough was made up into dumplings.

Where was the dough? — It remained in a pan before the fire for the purpose of rising, but I observed the dough never did rise.

Did you take off the cloth to look at it? — I did. My observation was that it had not risen, and it was in a very singular position, in which position it remained until it was divided into dumplings. It was not put into the pan as I have observed dough; its shape was singular; it retained that shape to the last.

It remained heavy all the time? — Yes, not rising at all. I am confident it never was meddled with, after it had been put there.

At about what time was the dividing of the dumplings to put them into the pot? — About 11.40 am. I was not in the kitchen at the time.

How late before you had seen it? — About half an hour before that time.

The Trial.

Charlotte Turner

A JUROR: Did you remark to the prisoner the singular appearance of the dough? — I did not remark to her the singular appearance. I told her it had never risen. The prisoner said it would rise before she wanted it.

Mr GURNEY: How many dumplings would there be? — Six.

It was afterwards divided into six dumplings? — Yes. The prisoner had divided it into six dumplings.

About 3.00 pm, did you sit down to dinner? — I did. These six dumplings were brought upon the table.

Did you make any observation upon their appearance? — I did. I told the other servant they were black and heavy, instead of being white and light.

Who sat down to dinner with you? — My husband, Mr Robert Gregson Turner, and his father, Mr Orlibar Turner. I helped them to some dumplings and took a small piece myself.

How soon afterwards did you find yourself ill? — I found myself affected in a few minutes after I had eaten. I did not eat a quarter of a dumpling. I felt myself very faint and in excruciating pain – an extreme burning pain which increased every minute. It became so bad I was obliged to leave the table. I went upstairs.

A JUROR: You ate nothing else? — Yes, I ate a bit of rump steak.

Who cooked that? — Eliza. When I went upstairs, I perceived my sickness had increased and my head was swollen extremely. I retched very violently.

Mr GURNEY: How soon after you had been upstairs did you find any of your family ill? — I was half an hour alone and wondered that they did not come to my assistance. When I came down, I found my husband and father very ill, both of them. I was very sick and ill, retching from 3.00 pm to 9.00 pm. At 9.00 pm it abated but did not cease. My head was swollen and my tongue and chest were swollen. We called in a gentleman who was near, and afterwards Mr Marshall, the surgeon.

You applied for the nearest assistance you could get? — Yes.

Cross-examined by Mr ALLEY.

This happened about six weeks after the girl came to live with you? — Yes.

You had no other cause of complaint except that you forgave her? — No.

On that day the coals had been delivered, had they not? — I do not think it was that day. The girl is here that received them. It could not be that day – she had no occasion to receive the coals.

The prisoner herself was taken ill, was she not? — I have heard so.

Fenning.

Orlibar Turner

Mr ORLIBAR TURNER, sworn and examined by Mr GURNEY.[168]

You are the father of Mr Robert Gregson Turner? — I believe I am.

On Tuesday 21 March, were you at your son's house in Chancery Lane? — I was; I dined there.

Your dinner consisted of yeast dumplings, beef steaks and potatoes? — It did.

After some time did Mrs Turner leave the room indisposed? — She did, sir.

After she was gone upstairs, you did not know that she was ill? — Not at the time she left the room.

Some time afterwards, did your son leave the room and go downstairs? — He did, sir, and I followed him very shortly. I had gone into the parlour below. I came into the passage. I met my son in the passage, at the foot of the stairs. He told me he had been very sick, and had brought up his dinner. I found his eyes were exceedingly swollen – very much indeed. I said I thought it very extraordinary. I was taken ill myself in less than three minutes afterwards. The effect was so violent that I had hardly time to get into the back yard before my dinner came up. I felt considerable heat across my stomach and chest, and pain.

What was the vomiting? Of the common kind? — I never experienced anything before like it for violence. I was terribly irritated.

How soon after did you observe any other of the family ill? — It was not more than a quarter of an hour when my apprentice, Roger Gadsden, was very ill in a similar way to myself.

Was your son sick also? — He was.

And while you and your son were sick and Gadsden was sick, where were you? — I was repeatedly in the parlour and the back yard. My son was up and downstairs at intervals. Gadsden, I believe, was in the kitchen below.

Did you observe the prisoner? Did she give you any assistance? — Not in the smallest. We were altogether alarmed. It was discovered that she did not appear concerned at our situation.

I need not ask you whether the appearance of you and your son, and all of you, must not be most distressing? — It was; more so than ever I witnessed in my life.

Did you observe whether the prisoner ate any of the dumplings that she had made? — I did not.

I take it for granted that you had suspicion of arsenic? — I had; I made a search the next morning.

---

168   Orlibar Turner, born [unknown]; married 21 September 1784 to Margaret Porter at St Andrew's, Holborn; died [unknown].

The Trial.

Sir JOHN SILVESTER: You expected it was poison? — I did.

Mr GURNEY: Did you observe the brown dish or pan in which the dumplings had been mixed? — I did – on the next morning, on the Wednesday morning.

Did you find anything in that pan that appeared to be the leavings of the dumplings? — I did: it sticked round the pan. I put some water into the pan and stirred it up with a spoon with a view to form a liquid of the whole. I found – upon the pan being set down for a moment or two, or half a minute, upon taking it slowly and in a slanting direction – I discovered a white powder at the bottom of it. I showed it to several persons in the house. I kept it in my custody.

Did you show it to Mr Marshall? — I kept it in my own custody for that purpose. I locked it up until Mr Marshall came. No person had access to it.

Had any arsenic been kept in any office in the house? — It had.

In what place? — In a drawer in the office, fronting the fireplace in the office.

What was it in? — In two wrappers, tied round very tight: the words, 'Arsenic, deadly poison' wrote on it.

Do you know whether the prisoner can read? — I believe she can both read and write.

[To Charlotte Turner.] Is that so, Mrs Turner?

CHARLOTTE TURNER: Yes, she can read and write very well.

Mr GURNEY: [to Orlibar Turner.] Mr Turner, was that drawer locked or open? — It always remained open. Any person may have access to it.

Who lit the fire in that office, do you know? — It was the prisoner's duty to do so.

Would she probably resort to there for paper to light the fire with? — Waste paper was kept in that drawer; she might properly resort to that drawer for paper to light the fire.

Had that parcel of arsenic been missed before that time? — I saw it there on 7 March, never after that time. I heard of it being missed about a fortnight before 21 March.

Did you make any observation about the appearance of the knives and forks? — I observed that the knives and forks we had to eat the dumplings with were black. There was no vinegar in the sauce at all. I have two of them in my pocket now, to show [two knives produced]; they have been in my custody ever since. I saw them with that blackness upon them the next day – it appeared upon them then. There is some little rust upon them now.

Did you, either on the day that this took place or afterwards, speak to the prisoner about these yeast dumplings – what they were made of? — I

Orlibar Turner

Fenning.

Orlibar Turner

did, the next day. I asked the prisoner how she came to introduce any ingredients into the dumplings that had been so prejudicial to us. She replied that it was not in the dumplings, but that it was in the milk that Sarah Peer brought in. I had several discourses with her on that day upon this subject, during the whole of which she persisted that it was in the milk, as before described.

What had that milk been used for, sir? — The sauce only. The prisoner made the dumplings with the refuse of the milk that had been left at breakfast.

Did the prisoner tell you what use had been made of the milk that had been fetched by Sarah Peer? — She did not. I asked her if any person but herself had mingled or had anything to do with the dumplings. She expressly said no.

Cross-examined by Mr ALLEY.

In the conversation you had with the prisoner, did not you tell her that, two weeks before, you had missed the poison? — I did not.

You say it was her duty to light the fire in the office. Did the clerks keep the door locked when they were not there? — I do not know.

Roger Gadsden

ROGER GADSDEN, sworn and examined by Mr GURNEY.[169]

You are an apprentice to Mr Turner? — I am.

Do you remember seeing, in a drawer in the office, a paper with 'Arsenic, deadly poison' on it? — I do, sir. The last day I saw it was Tuesday 7 March. I missed it in a day or two after.

Did you mention in the office that you had missed it? — I did, sir.

On Tuesday 21 March, did you between 3.00 pm and 4.00 pm go into the kitchen? — I did. I had dined at 2.00 pm.

When you went into the kitchen, did you observe anything there that came from the parlour table? — I observed there a plate on the table. On it was a dumpling and a half. I took a knife and fork up and was going to cut it, to eat of it. The prisoner exclaimed, 'Gadsden, do not eat that! It is cold and heavy. It will do you no good.' I ate a piece about as big as a walnut, or bigger. There was a small quantity of sauce in the boat: I took a bit of bread and sopped it in it, and ate that. This might be 3.20 pm.

How soon after that time did any of the family become ill? — I went into the office. Mr Robert Turner came into the office about ten minutes after and said he was very ill. They were all upstairs in the parlour. Not

---

169   Roger Gadsden, born March 28 1799; died on or before 22 February 1864. A fifteen-year-old at the time of the incident, and a sixteen-year-old at the time of the trial. Later a solicitor with a large family and resident in well-to-do areas of London and its environs.

The Trial.

the least alarm of anybody being ill then.

How soon were you taken ill? — About ten minutes after that, but not so ill as to vomit. In consequence of the distress the family were in, I was sent off to Mrs Turner, the mother. I was very sick going and coming back. I thought I should die.

Had the prisoner made any yeast dumplings for you the night before? — She had, for supper. I and the other maid, and herself, partook of them; they were quite different from these dumplings in point of colour and weight, light and white and very good.

A Juror: When the poison was missed, did you make any inquiry about it of the prisoner? — I did not.

Cross-examined by Mr ALLEY.

Do you usually keep the door locked when you are out of the office? — No.

Re-examined by Mr GURNEY.

Who made the fire in the office? — The prisoner. No person could go into the office until I did. Any person might go in and out in the day. At night it was locked.

What was kept in the drawer in which the arsenic was kept? — Loose paper.

Sir JOHN SILVESTER: Then your seeing her go to that drawer – it would not strike you as anything extraordinary? — No. I should not watch her to see what she did there.

Roger Gadsden

MARGARET TURNER, sworn and examined by Mr GURNEY.[170]

Upon this melancholy occasion, you were sent for? — I was.

When you arrived, you found your husband, son and daughter extremely ill, did you not? — I found them extremely ill.

I believe, madam, you found the prisoner ill and vomiting? — Very soon after I was there, she was sick, and vomiting.

Did you say anything to her while you were there that day respecting the dumplings? — I exclaimed to her, 'Oh, these devilish dumplings!' supposing they had done the mischief. She said, 'Not the dumplings, but the milk, ma'am'. I asked her what milk she meant. She said, 'The halfpennyworth of milk that Sally had fetched to make the sauce'.[171]

Margaret Turner

---

170 Margaret Turner, born Margaret Porter [date unknown]; married as a minor with the consent of her father Richard Porter on 21 September 1784 to Orlibar Turner at St Andrew's, Holborn; died [date unknown].
171 'Sally' *sic* in transcript. Read: Sarah Peer.

Fenning.

Margaret Turner

Did she say who had made the sauce? — My daughter. I said, 'That cannot be, it could not be the sauce'. She said, 'Yes, Gadsden ate but a very little bit of dumpling, not bigger than a nut, but he licked up three parts of a boat of sauce with a bit of bread'.

[To Charlotte Turner.] Was any sauce made with the milk that Sarah Peer had fetched?

CHARLOTTE TURNER: It was. I mixed it and left it for Eliza to make.

Robert Gregson Turner

ROBERT GREGSON TURNER, sworn and examined by Mr GURNEY.[172]

Did you partake of the dumplings at dinner? — Yes, I did.

Did you eat any of the sauce? — Not a portion of it whatever.

Were you taken ill, sir? — Soon after dinner I was, sir. I first felt an inclination to be sick: I then felt a strong heat across my chest. I was extremely sick.

Did it produce any swelling in you? — I was exactly as my father and wife were: sick, except stronger symptoms. I had eaten a dumpling and a half. I suffered more than any person.

Were your symptoms, and those of the others, such as could be produced by poison?[173] — I should presume so: all taken in the same way and pretty near the same time.

Sarah Peer

SARAH PEER, sworn and examined by Mr GURNEY.[174]

You are a servant to Mr Turner? — Yes.

How long have you lived in the family? — Near eleven months.

Do you recollect the circumstance of warning being given to the prisoner some time after she came? — I do, sir.

Did you hear her say anything after that respecting your mistress? — I heard her say that she should not like Mr or Mrs Robert Turner any more.

On the morning of 21 March, did you go for any milk? — Yes, after 2.00 pm. After I had had my dinner.

What had you eaten for dinner? — Beef steak pie. I had dined with the prisoner. I ate none of the dumplings myself.

Had you any concern whatever in making the dough for the dumplings? — No, sir.

---

172   Robert Gregson Turner, born on or before 11 December 1791; married 24 May 1814 to Charlotte Churchman at St Matthew's, Ipswich, Suffolk; died [date unknown].

173   An interesting variation on this question (but one which corresponds less naturally with the answer provided by the witness) is given in the *Proceedings of the Old Bailey*: 'Were your symptoms any other but such as would be produced by poison?'

174   Sarah Peer, perhaps born circa 1789; perhaps died on or before 19 January 1830.

The Trial.

Sarah Peer

Or the sauce? — No, sir.

Were you in the kitchen when the dough was made? — No, sir. I never meddled with it or put anything to it. I never was in the kitchen until I went up to make the beds, a quarter after eleven, until I came down again.

You, I believe, had permission of your mistress to go out that afternoon? — It was directly after I took up the dumplings, and then I went out directly. I came home at 9.00 pm exactly.

In eating of the beef steak pie, had you partaken of any of the crust? — Yes. I was not at all ill. I had eaten some dumplings she had made the night before. I never tasted any better. They were all made out of the same flour.

Had you had any difference with your mistress any time? — No.

Cross-examined by Mr ALLEY.

Were not the coals delivered in the house that day? — No.

Then it is not true that you were set to watch the coals coming in? — No.

As the dumplings were taken out of the pot, you went out? — Yes.

Had the prisoner and you been on good terms? — At times, sir.

When was the last quarrel? — Two or three days before, she had taken something out of my drawer for a duster. I said I did not like to lead that life: without, she altered her temper.

How long before that had you quarrelled with her? — About a week, or a week and a half.

What might that quarrel be about? — I cannot say.

Was it the habit of your house for the servants to take it turn about to go out of a Sunday? — Yes.

Who did you go to visit on Tuesday? — My sister, at Hackney

When had you been to your sister's before that? — About a month.

Whose turn was it to go out before this Tuesday? — Mine.

The prisoner lived seventeen weeks in your master's house. Did it happen that you ever went to visit your sister but on a Sunday? — Never, except on that day.

I suppose you occasionally went into the office where these young men were? — Very seldom.

You knew the waste paper was kept in the office? — Yes, but mistress always kept it upstairs in the dining room for my use.

You knew there was waste paper in the office? — No, sir. I never touched any there. I did not know it for a certainty. There might be waste paper there, but I never touched it.

Did you not know there was poison kept there? — No. I never went to the drawer in the office, nor never knew there was poison kept there to

Fenning.

Sarah Peer

kill rats and mice.

Re-examined by Mr GURNEY.

You went to see your sister that lived at Hackney? — Yes.

And the reason you went away as soon as you took the dumplings up was to arrive there and see your sister in time? — Yes.

Were the yeast dumplings made the night before different, or not? — Very different, and good, and of a different shape.[175]

Orlibar Turner

Mr ORLIBAR TURNER, recalled.

Sir JOHN SILVESTER: Did you keep this arsenic to poison the mice that infested the office? — Yes: it was only to be used in the office to destroy the mice and for no other purpose. This poison had not been used before for a year and a half.

William Thiselton

WILLIAM THISELTON, sworn and examined by Mr GURNEY.[176]

WITNESS: I am an officer of Hatton Garden police office.

MR GURNEY: Did you take the prisoner into custody? — I did, on 23 March, the day before Good Friday.

While she was sitting in the room in the office, did she say anything respecting the poison or the yeast? — I asked her whether she suspected there was anything in the flour. She said she had made a beef steak pie that day with the same flour that she made the dumplings with; that her and her fellow-servants, and one of the apprentices, had dined off the pie. I then observed, if there was anything bad in that flour, it must have hurt them as well as her. She said she thought it was in the yeast; she saw a red sediment at the bottom of the yeast after she had used it.

Joseph Penson

JOSEPH PENSON, sworn and examined by Mr GURNEY.[177]

You are a servant to Mr Edmonds, the brewer in Gray's Inn Lane? — Yes.

Were you in the habit of taking table beer to Mr Turner's? — Yes.

---

175 The *Newgate Calendar* adds an interesting detail: 'While the trial was proceeding, William Fenning, the father of the prisoner, went to a public house and got a person (for he was too agitated himself) to write on a slip of paper that on 21 March he went to Mr Turner's, his daughter having sent for him in the morning, and that Sarah Peer told him Eliza had gone of a message for her mistress, whilst, at the same time, she was in agonies below stairs from the effect of having eaten of the dumplings; he then went home, and thought no more about it. When this note was written, it was handed to Mr Alley, who, standing upon tip-toe, showed it to the recorder, who leaned over and looked at it.'

176 William Thiselton, perhaps born 21 February 1783; perhaps died on or before 5 March 1826.

177 Perhaps read: Joseph Parson.

The Trial.

Had the prisoner made any application to you respecting yeast? — Yes, she asked me on Thursday. I told her if I came that way on Saturday I would bring her a bit; if not, on Monday. I brought the yeast on Monday morning. I took it out of the steelyards where the casks lay. It was the same yeast what the bakers have.

Joseph Penson

Cross-examined by Mr ALLEY.

When you brought the yeast to the house, you gave it to the housemaid, not the prisoner? — I gave it to the housemaid. She brought me a pot; I put the yeast in it.

SARAH PEER, recalled.

Sarah Peer

Sir JOHN SILVESTER: What did you do with the yeast? — I emptied it into a white basin. I told Eliza that the brewer had brought the yeast. She took the basin. I saw no more of it.

Mr JOHN MARSHALL, sworn and examined by Mr GURNEY.

John Marshall

WITNESS: I am a surgeon. On the evening of Tuesday 21 March, I was sent for to Mr Turner's family in a great hurry. I got there about 8.45 pm. I found Mr Turner and Mrs Turner very ill. All the symptoms attending the family were such as would be produced by arsenic. I have no doubt of it, by the symptoms. The prisoner was also ill – by the same, I have no doubt.

Mr GURNEY: Did Mr Orlibar Turner show you a dish or pan the next morning? — He did. I examined it. I washed it with a tea-kettle of warm water. I first stirred it and let it subside. I decanted it off. I found half a teaspoonful of white powder. I washed it a second time. I decidedly found it to be arsenic.

Will arsenic, if it is cut with a knife, produce the appearance of blackness upon the knife? — I have no doubt of it.

Did you examine the remains of the yeast? — There was not a grain of arsenic there; and I examined the flour tub – there was no arsenic there.

*

Mr GURNEY: That is the case on the part of the prosecution.

****

Evidence for the Defence.

The PRISONER: I am truly innocent of the whole charge, as God is my witness. I am innocent; indeed I am! I liked my place. I was very

Eliza Fenning

Fenning.

Eliza Fenning

comfortable.

Gadsden behaved improper to me. My mistress came and saw me undressed – she said she did not like it. I said, 'Ma'am, it is Gadsden that has taken liberty with me'. The next morning I said, 'I hope you do not think anything of what passed last night'. She was in a great passion and said she would not put up with it. I was to go away directly.

I did not look on Mrs Turner as my mistress but the old lady [Mrs Margaret Turner]. In the evening, the old lady came to town. I said, 'I am going away tonight'.

Mrs Turner said, 'Do not think any more of it: I don't'. She asked Mrs Robert Turner if she was willing for me to go. She said, No, she thought no more about it.

As to my master saying I did not assist him, I was too ill. I had no concern with that drawer at all: when I wanted a piece of paper, I always asked for it.

John Woodderson

JOHN WOODDERSON, sworn and examined by Mr ALLEY.

Witness, of 44 Eagle Street, Red Lion Square, deposed that he had known the prisoner upwards of eleven years and that she was an honest, sober, industrious, good girl.

Mrs Hutchinson

Mrs HUTCHINSON, sworn and examined by Mr ALLEY.

Witness, of 19 Little Queen Street, late of Red Lion Passage, and in whose service William Fenning lived previous to the business being taken by Mr Rabbeth, his present master, deposed that she had known the prisoner several years and gave her an excellent character.

Mrs Hinson

Mrs HINSON, sworn and examined by Mr ALLEY.

Witness, of the Orange Tree, in Orange Street, Red Lion Square, deposed that she had known the prisoner between eight and nine years and in speaking to her good character generally observed that she had been attended by her whilst ill and that she could not have received more attention from one of her own children.

Richard Maze

RICHARD MAZE, sworn and examined by Mr ALLEY.

Witness, of 6 Orange Street, Red Lion Square, also deposed to his knowledge of the prisoner and her good character and disposition.

John Smith

JOHN SMITH, sworn and examined by Mr ALLEY.

Witness, of 8 The Colonnade, Brunswick Square, deposed that he had known the prisoner well for several years and particularly as to her good character and behaviour during the time he had known her from his

The Trial.

intimate acquaintance with her parents.[178]

[Whilst the trial was proceeding, William Fenning, the father of the prisoner, went to the Pitt's Head public house in the Old Bailey, opposite the Sessions' House. He was anxious to get the statement that follows committed to paper, but being unable to do it himself from the agitation of his mind and his hand trembling very much, he there asked the witness John Woodderson to write for him – who, from the same causes, being equally incompetent, Fenning applied to another person in the room, a stranger, and asked him if he could write. He said he could, and then, upon the solicitation of Fenning, wrote in ink, on both sides of a small scrap of paper which Fenning gave him, to the following effect: 'That he, William Fenning, in consequence of being sent for by his daughter, the prisoner, in the afternoon that the affair happened, went to Mr Turner's between nine and ten o'clock in the evening. He had intended to go before, but forgot it, and had gone home after shutting up shop, when, recollecting himself, he said to his wife [that] Eliza had sent for him, but he had forgotten to go, and would go then. He accordingly went to Mr Turner's and rang at the bell, and the housemaid came to the door, and said, "I suppose you want Eliza". He said, "No, I don't want to see Eliza. I understand my daughter wishes to see me." She replied, "No, you cannot see your daughter, for she is sent out upon a particular message for my mistress". Upon that, Fenning observed it was of no consequence, that his daughter knew where to find him if she wanted him, and probably he would call again tomorrow, and then went away.'

When the note was written, it was given into court to be handed to Mr Alley, the prisoner's counsel. Mr Alley, after reading the paper, stood up on tiptoe on the seat, and showed it to the Recorder, who leaned over and looked at it, and they appeared to be consulting upon the contents of the paper. No further notice was taken of this paper, either by the Recorder or Mr Alley.]

ROGER GADSDEN, recalled.

The PRISONER: No, my lord, it's not that apprentice boy – it's not

John Smith

Roger Gadsden

---

178   Hone, writing as Watkins in *The Important Results of an Elaborate Investigation into the Mysterious Case of Elizabeth Fenning*, states that 'this witness was proceeding to relate a conversation with the prisoner, two or three days before the poisoning, which he considered as counter-circumstantial to certain testimony delivered upon oath for the prosecution, and in particular that he had met the prisoner on the Saturday preceding the day of the poisoning, which was on a Tuesday, and asked her where she lived and how she liked her place; and that she told him, and expressed her entire satisfaction with her situation'. However, they state, 'the Recorder would not suffer the witness Smith to proceed – he would not hear him – he said it was *not evidence*'.

Fenning.

Roger Gadsden

the younger apprentice I want – it's Thomas King that I want – the elder apprentice, who knows that I never went to the drawer in my life, for when I asked for paper, he always gave it me. And if he was here, he dare not deny the truth to my face, and I wish him to be sent for.

Sir JOHN SILVESTER: You should have had him here before.

The PRISONER: My lord, I desired him to be brought, and I wish him to be sent for now.

Sir JOHN SILVESTER: No, it's too late now. I cannot hear you. [To the witness.] You say the prisoner used to light the office fire? — Yes. I and my fellow-apprentice have seen her go to that drawer many times.

William Fenning

WILLIAM FENNING, entering the witness box.

WILLIAM FENNING: [Greatly agitated.] I am the father of the unfortunate girl, my lord. If you won't hear her, I hope you will hear me.

[Witness was proceeding to relate, amongst other circumstances, his having been denied access to his daughter, in the manner mentioned in the note delivered to Mr Alley and shown to the Recorder, and to state that his daughter, when he was denied, was lying in great agony below stairs from the effects of the poisoned dumplings.

The Recorder would not suffer the prisoner's father to go on – he put his hand out, and motioned to him to leave the witness box – he told him he could not hear him – it was too late – he must go down.

Finding that the recorder would not hear him, and being ordered down, the father of the prisoner left the witness box.]

Summing-Up.

[The Recorder, in summing up the evidence made remarks as he went on, and dwelt particularly on the prisoner's declaration to Sarah Peer that she should not like Mr and Mrs Turner any more; on her repeatedly requesting her mistress to let her make yeast dumplings; particularly her telling her mistress, when she complained they did not rise, that they 'would rise time enough', and on her telling Gadsden not to eat of the dumplings that had come downstairs – that they were cold and heavy, and would do him no good.

The Recorder observed that, vellum and parchment being very valuable, arsenic was kept to preserve these valuable things from the vermin called rats and mice; and that it was evident that the prisoner at the bar could not be ignorant of the poison, because it was written on *'Arsenic, deadly poison'*; and as this girl had an education, and could read and write, she could not be ignorant of the poison.

The Recorder concluded his charge in the following words, or words

The Trial.

to the like effect:]

Sir JOHN SILVESTER: Gentlemen, you have now heard the evidence given on this trial, and the case lies in a very narrow compass. There are but two questions for your consideration, and these are whether poison was administered, in all, to four persons, and by what hand such poison was given. That these persons were poisoned appears certain from the evidence of Mrs Charlotte Turner, Orlibar Turner, Roger Gadsden, the apprentice, and Robert Turner: for each of these persons ate of the dumplings, and were all more or less affected – that is, they were every one poisoned.

That the poison was in the dough of which these dumplings were composed has been fully proved, I think, by the testimony of the surgeon who examined the remains of the dough left in the dish in which the dumplings had been mixed and divided; and he deposes that the powder which had subsided at the bottom of the dish was arsenic.

That the arsenic was not in the flour, I think, appears plain from the circumstance that the crust of a pie had been made that very morning with some of the same flour of which the dumplings were made and the persons who dined off the pie felt no inconvenience whatever: that it was not in the yeast nor in the milk has been also proved; neither could it be in the sauce, for two of the persons who were ill never touched a particle of the sauce, and yet they were violently affected with retching and sickness.

From all these circumstances it must follow that the poisonous ingredient was in the dough alone; for, besides that the persons who partook of the dumplings at dinner were all more or less affected by what they had eaten, it was observed by one of the witnesses that the dough retained the same shape it had when first put into the dish to rise and that it appeared dark, and was heavy, and in fact never did rise.

The other question for your consideration is by what hand the poison was administered; and although we have nothing before us but circumstantial evidence, yet it often happens that circumstances are more conclusive than the most positive testimony. The prisoner, when taxed with poisoning the dumplings, threw the blame first on the milk, next on the yeast, and then on the sauce; but it has been proved, most satisfactorily, that none of these contained it, and that it was in the dumplings alone, which no person but the prisoner made.

Gentlemen, if poison had been given even to a dog, one would suppose that common humanity would have prompted us to assist it in its agonies; here is the case of a master and mistress being both poisoned, and no assistance was offered.

Gentlemen, I have now stated all the facts as they have arisen, and I

Sir John Silvester

Fenning.

Sir John Silvester leave the case in your hands, being fully persuaded that, whatever your verdict may be, you will conscientiously discharge your duty both to your God and to your country.

****

The Verdict: Guilty.
Sentence: Death.

Appendices.

APPENDIX I.

Examination at Hatton Garden.

On Thursday 30 March 1815, Eliza Fenning underwent a final examination at the Police Office, Hatton Garden, charged with attempting to poison the family of Mr Turner, law stationer, number 68 Chancery Lane, on the twenty-first instant.

Orlibar Turner deposed that, on Tuesday the twenty-first instant, on returning to town from his house in Lambeth, he was induced to dine at his house in Chancery Lane with his son and daughter in law. They had for dinner some yeast dumplings, with rump steaks and potatoes. They had nearly dined when Mrs Charlotte Turner, finding herself extremely unwell, retired to her room above stairs, and upon inquiry they found her complaining of violent sickness. Robert Turner and himself were soon afterwards taken very ill, and vomited dreadfully. The apprentice, Roger Gadsden, went into the kitchen and, seeing the remnant of the dumplings, was desirous of eating a part of them, but the prisoner, Eliza Fenning, endeavoured to dissuade him from it by saying they were cold and heavy, and would do him no good. He, however, did eat a small portion of them, and was afterwards seized with violent vomitings also. The prisoner made no inquiry, nor did she do anything to assist, but partook afterwards of the same dumplings, although she had had her dinner before, and was in consequence seized with similar vomiting. Having suspicion, he endeavoured to find arsenic in the house, but failed in so doing. A quantity of arsenic had for many months been deposited in a drawer in the office, tied up in wrappers, and written on, 'Arsenic, deadly poison', which had been missed about three weeks. This was kept, to be occasionally used to destroy mice, in the office drawers, where parchments and papers of consequence were deposited. Witness went into the kitchen, where seeing a brown dish or pan, in which the dumplings had been mixed, with water in it, he immediately examined it, and discovered, at the bottom of the dish, a powder which appeared to have separated from the dough which had remained in the dish. He took the dish, with its contents, and kept it for the examination of Mr Marshall and Mr Ogilvy, two medical gentlemen. The prisoner had lived in the family about five or six weeks, and admitted that no one but herself made the said dumplings.

John Marshall, surgeon, of Half Moon Street, Piccadilly, deposed that, about nine o'clock in the evening of Tuesday, the twenty-first instant, he was called to the family of Mr Turner. He found the prisoner, Eliza Fenning, lying on the stairs, apparently in great agony, and was informed she had vomited much. After

Fenning.

attending to her, he went upstairs, and found Mr Robert Turner and his wife in bed, each of them retching violently, Mr Robert Turner complaining of violent and excruciating pain in the stomach and abdomen. Witness was satisfied from the symptoms he saw in Mr and Mrs Robert Turner, Mr Orlibar Turner, the prisoner Eliza Fenning, and the apprentice, that they were affected by poison, and, he believed, arsenic. He had examined the dish and its contents, shown to him by Mr Orlibar Turner, and found a quantity of arsenic at the bottom of it. He separated it from the dough by the usual method, dissolving the dough in warm water, by which the arsenic fell to the bottom.

Charlotte Turner, the wife of Robert Turner, deposed that the prisoner lived with her about six weeks as a cook. About three weeks ago, witness had some dispute with the prisoner, on account of some indelicacy in her conduct, and gave her warning to quit, but afterwards took compassion on her, and changed her mind. The prisoner had frequently, within the last fortnight, teased her to let her make some dumplings for dinner, adding, 'You cannot believe how well I can make them'. Monday, the twentieth, she told witness that the brewer had brought some yeast, which she ordered without witness desiring her. Witness, in consequence, ordered her to make the dumplings she had been so long talking of for next day's dinner. Tuesday, the twenty-first, the prisoner went to Brooks Market for some beef steaks for dinner. She made a beef steak pie for dinner for herself and Sally, her fellow-servant, and the two apprentices. They had their dinner at two o'clock, and she made the dumplings for the family's dinner. Witness saw the dough after she mixed it up, and firmly believed the deleterious ingredients were then mixed in it, from its appearance being flat, black, and heavy.

Margaret Turner, wife of Mr Orlibar Turner, deposed that, on the evening of the above day, she was sent for to her house in Lambeth to come to town immediately. Witness arrived in Chancery Lane about eight o'clock, and found the family as already described. Witness, seeing the prisoner at the stair foot, made an observation respecting the dumplings, when the prisoner attributed it all to the milk that Sally had fetched, and of which Mrs Robert made the sauce.

Mr Robert Gregson Turner corroborated his father's evidence, with the addition that he was worse than any of them from eating the dumpling, he not having tasted any of the sauce.

Roger Gadsden, the apprentice, corroborated Mr Turner, sen.'s, evidence.

Sarah Peer, the housemaid, deposed that she had lived eleven months in Mr Turner's family. She recollected hearing the prisoner say, after her mistress gave her warning, that she should never like them any more. Witness, by desire of the prisoner, brought her a halfpenny-worth of milk to make the sauce, as she said she had not enough. Witness never entered the kitchen all the time the prisoner was getting the dumplings ready. Having leave to spend the day out from dinner time, she was busy upstairs making the beds, &c. The servants and apprentices

Appendix I.

dined at two, after which witness brought up the dinner as handed to her by the prisoner. She never tasted the dumplings, as she went out when the family sat down to dinner, and did not return until nine o'clock.

William Thiselton, the office, deposed that he apprehended the prisoner. He searched her person and box, but found nothing of a suspicious nature. She told him in the Office that she believed it to be in the yeast, as she perceived a white settlement at the bottom; or that the other girl, who was very sly and artful, might have put it in the milk.

She was committed for trial.

APPENDIX II.

The Petition for Royal Clemency.[179]

Editor's note.

The degree of literacy evident in this petition (transcribed here as per Watkins) suggests that Eliza received significant guidance from her supporters in its composition. Compare her unedited letter (Letter 33) in Appendix VII.

To His Royal Highness the Prince Regent,
in Council Assembled.

The humble Petition of Eliza Fenning, a Prisoner now
under Sentence of Death, in Newgate,

Sheweth,

That your petitioner, who is only of the age of 20 years, about the commencement of the month of January last, lived in the character of cook with Mr. Orlibar Turner, of Chancery Lane, Law Stationer, whose family consisted of himself, Mrs. Margaret Turner his wife, Mr. Robert Gregson Turner his son, and Mrs. Charlotte Turner his son's wife, with two apprentices, and two female servants, one of whom was your petitioner. – That on the 21st of March last, your petitioner made some yeast dumplings, in which it was proved at the trial of your petitioner, that the poison of arsenick was contained, and that Mr. Orlibar Turner, his son, his son's wife, Gadsden, one of the apprentices, and your petitioner, all ate part of those dumplings, and were severally taken ill by the effect of the arsenick contained in them.

That your petitioner being the cook-maid, who made the dumplings, was suspected by her master of having by design put the arsenick into the flour, and was accused at the Police Office, Hatton Garden, before the magistrates; by whom, after two examinations your petitioner was committed to Newgate.

That your petitioner was indicted at the last Old Bailey Sessions, charging her, that on the 21st day of March last, she feloniously and unlawfully did administer to, and cause to be administered to, Orlibar Turner, Robert Gregson Turner, and Charlotte Turner his wife, certain deadly poison, called arsenick, with intent the

---

179 Watkins, 71-72.

Fenning.

said persons to kill and murder.

That your petitioner most solemnly declares, in the presence of that Being, whose omniscience prevents all concealment, that she is totally innocent of the crime laid to her charge.

That your petitioner has been applied to, and solicited by some of her nearest friends, to declare her guilt, if she really were guilty; but as your petitioner is totally unconscious of any crime, she could only declare her innocence: – that from whatever causes her indisposition proceeded, it extended to her master, the son and his wife, and the apprentice Gadsden.

That your petitioner, who, by the sentence of the law, is condemned to enter into an awful eternity, would have gladly confessed her guilt, if she had offended, as she knows that contrition is the sure ground of that humility, without which she could not expect the pardon of an offended God. But your petitioner, in sacred truth, has nothing to confess on the accusation against her, but is utterly innocent of the crime laid to her charge.

And your petitioner most humbly hopes that she may receive the Royal pardon from the conviction under which she had been sentenced, and that she may be restored to society, and to those friends who have kindly interested themselves for her; and your petitioner shall ever pray for the gracious providence of Almighty God upon your Royal Highness and your Royal Family.

APPENDIX III.

The Coal Merchant's Records.[180]

Editor's note.

The coal merchant's records are of great significance for two reasons. The entry produced here not only proves that there was a delivery of coal to the Turners' home in Chancery Lane on the day of the poisoning, but also Charlotte Turner and the maid, Sarah Peer, were untruthful when they testified in court that no coal was delivered that day. Was this an honest mistake, or a deliberate lie?

The latter explanation is certainly tempting. The Turners were motivated to convince the jury that Eliza had at no time left the dumpling mixture unattended, allowing covert access to the kitchen to any person intent on poisoning the family; they were not keen to introduce the exculpatory possibility of an alternative assailant. Eliza herself found Thomas King in the kitchen while she was cleaning knives in a back room – he, of course, was never questioned about the reason for his being there. Eliza's various domestic duties and her scrupulous checking of deliveries would have given anyone with malevolent fantasies plenty of time to sprinkle some arsenic on the dumpling mixture which Eliza had set by the fire to rise.

John Watkins hints that, between Eliza's conviction and her execution, Orlibar Turner accessed the coal merchant's record of deliveries for the day of the poisoning, which proved beyond doubt that his daughter-in-law and the maid had lied, and chose to withhold his discovery from the authorities:

After Mrs Turner and her housemaid had sworn as they did that the coals did not come in that day, and that Elizabeth Fenning did not receive them, if it was proved, by subsequent evidence, that the coals did come in that day, and that Elizabeth Fenning was the person who did receive them, and was absent from the kitchen, there cannot be a thinking person who will believe that any jury would have found Elizabeth Fenning guilty upon such evidence.

But, having been found guilty upon that evidence, will it be believed that Mr Turner, having possessed himself of the knowledge of the most important fact of the delivery of the coals that day, by reference to Mr Wood's books and by a certificate which he obtained from the Coal Meters' office, yet did not take any steps in consequence of such information to prevent the execution of the unhappy

---

180   Watkins, 18.

Fenning.

girl, who had been convicted principally upon the evidence of Mrs Charlotte Turner and Sarah Peer?[181]

Orlibar Turner's deliberate inaction was surely an attempt to protect his son, Robert, who had publicly threatened to poison his family and himself. Orlibar must have known that Eliza's absence from the kitchen whilst taking delivery of the coal would have provided the perfect opportunity for his son to carry out his terrible threat. This idea could not be countenanced, and, by the time the coal merchant's books were seen by anyone who felt favourably towards Eliza – or even favourably towards the idea of justice and equality before the law – it was too late, and she had been hanged.

Extract from the ledger of Mr Wood, of Eaton Street, Pimlico, coal merchant, which is in conformity to his day-book.

Copy.

Mr Orlibar Turner.

1815.		£.	s.	d.
Feby. 14.	1 Chaldron Coals at 65s.	3	5	0
	Shooting and Meting.	0	1	11
March 21.	1 Chaldron Coals at 65s.	3	5	0
	Shooting and Meting.	0	1	11
April 25.	3 Chaldron Coals at 65s.	9	15	0
	Meting 1s 6d. Shooting 4s 3d.	0	5	9
July 29.	5 Chaldron Coals at 60s.	15	0	0
	Meting 2s 6d. Shooting 7s 1d.	0	9	7

Copy.

Westminster Land Coal-Meters' Office, Northumberland Street, Strand.

John Baker and Alexander Tullock, Principal Meters.

This is to certify that the under-mentioned Quantity of Coals are entered in the Books of this Office, and were measured under the Inspection of the sworn labouring Land Coal-Meter, whose name is under-written.

---

181 Watkins, 125-126.

Appendix III.

1815. Coals Meted for Mr J. Wood.

To Mr Turner.

March 21st, Twelve Sacks.

Carman, Benj. Edwards.

Meter, William Brown.

Examined at the Office the 28th August 1815, by John Brookes.

APPENDIX IV.

Affidavits of Samuel Davis and William Fenning.[182]

It seemed expedient, as the prosecutors' cook, Elizabeth Fenning, had been hanged upon the evidence of the Turners, of their housemaid, Sarah Peer, their apprentice, Roger Gadsden, their acquaintance, Mr Marshall, the surgeon, and the police officer, William Thiselton, that the father of Elizabeth Fenning should not be left to sorrow over the unburied body of his child without disturbance on the part of her prosecutors. Accordingly, two days after the execution, a turnkey of Newgate was selected to make the following affidavit against the afflicted parent:

Copy.

London, to wit. Samuel Davis, one of the principal turnkeys of his Majesty's Gaol of Newgate, maketh oath and saith that at an interview which lately took place between the late convict Elizabeth Fenning, who was executed on Wednesday last, and her father (at which interview this deponent and the Rev. Mr Cotton, chaplain of the said prison, were both present), and on several other interviews between them prior to her execution, her said father urgently entreated her in the following words, or words to the like effect: (that is to say) 'Oh! my dear child, when you come out on the gallows, tell everybody that you are innocent, and then I can walk the streets upright, as a man; but if you say you are guilty, I shall never be able to hold up my head among the public any more'.

(Signed) Samuel Davis.

Sworn at the Mansion House, in the City of London, the 28th day of July 1815.

(Signed) Samuel Birch, Mayor.

The prosecutors, having procured this affidavit to be made, now procured it to be inserted in different daily papers. It was carried to the newspaper offices, with introductory observations, which not even persuasions or payment could obtain admission for in the shape wherein they were originally tendered. Some of the papers rejected the observations entirely; others omitted the grosser part of this attempt at public delusion, and modified the preamble at pleasure. But the newspapers were not the only vehicle for the extension of the ill-timed attack upon poor Fenning. The turnkey's affidavit was printed in the shape of a handbill,

---

182   Watkins, 104-111. Minor changes have been made to the original spellings and punctuation where necessary.

Fenning.

thrown into houses, dropped upon shop counters, exhibited in windows, and circulated as widely as the prosecutors thought proper to circulate it.

Though these measures were resorted to, no step was taken by the father whilst his child lay above ground. He took no advantage of the mode and moment selected for attacking him to repel that attack. He did not do what he might have done; what, from the conduct of the prosecutors, it might have been supposed he would do; what it was natural to expect that the sight of his executed daughter would have prompted him to do: he abstained from making a public appeal. Though goaded by this unmanly and cruel attack, he chose to forbear the publication of any statement that might have visited the sins of the turnkey's affidavit tenfold upon his daughter's prosecutors. He buried her body before he uttered a syllable to the world to repel the odium he had sustained.

On 1 August, the day after the funeral, William Fenning applied to Mr Kinnaird, a Middlesex magistrate, to swear him to an affidavit in answer to the turnkey's: Mr Kinnaird refused to administer the oath, on the ground that persons daily assembled before Mr Turner's house. In the evening, he applied at Hatton Garden Office, attended by a friend or two, for the same purpose. The affidavit was handed to one of the police officers, in the outer office, who said, 'You'll not get this sworn here, I can tell you; the magistrate will not swear any affidavit of yours'. This officer loitered to read it, and then went into the justice-room with Fenning and his friends, and gave the affidavit to the magistrates' clerk. As soon as Fenning saw the clerk, he exclaimed, 'No! I shall not get it sworn here, I see; there'll be no justice here for me'.

His friend asked him why he said so. 'Why, sir, that gentleman,' he replied, 'who is the clerk, is a particular friend of Mr Turner's, and is against my daughter.'

'What is his name?'

'Mr Shearman: he lives in Hart Street, Bloomsbury, and visits at Mr Turner's: he took down what they said against my daughter when she was examined here.'

'Are you sure of that?'

'I am, sir, and he'll take care I shall not have my affidavit sworn here.'

'Well, we shall see.'

'We shall, sir,' said Fenning, 'and you will see what I tell you to be true, for it's not likely that the gentleman that was against my daughter all along will be for her now'.

It appeared, upon explanation, that Mr Shearman, the clerk to the magistrates, who took the depositions on the examinations of Elizabeth Fenning, became Mr Turner's attorney, and prosecuted her to conviction. As Fenning had anticipated, Mr Shearman addressed the magistrate across the table, to induce him to refuse swearing Fenning to the affidavit against that which his client had procured to be made by the turnkey. It was in vain that Fenning remonstrated: the magistrate

Appendix IV.

would not swear him, and Mr Shearman returned him the affidavit. The poor fellow, upon going away, whispered [to] Mr Shearman, loud enough to be overheard by some of the bystanders, 'I think, sir, you are a particular friend of Mr Turner's; you visit him?' Mr Shearman heard the remark – and was silent.

On the next day, 2 August, Fenning was sworn to his affidavit before the Right Hon. the Lord Mayor, at the Mansion-House. It is as follows:

Copy.

Middlesex. William Fenning, of no. 14 Eagle Street, Red Lion Square, maketh oath and saith that he hath read a certain printed paper which he hath been informed and believes has been most extensively distributed, and placed in shop windows, and other conspicuous places, by, through and under the direction of Mr Turner's family, and certain persons connected with the police or magistracy of the said County of Middlesex; which said printed paper is, or purports to be, an affidavit, or copy of an affidavit, sworn before the Lord Mayor at the Mansion House on the 28th day of July 1815, by Samuel Davis, one of the principal turnkeys of his Majesty's Gaol of Newgate, wherein the said Samuel Davis deposes or swears in the following words: (that is to say) 'That at an interview which lately took place between the late convict, Elizabeth Fenning, who was executed on Wednesday last, and her father (at which interview this deponent, and the Rev. Mr Cotton, chaplain of the said prison, were both present), and on several other interviews between them prior to her execution, her said father urgently entreated her in the following words, or words to the like effect: (that is to say,) "Oh! my dear child, when you come out on the gallows, tell everybody that you are innocent, and then I can walk the streets upright, as a man; but if you say you are guilty, I shall never be able to hold up my head among the public any more."' And this deponent further saith that he, this deponent, did not, at any interview which lately took place between this deponent and his daughter Elizabeth Fenning; nor did he, this deponent, at any other interview or interviews between them, prior to her execution, urgently or otherwise entreat or admonish her in the following words, or words to the like effect: (that is to say) 'Oh! my dear child, when you come out on the gallows, tell everybody that you are innocent, and then I can walk the streets upright, as a man; but if you say you are guilty, I shall never be able to hold up my head among the public any more'; but that this deponent did repeatedly and most earnestly entreat his said daughter, in words to the following or the like effect: (that is to say) 'Oh! my dear child, when you come out on the gallows, if you are not guilty, tell everybody that you are innocent'. And this deponent further saith that he hath upon various occasions earnestly entreated and solemnly conjured his said daughter to declare all, if anything, that she knew respecting the poisoning of the family of the said Mr Turner; and, notwithstanding many and repeated injunctions on his this deponent's part that she should make a full and open confession (if guilty) of the crime alleged against her, she, on all such

Fenning.

occasions up to and including the last interview he had with his said daughter previous to her execution, did totally deny all knowledge or participation of or in the said crime, and solemnly affirmed her innocence upon all and every such occasion or occasions as strongly as this deponent is informed and believes she did to the Rev. Mr Cotton, the Ordinary of Newgate, a few minutes previous to her ascending the scaffold, when she emphatically declared in words to the following or the like effect: (that is to say) 'Before the just and Almighty God, and by the faith of the Holy Sacrament I have taken, I am innocent of the offence with which I am charged'.

(Signed) William Fenning.

Sworn at the Mansion House of the City of London, this second day of August, 1815.

(Signed) Samuel Birch, Mayor.

*

After the above affidavit had been sworn, it was suggested that, on account of its length, some of the newspapers might decline inserting it; another affidavit was then prepared, shortening the first part of the former, in the following manner:

Copy.

Middlesex. William Fenning, of no. 14, Eagle Street, Red Lion Square, father of Elizabeth Fenning, executed on Wednesday last on a charge of poisoning the family of Mr Turner, maketh oath and saith that he hath seen a printed paper purporting to be an affidavit of Samuel Davis, a turnkey of Newgate, which has appeared in almost all the newspapers; and this deponent saith that the facts therein stated are wholly false and untrue, and that, on the contrary, this deponent, at every interview with his said daughter, when her guilt or innocence was the subject of conversation, did most earnestly entreat and solemnly conjure his said daughter to declare all, if anything, that she knew respecting the poisoning of the family of the said Mr Turner; and, notwithstanding many and repeated injunctions on his, this deponent's, part, that she should make a full and open confession, if guilty, of the crime alleged against her, she, on all such occasions up to and including the last interview he had with his said daughter previous to her execution, did totally deny all knowledge or participation of or in the said crime, and solemnly affirmed her innocence upon all and every such occasion or occasions as strongly as this deponent is informed and believes she did to the Rev. Mr Cotton, the Ordinary of Newgate, a few minutes previous to her ascending the scaffold, when she emphatically declared in words to the following or the like effect: (that is to say) 'Before the just and Almighty God, and by the faith of the Holy Sacrament I have taken, I am innocent of the offence with which I am charged'.

(Signed) W. Fenning.

Appendix IV.

Sworn at the Mansion House of the City of London, this second day of August 1815.

(Signed) Samuel Birch, Mayor.

*

That Mr Turner was himself the procurer of the turnkey's affidavit is publicly evidenced by a letter that appeared in the public papers, in consequence of an address to the Rev. Mr Cotton, the Ordinary, strongly animadverting upon the affidavit and calling upon that gentleman for an avowal respecting it. The letter, which delivers up Mr Turner as the instigator of the affidavit, bears the affidavit maker's signature, and is as follows:

Copy.

Sir,

The writer of the letter to the Rev. Mr Cotton, in your paper of yesterday, has treated me very cruelly and unjustly by charging me with making an illegal affidavit to wound the feelings of a poor man, when, on the contrary, it was at the particular desire of Mr Turner that I made that affidavit, which is nothing but the truth, for the purpose of saving Mr Turner's house!

I do not pretend to say that Mr Fenning did not believe his daughter to be innocent; nor did I make the affidavit to wound his feelings, but to protect Mr Turner. And I respectfully assure you that, although turnkey of Newgate, I have as much feeling for the distress of my fellow-creatures as the writer of that letter.

I am your humble servant,

(Signed) Samuel Davis.

August 3, 1815.

APPENDIX V.

'Effects of Arsenic upon Yeast Dough' and 'Effects of Arsenic upon the Knives'.[183]

EFFECTS OF ARSENIC UPON YEAST DOUGH.

That part of the evidence relative to the weight and colour of the dumplings, and particularly of Mrs Charlotte Turner's evidence, manifestly tended to persuade the jury that their heaviness and blackness were in consequence of arsenic being in the dough; a persuasion, the effect of most loose and erroneous reasoning, and entirely devoid of rational support.

If the dumplings were poisoned at all, and there is no evidence that they were – if they were poisoned with arsenic, and no witness proves that there was a single grain of arsenic in the dumplings: – but admitting that they were, the reasonable presumption is that the arsenic was not incorporated in the dough at the time of the making, but that it was sprinkled or strewed on after the dough was put before the fire to rise.

Now, it is by no means difficult to incorporate arsenic with dough prepared for dumplings, commonly called yeast dumplings, after the first mixing of the ingredients, so as to render the dough poisonous to any person who may eat of it. The colour of arsenic is not different from the colour of flour: one resembles the other so closely that none but a person acquainted with the peculiar characteristics of arsenic can distinguish it from flour, even when casually sprinkled, still less when the two substances are mixed together.

Arsenic mixed with dough containing yeast will not prevent the mixture from rising, although the quantity of arsenic exceed two thirds of the mass. It is generally known that yeast contains a large quantity of carbonic acid gas in a concentrated state: the effect of heat extricates the bubbles of gas, and in the act of extrication distends the dough, until all further attraction for caloric, or heat, ceases, by the total absence of gas. In this state, if the mass be confined at its sides, its surface will become elevated, and present the appearance of what is termed rising.

It is evident that to prevent dough from rising, the extrication of carbonic acid gas by caloric, or heat from the fire, must also be prevented; and this can only be done by saturating the gas with an alkali; thereby breaking down the chemical aggregation, which is produced by the affinity of an acid to an alkali.

---

183 Watkins, 68-70.

Fenning.

Arsenic not being an alkali, and therefore incapable of saturating carbonic acid gas, it cannot prevent dough, or any other matter containing carbonic acid gas, from rising, when exposed to the action of caloric, or heat.[184]

Hence it is clear that so much of the Recorder's charge to the jury as instructed them that the heaviness and black appearance of the dumplings were occasioned by the arsenic, was nugatory, and unsupported by fact or experience.

EFFECTS OF ARSENIC UPON THE KNIVES.

That arsenic did not blacken the two knives produced by Mr Orlibar Turner on the trial, out of the three used upstairs at dinner, is as certain as that Mr Marshall swore it would blacken them.[185]

A yeast dumpling, compounded with a very large proportion of arsenic, was boiled, and afterwards cut to pieces with a knife purposely cleaned. The knife was carefully put by, with whatever of the dumpling remained on its sides after the cutting: when dry, the crumbs were removed, and there was not the least blackness on the knife.

A gentleman of chemical eminence, in the city, put more arsenic into a pint of water than could be held in solution, and boiled it at a sand heat. A clean knife, being placed in the water whilst hot, remained there until it was cold. The knife was then taken out wet, and remained untouched until the blade became perfectly dry. It was in no way whatever discoloured.

Arsenic, moistened with water, has been formed into a sort of paste, and placed upon the blade of a knife to dry there, without producing any discolouration on the surface of the blade.

Arsenic, moistened with water, has been rubbed upon the blade of a knife with the fingers, and suffered to dry on without changing the colour of the steel.

The production of the two blackened knives, therefore, was no more proof of the presence of arsenic in the dumplings than Mr Marshall's testimony to that effect.

---

184 A footnote states, 'A variety of chemical experiments as to the effects of arsenic upon dough were made by a medical gentleman [Dr Thomas Wansbrough], and detailed at considerable length in a paper which was also sent in to the office of the Secretary of State for the Home Department, about the same time as the preceding papers; the results of those experiments were as above stated. Numerous applications by the gentleman himself, and at his request, both in writing and by attendance, have been made at Lord Sidmouth's office for those experiments, but without effect. If procured, they would have been published here; but neither the original paper, nor a copy of it, could be obtained.'

185 A footnote states, 'The impossibility of blackening knives with arsenic was also amongst the experiments submitted in the last-mentioned paper to the Secretary of State'.

APPENDIX VI.

The Opinions of Mr and Mrs Hardy.[186]

It would be difficult, perhaps, to adduce an object of grosser or more wanton calumny than the late Elizabeth Fenning. Her prosecutors themselves encouraged, by their silence, the circulation of the aspersions upon her when living, and entertained them after she had been executed. Their respectability, by which is understood their opulence, was pitted against the humble poverty of their servant maid, and all the masters and mistresses of families, whose credulity or idleness rendered them proper subjects for alarums, were incessantly devoted to the vociferous execration of the wickedness of servants, who poison those who give them bread and work. Thus a sort of general cry was raised for the hanging of Elizabeth Fenning as an example to all maidservants suspected, upon presumption, of murderous inclinations. In aid of this wise and salutary feeling, it was generally and positively affirmed that Elizabeth Fenning lived in a family which she attempted to poison twice before she went to live at Mr Turner's, and Mr Turner himself was in possession of that report three months before Elizabeth Fenning's execution, with the means in his power of ascertaining whether it was true or not.

As far back, perhaps, as that time before the execution, the report was stated to a person with such marks of certainty and conviction on the mind of the narrator, that the person to whom it was related gave his informant full credit for being well and truly informed, and thought nothing further of Elizabeth Fenning until, on 26 July, perceiving crowds of people hurrying past his door in one direction, and inquiring the cause, he was informed that 'the girl was going to be hanged for poisoning the family in Chancery Lane'. He then recollected what he had heard so long ago, and being now told that she persisted in denying her guilt at the time she was locked up in her cell the night before, he went into the Old Bailey for the purpose of seeing how this hardened being would quit the world. He was much surprised to observe a young girl suffer death with immovable firmness, and was shocked at the depravity of a heart that could cease to beat in this world without avowing the horrible crime of a third hardened attempt to commit murder. He mentioned in the course of the morning to several persons the extraordinary obduracy of the girl he saw executed; and, upon a doubt being expressed of her guilt, he related her alleged attempts to poison the last family she lived in,

---

186 Watkins, 132-145.

Fenning.

previous to going into Mr Turner's service. In the course of the day, during his absence from home, he was called on by a respectable gentleman, whom he was acquainted with, and who left a message that he was desirous of hearing anything respecting Elizabeth Fenning, and that he would call the following morning to see if he could obtain anything new.

The next morning, Thursday 27 July, on this person being called on by his friend, he related to him her attempts at poisoning, which he had been so credibly informed of some months before. His friend doubting the fact, to assure him of it, he insisted on his accompanying him to a Mr C., the person who related it to him. On their way, his friend mentioned certain circumstances which induced him to imagine that Mr C. might have been mistaken. When they saw Mr C., he was desired to state what he had before related, as above mentioned, respecting Elizabeth Fenning's trying to poison the family she lived with before she went to Mr Turner's. Mr C. said he had since heard some things which made him think that it was possible she was not guilty; he was, however, desired to give his authority for the positive statement he had before made of Elizabeth Fenning's alleged nefarious attempt. Mr C. named a tenant of his, a Mrs B., who, he said, was then ill. The person, however, who had brought his friend to Mr C. to witness what took place, was determined to trace the report to its source, and persisted in seeing Mrs B., who, when seen, said she had certainly related it to Mr C., and that she herself had been told it by two or three persons; and at length named a young woman, who lived with a Mr King, who had a son apprentice to Mr Turner, as her particular informant. Mr King, she had heard, lived in some street in the Strand, near the New Church, but could not tell where. The person and his friend, after much search, found Mr King, a dyer, at 44 Essex Street. They told Mr King they wished to ask a question of his daughter, which he complied with; and when she, with her mother, appeared, she was asked what she had related to Mrs B. respecting the before-mentioned report. Miss King seemed surprised at the question, and, after a little explanation, her father said he believed it was not his daughter, but his shopwoman whom they wanted. He called her up and, the same question being put to her, she said that she had told Mrs B. that Elizabeth Fenning had twice attempted to poison the family she had lived with before her going to Mr Turner's; and she related some other particulars. Being asked where she had obtained that information, Mr King and she gave an account to the following purport:

The latter end of April last, Mr King's shopwoman went to Mr Peck's, grocer, 175 Strand, on an errand for the family. Whilst there, a young man of Mr Peck's related that Mr Turner's servant, who had poisoned the family, had twice attempted to poison the family she lived servant to before she went to Mr Turner's; that her second attempt was made by putting arsenic in a pot of porter, which was detected; that she was instantly turned away; and that the family she lived with, and so attempted to poison, was Mr Hardy's, a grocer, in Portugal Street. As soon

Appendix VI.

as Mr King's shopwoman returned home, she told Mr King what she had heard, and, it being new to him, he desired her to go back to Mr Peck's and inquire there from whom they got the intelligence. She accordingly made the inquiry, and was answered, they had it from Mr Hickson, the oilman. Mr Hickson's female servant happening to be in Mr Peck's shop, and hearing the inquiry and answer, invited Mr King's shopwoman to go home with her to her master, Mr Hickson, and they both left Mr Peck's for that purpose. At Mr Hickson's, Mr King's shopwoman saw a person whom she took to be Mr Hickson, who related to her the circumstances as she had heard them at Mr Peck's, and she then went home and acquainted Mr King with what she said Mr Hickson had told her.

Mr King here stated, that from his connexion with Mr Turner, his son being apprentice to him, he had thought it his duty to make Mr Turner acquainted with the circumstances as they had been related by his shopwoman, and he immediately went to Mr Turner and informed him of the particulars, to the above effect.

The person who, with his friend, had thus called upon Mr King and obtained this information then proposed that, for the purpose of further elucidation, Mr King's shopwoman should go with them to Mr Hickson's, which Mr King assented to.

Mr Hickson is an oilman, at 170 Strand, near Surrey Street. He was not at home. His servant girl was seen, who corroborated everything related by Mr King's shopwoman as having taken place in Mr Peck's shop, the second time of Mr King's shopwoman's going there; and Mr Hickson's servant said that when she brought Mr King's shopwoman home with her, her master, Mr Hickson, was in the shop, and she told him that the young woman then with her wanted to ask him a question, and that she herself went downstairs with the grocery she had been buying for the family, and left Mr King's shopwoman with her master.

After waiting some time, Mr Hickson came in, and was briefly informed of the object of the visit. In answer to various questions, he said he could not tell anything about such a report. He had heard 'many reports'. He certainly knew Mr Hardy, the grocer, in Portugal Street, and he certainly had some conversation with him about the girl, but he 'could not exactly tell what'. He had no 'recollection whatever' of the report alluded to having been mentioned by Mr Hardy; nor did he believe it was; nor did he remember that such an inquiry had been made of him as Mr King's shopwoman stated.

Mr Hickson's servant, being again called, related, in the presence of her master, what she had before said, and that she had introduced Mr King's shopwoman to her master as before mentioned, and left them together, and went downstairs; but what either her master or the young woman said she did not hear, as she was in haste to take her grocery into the kitchen.

Mr King's shopwoman said she was not accustomed to go to Mr Hickson's. She could not say whether Mr Hickson was the gentleman she saw or not; but the gentleman that she did see, when taken there by Mr Hickson's servant, and

Fenning.

whom she supposed to be Mr Hickson, was the person who had corroborated the information she received, as before related.

Much conversation then ensued with Mr Hickson, and different questions were put to him as to his conversation with Mr Hardy, the first time he saw him after the poisoning of Mr Turner's family. Mr Hickson at length said that Mr Hardy had told him something about the tea-kettle being poisoned when the girl lived there. This was all that could be obtained from Mr Hickson, who, upon understanding that it was intended to see Mr Hardy, recommended it as a necessary measure for procuring precise information.

The person and his friend who were pursuing these inquiries in order to trace the report then went to Mr Hardy, grocer, 20 Portugal Street, Lincoln's Inn Fields. Mr Hardy was in the shop weighing tea. He was asked to state what the conduct of Elizabeth Fenning was whilst she was in his service and what he knew of her. Mr Hardy said that if he was asked his opinion of her, he had only to say that he had no doubt she was guilty of poisoning Mr Turner's family; no doubt of it whatever. He was answered that it was her behaviour whilst in his family that information was wanting upon. Mr Hardy said that she was a bad girl; a bold, sly, artful, designing girl. She first come[187] there on a Saturday night, late, with a lie in her mouth; with an excuse about not being able to get her clothes from her mother's that night, which was a lie. It must have been eleven o'clock that Saturday night as she came, and if he had been Mrs Hardy, he would never have let her enter the doors at that time of night; he told Mrs Hardy so then, and a many times afterwards. He did not like the girl at all. She was fond of hearing herself talk and gossip and he never liked her from the first moment as she came into the house.

Mr Hardy was then asked to communicate the particulars of the attempts made by Elizabeth Fenning to poison his family. Mr Hardy said, as to that, he had nothing to say; he knew nothing about it, and could tell nothing about it; he had nothing to say about it at all. Whilst she was there, he had a bad opinion of her; a very bad opinion, and never did like her. She was a hoity-toity, wild, giddy, unsettled sort of a girl, curious and inquisitive, and minding what did not concern her; and nothing that nobody could say would never persuade him but what she was a very bad girl indeed.

Mr Hardy was here particularly pressed to relate what he knew, if anything, as to Elizabeth Fenning's attempts at poisoning his family; and during this part of the conversation Mrs Hardy came from the parlour behind the shop, and began to join in it. Upon this topic both Mr and Mrs Hardy were evidently sore: Mr Hardy said he had nothing to say about it, and Mrs Hardy said so too.

---

187 Mr Hardy is presented throughout Hone's account (published under the name of Watkins) as a man whose grasp of grammar was incompletely developed, or subject to deterioration depending on the level of animation to which he rose. Mrs Hardy is not suggested to be any better.

Appendix VI.

Mr Hardy was asked if he knew Mr Hickson, the oilman, in the Strand. He said he did, and inquired, 'What of Mr Hickson?' He was requested to relate the conversation that he had with Mr Hickson, the first time they met after the poisoning of Mr Turner's family. Mr Hardy said he had nothing to relate of any conversation with Mr Hickson; he could not tell anything at all about it; and he desired to know the reason of the inquiries put to him. Mr Hardy was briefly informed of the report that had been circulated of the girl's attempting to poison his family; that it had been traced to Mr Hickson's; that Mr Hickson had been seen, who had referred to Mr Hardy as the person best adapted to state what had taken place in his own family.

Mr Hardy said he had nothing to state, and persisted in not being able to recollect anything he had said to Mr Hickson. He was asked about the poison in the porter, which he disclaimed all knowledge of and said it was utterly false. He was then asked respecting any other attempt at poisoning whilst the girl lived with him. Both Mr and Mrs Hardy refused to say anything more about the girl whilst living with them; and Mrs Hardy, on her husband being questioned, said he knew nothing at all about it, and they, neither of them, had anything to say about it, and persisted in refusing to say anything more.

Notwithstanding this declaration, Mr Hardy was requested to state what he knew respecting the poisoning of a tea-kettle whilst Elizabeth Fenning lived in his service. Mr Hardy declined saying anything upon the subject. He was then asked to relate what he had said to Mr Hickson respecting Elizabeth Fenning poisoning their tea-kettle; and he was informed that Mr Hickson had, that morning, mentioned the circumstance of the tea-kettle upon the reports relative to the alleged poisoning in his, Mr Hardy's, house, being traced to Mr Hickson's.

Mr Hardy, upon this being told him, observed, that in consequence of what had been said, he would relate what he knew about the tea-kettle, but Mrs Hardy interrupted him, and would not let him speak: she said, that it was she who knew about the tea-kettle, that Mr Hardy knew nothing at all about it but what she had told him, and if anything was to be told, she would tell all about it. Mrs Hardy accordingly proceeded to relate as follows:

'One day, I went into the parlour, and the tea-kettle was upon the fire, and I see the tea-kettle a-frothing at the mouth. With that, I says to myself, "Lord bless me!" – says I – "What can make the tea-kettle froth at the mouth?" Thinks I to myself, "I've heard of pizen being put into tea-kettles"; and still the tea-kettle kept on frothing at the mouth. With that I takes me the tea-kettle off the fire, and goes into the yard and empties it; and then I wrenches it out with cold water, and wrenches it again and again, and fills it with clean water; and then I comes in again and puts the tea-kettle upon the fire.'

Here Mrs Hardy paused.

'And pray, madam, what further took place then?'

Fenning.

'Nothing further, sir; that's all as I know about the matter; and now I've told you the whole truth.'

'Then, madam, after you had washed out the tea-kettle that contained, as you supposed, poison, what did you say to Eliza Fenning?'

'Lord bless me, sir!' said Mrs Hardy. 'I don't say it was Eliza Fenning as did it; it mought have been her, or it mought not; I don't know as she lived with us at the time; she mought, or she mought not; or it mought have been a year before, or a year after she lived with us; I am sure I can't say; but this I know as Mr Hardy never had no peace of mind whilst Eliza Fenning lived here, nor never would let me rest till we got rid of her.'

'But, madam, whether it was Eliza Fenning or not that lived with you when the tea-kettle was poisoned --'

'Lord bless me!' says Mrs Hardy. 'I don't say it was pizened.'

'But whether it was or not, madam, as the frothing of the tea-kettle led you to think about poisoning, and made you suspicious and empty it, what did you say to the servant girl after you had emptied the kettle and put it on the fire?'

'What did I say, sir?'

'Yes, madam; what remark did you make to the servant girl who then lived with you about the frothing of the tea-kettle?'

'Lord bless me, sir! I said nothing. What should I say? I thought no more about it – not I. But it was a very strange thing; and so I thought! I said nothing about it to nobody:-I did not even tell Mr Hardy of it; not till after as I heard as Mr Turner's family had all been pizen'd, and found as the girl as did it lived with us; and then, when I heard that, I up and told Mr Hardy about the tea-kettle; for Mr Hardy never knew of it before.

Mr Hardy said, no; he never had; that was the first time that Mrs Hardy told him of it.

This being everything that Mr and Mrs Hardy could say about the tea-kettle, they were both requested to state particularly any and every circumstance of the girl's conduct that was improper whilst she was there.

Mr Hardy said, that she was altogether a girl that he never did or could like. He said, God forgive him! He suspected her from the very moment she first came into the house. Many servants that had lived with him and robbed him, and he never had no suspicion of them as he had of this girl. And, from the very first moment as he set eyes upon the girl, he could not bear her; there was something about her as made him think she was not a fit girl for them, and he told his wife so; and, what was more, as Mrs Hardy did not think proper to get rid of her, he told Mrs Hardy that he never would go out of a Sunday and leave the house alone with the girl in it by herself. There was a chap as came after her when she was there, and he did not approve of it: he knowed nothing of who he was, nor what he

Appendix VI.

was, but he did not like his looks; and, as to inquiring who he was, it was nothing to him, for he was determined she should not stop long; and so, all the while she was there, he and Mrs Hardy never went out together on a Sunday; but when he went out, Mrs Hardy stopped at home, and when Mrs Hardy went out, he stopped at home, for he was determined he would not have the house left.

Mr Hardy was asked if Elizabeth Fenning, whilst she lived there, had ever done anything to warrant these suspicions? He said, no, he could not say as ever she had, but he looked upon her as a deep, sharp girl, and she had got things he did not think she had come honestly by, and she was never easy but when she was reading, and was everlastingly inquisitive and prying. She made several attempts to get at his son's books. He was asked what sort of books they were – if he meant account books, or what other books? Mr Hardy explained by saying, no, they were printed books, such as his son read – his son's collection of books he meant – and the things as he meant she did not come honestly by was a couple of handsome volumes, all done over with gold at the back, not books fit for a servant girl to read: they belonged to what they called Fielding's Works. He asked her how she came by them. She said a mistress she lived with had given them to her, but was it likely that a mistress would give a servant a couple of such books as them? It was not likely, and he did not believe it.

Mr Hardy was asked if the girl did get at his son's books. He said, no, she never did get at them – for why? He took good care of that – he always kept them locked up, or else she would have got at them, no doubt – but this he must say, that she was a sly, quick, clever, artful girl, as sharp as a needle, and was of that inquisitive deep turn, that his mind always misgave him whilst she lived there; and then there was the books as she used to read, he did not like it – and she was a girl that he did not like, for he never know'd no good come of servants reading; and he had no doubt that she poisoned Mr Turner's family, and was rightfully hanged – no more than he stood there – not as she had never done no harm to him or his – but she was a girl as he never could fancy, God forgive him! He could not tell why nor wherefore – and then, as to her lies, why the reason as she went away was this. He sent her one night, between ten and eleven o'clock, to the public house for a glass of mixed liquor, and she stopped so long that it was out of all reason, and when she came back she said as they had not got the water hot. However, he know'd it was a lie when she said so, so he told her his mind; and, a night or two afterwards, he sent her again, and she stopped again; so when she come to the door, he went to let her in, and there was she with the glass in her hand. "'And pray, madam,' says I, 'where have you been?' 'I've been to the public house,' says she. 'Yes,' says I, 'you have, madam – pray walk in.' She made the same excuse as before, that the water was not hot. So the next morning I goes to the public house, and then I finds as the water was hot! And that instead of coming home as soon as the liquor was made, she stopped there gossiping. With that,' said Mr Hardy, 'I was determined, as I had catched her out in a lie, that

Fenning.

she should not stop no longer, and I told Mrs Hardy so, and I set her off directly, without any warning, and glad I was when she was gone, for all the while as she was in the house I never had no peace.'

Mrs Hardy was asked, where she had Elizabeth Fenning's character from. She said, from Mrs Stokes of Walworth, and that she had a very good character with her from Mrs Stokes, who said if she had been in want of a servant she would gladly have taken her again. Mrs Hardy further said that it was a pity the girl had ever come to them, for Mr Hardy had such a dislike of her from the first time of her coming that he never was easy whilst she was there – that she could not but say she was a good, cleanly, industrious girl that did her work well, and she knew no particular harm of her; but, as she told lies, Mr Hardy had certainly turned her out of doors at a moment's warning. 'And indeed,' said Mrs Hardy, 'it was a very disagreeable thing, for I never went out of a Sunday with Mr Hardy all the while the girl was here.'

Mr Hardy said he was as certain as ever he could be she poisoned Mr Turner's family, and he should always say so; 'She was a bad one, depend upon it,' and he repeated he never did like her from the very first moment she came into his house; and, God forgive him!, he could not tell for why nor wherefore.

Thus ended the interview with Mr and Mrs Hardy. It would be a waste of time and patience to make a single remark upon the likings or dislikings of such a man as Mr Hardy, or upon any one part of the interview. But it is essential to state that Mr Redit, of King's Road, Bedford Row, who knows Mr Turner, and who certainly is not favourable to Elizabeth Fenning, was informed by Mr Hardy himself, who was his grocer, that after Mrs Hardy found her tea-kettle frothing at the mouth, she actually charged Elizabeth Fenning with putting something into the tea-kettle, and that she denied putting in anything. Mr Redit is a respectable solicitor. He had been informed so by Mr Hardy, long before the execution. The interview above narrated at length took place, it must be recollected, the day after the execution; and Mrs Hardy then, when closely pressed to relate what she said to Elizabeth Fenning when her tea-kettle frothed at the mouth, affirmed that she did not know that Elizabeth Fenning was the servant that lived with her at the time – which was no doubt true; that she did not tell it to the servant girl, whoever she might be, that did live with her – which there is as little doubt of; that she told nobody of her disordered tea-kettle until after the affair at Mr Turner's; and that then, for the first time that she told anybody, she told – her husband.

APPENDIX VII.

The Letters of Eliza Fenning.

Editor's Note.

Eliza's letters are collected here for the first time. Many of them were reprinted by John Watkins, but others slipped his net and were published elsewhere. Unless otherwise indicated, these transcriptions (and most of the editorial comments in square brackets) are those given by Watkins. Almost all of the letters are dated, but a few undated letters appear at the end of the collection.

Letter 1.

New Clerkenwell Prison,
March 29, 1815.

Dear E—d,

You may be truly surprised at me for not writing or sending to you; but, no doubt, you have heard what has happened to me, for I now lay ill at the infirmary sick ward at the New Clerkenwell Prison; for on last Tuesday week I had some yeast dumplings to make, and there was something in which I can't answer for, and they made four of us, including myself, dangerously ill; and because I made them, they suspect me that I have put something in them, which I assure you I am innocent of; but I expect I shall be cleared on Thursday, if in case I can attend. My mother attends me three times a day, and brings me every thing I can wish for: but, Edward, I shall never be right or happy again, to think that I was ever in a prison; but if I was to die, I still should be happy to think I die innocent. If it be no trouble to you, I wish you would answer this quick though I am in prison, and send directly.

Your's truly,

Eliza Fenning.

Fenning.

Letter 2.

Clerkenwell Prison,
31st March, 1815.

Dear E—d,

This is the second time that I have wrote to you, and I feel very unhappy at your not answering my letters: but, I suppose, as you have heard what has happened to me, you don't care to take any notice of me now; but I never should disgrace you, as I suffer innocent; but I trust in God I shall get the better of my enemies yet: but I assure you, never did I suffer so much in all my life as I do now; but I have one comfort left, to think I saved your picture and letters, and I have got them with me; for when I had my box searched they took them from me, and I paid the officer five shillings to recover them again. I came in a coach on Thursday to Hatton Garden, but it being not settled, I have gone back again to have another hearing; but I shall in the course of another week be cleared. I saw William on Thursday, and he informed me that you went to the ball on Thursday, and I am glad to hear that you can spend your time so agreeably with another; but still, Edward, its more than one would expect, as you must very well know what I feel to be away from you; but if you was in my case, I think I should spend my time a little better than going to such diversions; but, perhaps, its all for the best. My mother and father come constantly to see me, for I should have been dead had they not attended me, as I kept my bed four days; but thank God I have got better, and if you have any respect whatever, I should be happy if you will write as soon as possible.

Direct for me, at the New Clerkenwell Prison,

Don't fail.

Letter 3.

Tuesday, 3d [4th] of April.

Dearest E—d,

It was my full intention of writing to you, as I wish to inform you of every particular that will happen; for if I had not been removed from Clerkenwell prison, I should have been confined in there most likely a twelve-month; but thank God I shall stand my trial at the Old Bailey, where I shall have a Counsellor to plead for me; so I have nothing to fear, as my conscience tells me that am not guilty. But pray do not tell your fellow-servant any thing more, unless he reads it in the papers. I really was ashamed of seeing the young man in such a place, and more so, as he had two more with me [him?]. I certainly appeared with good spirits, though you may easily guess what spirits I have to be confined in such a place as Newgate; but I have paid the fees, and so I have a room with another to

Appendix VII.

be in, where I can see my mother, or any friend when they come to see me; but I expect to have it settled on Monday at the least. But I have been informed that you got acquainted with another young woman; but I am not apt to be jealous, therefore I shall think no more about it; but I firmly believe you are still true and faithful to me; and as to me, I have fixed my mind and heart entirely on you.

Pray send me a line or two on Friday, if you can spare time.

I am, dearest E—d,

Your affectionate and true
Eliza Fenning.

Letter 4.

Tuesday the 11th [April,] 5 o'Clock.

Dear E—d,

I attended my trial on Tuesday, and they have, which is the most cruellest thing in this world, brought me in guilty, because I had the fire to light in the office where the arsenick was kept, and my master said that I went often into the office for things, and so, on that account, they suppose that I must have taken the arsenick out of the drawer, which is the most horrid thing I ever can think of; for was I to die this instant I am sure I should be happy in thinking I am innocent. But God reward them for all they have done towards me: but I can't tell my fate as yet as the sessions won't be over till Saturday, and then I shall know on Monday. But, Edward, let me advise you to for ever forget me, as most likely you will often have it thrown up in your face, for I am, Edward, I believe, now for ever shut from the world. I still have some comfort left, when I can see my parents as yet; but pray make your mind happy, and get some one else that will never bring any reflection on you. I shall never think of marrying any person excepting yourself; but I must for ever give up any thought of such, as it may hurt your character; but I still love and respect you. Pray write soon.

From your much injured and afflicted
Eliza.

Don't forget.

Fenning.

Letter 5.

Newgate, 9 o'Clock, 13th [April.]

Dearest E—d,

I received your kind and dear letter, which still more endears you to me: but oh, Edward! if I was sure that I should see you but once, I am certain that I never should hold up my head again. But don't think that I shall be denied of seeing you, though I may be confined most likely six months at least; but perhaps it is all for the best, for I am confident that it will make me both steady and penitent the rest of my life; though its hard to suffer innocent; but I shall in a little time be more composed, as I put my trust in God, for all his goodness to me, and do, dear Edward, do the same. Don't be unhappy, as you very well know how much I love and respect you, for no young woman can ever love you more than I do; and I am certain, at least I think so, that I have yours in return. I should not have wrote so soon to you, but I don't like to see your mother as yet, till I am settled. Don't be angry at me for not wishing to see your kind mother, for the case is, that I have not got my things away from my place as yet, and I have got nothing to come down to appear respectable in; so for that reason I wish to put it off till next week: but pray come, dear Edward, on Sunday, about three o'clock, and you can stop till five; for you can come any Sunday at these hours, and come into my room: but you must ask to see Mrs. Nicols, at the gate where you saw them girls. I am happy to hear you still respect my picture, but I had a misfortune, on the day I had my trial, to break the glass of yours, as I constantly wear it; for I was taken out very unwell, for it so overcame me, that I felt as if I was dying; so that I must trouble you to get it repaired, for I can't trust any one else with it. Adieu.

From your affectionate and true
Eliza.

Letter 6.

April the 16th, 1815. Newgate.

Dearest and beloved Father and Mother,

This is from your poor and only, unhappy child, who is going to suffer: but be happy, as I told you that I am innocent. O mother! believe me for the last time, that I die innocent of the crime I am charged with: but I entreat you to bury me with my two brothers; and likewise another request I have, that is, to put Edward's picture in the coffin with me: don't refuse, as I never shall rest happy, but let me beg of you not to forget, or perhaps I shall come to you, for Edward is my first and only love, and he always gave me the best of advice. But I am happy to think I can make my peace with God; but let me request of you both to put your trust in God, and never fear, as I die happy, though its cruel to come to

Appendix VII.

such untimely end. Oh! I am innocent, dearest parents. Pray for your only child, and dear child.

I am, dearest Father and Mother,
Your only child in death. Farewell for ever.
Eliza Fenning.

Dear Father and Mother,
No.5, Tash Court, Tash Street, Gray's Inn Lane, Holborn.

Letter 7.

Sunday, the 23d, [April] 8 o'Clock.

Dear E—d,

I received your note on Sunday, but I was surprised at not hearing from you before, and I wish to inform you that I received it safe from Catherine, who went for it for me, for your fellow-servant called on me on Sunday, and I was very happy to see any person from you. And now, dear Edward, you may make your mind easy concerning me, for I certainly shall suffer, at least I have no other hopes whatever; so pray put your trust in God, that no accident whatsoever may happen to you. I am making my peace with God, and hope to be in a better world, as I shall leave this world innocent of a crime that's alleged against me: but its dreadful to think what I suffer at such a thing being laid against me, when my conscience is thoroughly clear. Pray go to my mother and show her this letter, and there may be lines that may give her comfort that come from her poor unhappy child. Pray write soon to me. Don't forget.

From your unhappy and [illegible]
Eliza Fenning.

Adieu.

Letter 8.

25th April, 8 o'Clock, Night.

Dear E—d,

I received your letter on Wednesday night, and am happy to hear that you are coming out on Sunday, for most likely it will be the last time that you will see me in this world, and you must come by one o'clock, or else you can't get in, and ask, when you come to the gate, for Mrs. Foster, and then I will give you a note to give to the turnkeys, and then it will admit you. Do not disappoint me, as you may easily believe where my affection is placed; but I hope you will find another that will make you happy when I am no more. But I don't wish to hurt your feelings

Fenning.

but as little as I can, but I hope we shall meet in a better world, where no one can separate us: and I trust when you read this, that you will make your mind more composed concerning me, for you alone have often made my mind unhappy; but now all friends seem indifferent to me, since I know my unhappy fate. My last letter you need not send, as I have since seen my mother, for she has been so ill that I did not expect to see her any more,

I am, dear, dear E—d,

Your true and unhappy
Eliza Fenning.

Letter 9.[188]

[Written 'about the end of April'.]

Honoured Sir,

With due submission I most earnestly entreat of you to sign my petition, to save my life, which is forfeited for what I am not guilty of. Honoured sir, I do here most solemnly declare I never meant to injure you or any of your family. Picture to yourself the distressed mind of my dear parents, to see their only child suffer such an ignominious death; but innocent I am. May the blessed God give my ever dear parents strength to bear the dreadful affliction to see their only child suffer; but may you never feel the pangs of a broken heart, which your unfortunate servant endures. Prayers for you and your family.

Eliza Fenning.

P. S. If your goodness will comply with my request, I shall ever be bound to pray for you.

Letter 10.

[Sent the latter end of April, or beginning of May.]

Sir,

Pardon this liberty I take in writing to you; but its my particular wish to know if you have any hopes. I am a young woman that's under the sentence, and I am sure to suffer when the Report comes down. I heard something about your petition, which made me take this liberty. Please to send me word, for I feel much for you.

E. F.

---

188 Eliza's letter to Mr Turner – whether Orlibar Turner or Robert Turner is not known. Date as per Watkins (75).

Appendix VII.

Bottom [of] Master's side.
Mr. Oldfield, Condemned Cell.

Letter 11.

Felons' side, Newgate, 4 May.

Dear E—d,

You are the last person that I should think would behave to me as you do now; for I fully expected you on Sunday; but most likely you have other places to go to much better than to come and see me, though I am in Newgate. Other young men and women come and see me, and are surprised when I inform them that you seldom come near, or even send to me. Was you in my place, I never should have slighted you: but God bless you and yours as long as you live, is the prayer of Eliza, who once was yours, but now never shall be; for was the Lord to spare my life, though I have no hopes, I don't think I should ever like a man that would forget me, because I can't help myself now. Once more, God bless you! – Adieu! – from

Eliza Fenning.

You may answer this, just as you please.

Letter 12.

Friday night, 9 o'Clock. May 5, 1815.

Dear E—d,

I received your letter, and am surprised at your thinking that I wish to quarrel with you; but I think I have a just right to speak, when you promised me that you would come and see me, and then to disappoint me when there was no excuse; for you well know that my life is at stake, and one would suppose that a person that respected another, should feel happy in seeing them as often as time could permit them. I should feel sorry for you to get anger at coming at any other time than your Sunday; but I feel very much hurt at your being out, and could not spare one single hour with me: and as to your saying that you have many enemies, it's more than I know of, for there's no person has said any thing to me concerning you, that you should seem affronted at. If there's any person has done any services for me, that you know of, I am very thankful to you for so much kindness; but I trust in hopes that I shall repay you some time or another. I have not seen my father since, therefore I don't know any thing of your being with him, but I am glad that he is in such good friendship with you, for you can spend many hours with them, when I am no more – and pray make them as happy as you can, for, should

Fenning.

I suffer, it shall be my last prayer for you to go as often as you can; and I am certain that they will always respect you on the account of their daughter. Pray don't send any note with farewell again to me; for, though we never shall meet in the world again, it's cruel to say adieu as yet. God bless you, dear Edward, and all your friends, and may you never feel the pangs of a broken heart. You say that you shan't be out till Sunday week, and so I suppose I shall not see you any more, as I expect the report will be down every day – and now I wait with impatience to know my fate.

From your unhappy and forsaken
Eliza Fenning.

Once more write when you can spare time.

Letter 13.[189]

Newgate, 12 June, 1815.

My Lord,

When the life of an innocent person is at stake it needs no apology for intruding upon your Lordship's invaluable time: I therefore, with all humility, submit my Case to your Lordship's humane consideration, which cannot be doubted.

I protest, before God and man, that I am not guilty of the crime charged to me, although I feel the great difficulty of proving my innocence.

Mrs. Turner swore that I carried a pie to the baker's about 12 o'clock; that she went into the kitchen after my return, and gave directions to make the dough, which she found placed before the fire to rise, half an hour after such order; and further, that she saw the dough two or three times between half past twelve and three o'clock, until it was divided into dumplings; that it did not rise as usual, but kept a singular shape to the last; while, in another part of her evidence, she swore the dough was divided into dumplings 20 minutes before 12 o'clock.

Other instances might be mentioned to prove many mistakes, especially on the part of Mrs. Turner.

The particular and unusual orders Mrs. Turner gave not to leave the kitchen, and her assertion that she was sure no one was there, are circumstances your Lordship may think worthy of notice.

Thomas King (one of the apprentices, who was not examined at the Trial,) was in the front kitchen while I was in the back room cleaning the knives: I thought

---

[189] Eliza's letter to the Right Honourable John Scott, Lord Chancellor of Great Britain. Whether Eliza wrote the entire letter independently, or whether it was written by one of her supporters and merely signed by her, is not certain.

Appendix VII.

it was my mistress; but as I was going into the kitchen I met him, and asked what he had been doing. To which he made no reply, but went upstairs. Now, God forbid that I should impeach any person, I only relate this circumstance, as I am informed that arsenick, merely sprinkled over the dough, would infuse itself through the whole; and it appeared that the arsenick was put by Mr. Turner in a place open to any body.

It was stated by Mr. Turner, and Gadsden, the apprentice, that the arsenick was missed a fortnight before the occurrence: but, surely, if it had been me, the person who was the most likely to be accused, I should not have made any dumplings of the over-night, thereby inducing the apprentice to eat again; neither should I have omitted cleaning the utensils; and, least of all, to have eat of them myself, whereby I was affected as much as any of the family, as could have been corroborated by Surgeon Ogilvy: but although he attended the family five or six hours before Mr. Marshall, and might have stated other favourable circumstances, yet he was not examined on the Trial.

However eager I feel to live, and, above all, to avoid unworthy ignominy, I know not how to prove my innocence, most humbly craving your Lordship's humane attention, which I doubt not will cause investigation to be made in my unfortunate Case.

I am,
My Lord,
Your Lordship's unfortunate servant,
Eliza Fenning.

Letter 14.[190]

13 June.

Dear Friend,

Impressed with a just sense of your kindness towards me, I feel myself in want of words to express my gratitude for the same; but they ever will bear record in heaven in your favour, in the part you have taken in proving the injustice of the aspersions that was said of me; but, believe me, I shall for the future be very circumspect in every action, and keep myself as private as possible. I return you thanks, and hope you will not be offended at my making an objection to receive the Holy Sacrament, but I think I am not in a proper state of mind to receive it: situated as I am, with those that are in the same room, there is little time for the reflections that are proper for so sacred an occasion; but I trust that a merciful God, that knows the most secret thoughts of all hearts, will grant me grace, and

---

190 This letter is understood to have been addressed to Thomas Wansbrough.

Fenning.

renew me with a new heart, that my past and present sufferings may prove an acceptable sacrifice for my past faults, and that they may be so imprinted in my breast, that they may prove a sufficient monitor, to deter me from violating the laws of God, should I be so happy as to be once more restored to society again. For the particulars of your misfortunes I am sorry to hear, but hope they will end to your satisfaction; and I hope you will, with myself, pray to the Lord to forgive our enemies. For what you have done I shall always feel myself under the greatest obligation, as I am thoroughly convinced that you have acted from the sole motives of humanity.

Suffer me to remain

Yours, with due respect,
Eliza Fenning.

Please to write soon

Letter 15.[191]

22 June.

Sir,

I am sorry to think that you should have heard that I only fly to my book when Mr. Cotton is coming. Far be it from my heart to notice such observations as those, being fully convinced, in my own heart, that outward show is little, as the heart may be at work without a book: but all the books in my hand, if my thoughts were otherwise employed, will have little effect towards my salvation; for God is never mistaken in the character of his servants, for he seeth their heart and judgeth according to the truth. The time draws on when I must approach to the Divine Being, the Sovereign of whom I stand in awe; but yet, I trust to a kind Father of infinite mercy that he will pardon me all my sins: though they be like crimson, he can make them as white as snow; and, if it was not for the dreadful end, I should prefer to leave this world of wickedness, where is nothing but trouble and sorrow, and vexation through life, for, believe me, often is the smile of cheerfulness assumed while the heart aches within. I have one request to make of you, which is, if the report comes unfavourable, if I should wish to see you, that you will comply. If granted, I hope this will not hurt your feelings, as it would grieve me much, for I think I should really feel happy in seeing you.

Suffer me to remain

Yours, till death do me call,

Eliza Fenning.

---

191 Watkins (10 [appendix numbering]): 'The following is the letter which the *Observer* newspaper called "her first act of impurity."'

Appendix VII.

Letter 16.

25 June.

Sir,

I received your present, and believe me your advice will not be lost on me, as I look on your judgment and discrimination to be very just, and I trust in God to get me through this great trouble, as he can create and he can destroy, he can cast down and build up: but I believe I had better leave this dreadful place to go to a better world, than to be sent to another country with such depraved wretches; and not only that, but would be looked on as guilty go where I would, and leaving my dear parents would be the [greatest] hardship I could endure. Yet I leave every thing to the hand of a kind Providence to direct, for it says in Holy Scriptures, those whom the Lord loveth he chasteneth; and, believe me, I feel so happy in my mind that nothing, I am determined, will ever change or disturb me any more. I should be glad to see Mr. — when he calls again. I cannot inform you who paid the expenses of my affairs, as I do not know, as several were entire strangers to me. Mary-Anne Clarke is the person I sleep with, and she is the only one that has the least feeling; but we have not any other prisoners with as yet with us. As we are the four that are under sentence, Mr. Cotton does not think it proper to place any person with us. Believe me, I know nothing concerning the poison being in the pot of beer, as it never was told me before. Please to let me keep your letters. If the Lord should spare my life, I shall have them in remembrance of you; and if I am to leave this world, I will then deliver them up safe. And may God bless you, is the sincere prayer of your well-wisher. – I feel so indebted to you for your good ness, that I lament I can but express my gratitude to you. Suffer me yet to remain

Yours, till death,
Eliza Fenning.

I shall write often, as I have now got some paper in, for I forgot on Saturday to get some, and could not write till now.

Fenning.

Letter 17.[192]

27 June.

Dear Sir,

I wish to speak the whole sentiments of my heart to you; and now, without reserve, to convince you I feel perfectly prepared in respect of taking the sacrament, which I believe I can, when I know within my own breast I never injured any person; and more so, when I know myself innocent of the crime that is alleged against me. Though a poor servant, I always have trodden the paths of virtue. I know I am a wicked sinner, but hope through the blood of Christ to be washed from all my sins. Believe me it is a pleasing reflection to think I have not violated the sacred laws of God. Though cruel is my fate, I must not repine, as it is for some divine purpose the Almighty has ordained this trouble to come on me, to bring me to himself. If it should be so, I must pray to the Lord to give me strength to bear it. The awful moment I dread, is bidding an an [sic] eternal farewell. Think within yourself of dear parents, and sincere friends. What a scene may probably arise to my parents if I suffer! I now conclude as yours

Eliza Fenning.

Letter 18.[193]

June 27, 1815.

My Lord,

With deference I humbly beg leave to address your Lordship, at the same time am at a loss how to dare to venture such a presumption: but your Lordship's well known goodness and mercy, which has been repeatedly extended to many miserable creatures under calamities like myself, encourages me with all submission to state my real situation to your Lordship. I most humbly beg leave to inform your Lordship that I am under the awful sentence of death, on suspicion of poisoning Mr. Turner's family; which heinous crime I never was guilty of, I most solemnly declare to a just God, when I must meet my blessed Redeemer at the great and grand tribunal, where the secrets of all hearts will be known. Innocence induces me to solicit a fuller examination. I am the only child of ten; and to be taken off for such an ignominious crime, strikes me and my dear parents with horror. I therefore most humbly beg leave to solicit your Lordship's merciful

---

[192] The same letter is transcribed, with trivial differences, by Wansbrough (28-29), who says that it was shown to him by its recipient. The transcription given in the pamphlet attributed to Watkins is preferred, since the letter was apparently part of his own 'extensive collection' – or, perhaps more correctly, that of the pamphlet's true author, William Hone (Watkins, 1 [appendix numbering]).

[193] Eliza's letter to Lord Sidmouth, Secretary of State for the Home Department. This transcription is from the pamphlet attributed to Watkins; the transcription in Fairburn exhibits minor but immaterial differences.

Appendix VII.

interference in my behalf, to spare my life; and my parents will, with me, ever be bound to pray for your Lordship.

With due submission, I am your poor, but innocent servant,
Eliza Fenning.

Letter 19.

12 o'Clock, 29 June.

Sir,

I have not the least doubt of your assiduity in my behalf. God in his goodness has sent you to restore a lost child to her afflicted parents, which, should you succeed in, I am convinced your goodness of heart will think an ample recompense for all your trouble: for my part, all that I can say on that subject is, that my heart overflows with gratitude. Hope is one of the best sources in the time of our greatest troubles. – I have been poised up with it in all my afflictions. I should be much obliged to you to inform me what Mr. Cotton said in respect of me. I have seen him this morning, but he did not speak to me.

I remain

Yours, with due respect,
Eliza Fenning.

Letter 20.

29 June.

Sir,

I should have answered your letter sooner; but, believe me, I feel so agitated between hope and fear, that I really know not what I am doing three parts of the day, for your letter was so affecting that it has depressed my spirits much; particularly as you mention to wear mourning after my decease; which I take as a mark of great respect. Be assured it is not true concerning my being detected in respecting the poison in the beer, for when I come to recollect, Mr. Cotton mentioned it to me about a young woman who attempted to poison a family in Bath, and her name was similar to my own, but he has told me it was false. Be so good as to tell M— I wish to see him particularly, to inform him of something I have heard: but I am surely convinced that Mr. Cotton is a great enemy to me. I expect Mr. — to call to-day. The cards my mother brought made me angry, as I don't think them a proper amusement for any one. She brought them for one of the wards women. I now conclude, with sincere prayers towards your welfare, and hope you will never experience the pangs of a broken heart – for often in the

Fenning.

smile of cheerfulness assumed, when the heart aches within.

From your unhappy, though penitent,
Eliza Fenning.

———

Letter 21.

29 June.

Sir,

The only thing I wished to see Mr. — for, was, to inform him a report prevailed that I had made an attempt, prior to the last, of poisoning a family; but reports must not be minded in such cases as mine, where life is depending. Justice and truth only can take place in such weighty concerns.

Yours
E. F.

———

Letter 22.

[4 July.]

Sir,

By Mr. C—'s orders, I, with the others, attended prayers in the condemned room, where the men were likewise. In coming out, Mr. Oldfield called me, and said, he has learned, from good authority, from the Secretary of State's, there is not the least glimmer of hopes in saving my life. I made no reply, as Mr. Cotton was present. I thought it proper to inform you, as you wished to know if I had heard from him.

E. F.

———

Letter 23.

6 July.

I have seen my mother to-day – her heart was too full to inform me all; but, by hints, I need not flatter myself with hopes. Pray don't trouble yourself, as I fear all will have no effect: I know your goodness of heart, and will always pray for you, till the period arrives when I shall leave this world of woe. Please excuse my writing.

E. F.

———

Appendix VII.

Letter 24.

6 July.

Believe me, I feel so reconciled and composed in my mind, that I fear not what the ignorant or wicked can invent against me. Cruel and distressing is my case, to be drawn in innocent, and to be under the awful sentence; and hard must be the heart, that would not sympathize with the unfortunate. I fancied I had one consolation which I must now with tears give up – hopes of hearing from you, as I suppose there will be no letters able to pass in to me. I feel very unwell to-day, being low in spirits. Pray make yourself happy.

E. F.

Letter 25.

July, 1815.

Sir,

In the interim of speaking with you, I had not the least idea or suspicion the person who wrote concerning me was standing not far distant, and was endeavouring to learn our conversation, but did not succeed, or no doubt they would have acquainted Mr. Davis; and if they had, I neither care nor value what such depraved wretches would invent against me in any respect whatever. I am already too much injured to mind such trifling observations, and indeed would be sorry to degrade myself to make them my companions, much more to be so foolish as to place any confidence in them. Although my situation in life has been no other than a servant, and poor and unfortunate as I am now, I have every reason to set a greater value on myself, than to make them my equals in any respect whatsoever. In the mean-time, after you left me, I with little inquiries found my foe, it was —, the same who had stolen my shawl, and, though trifling, I gave four shillings to two of the girls to restore it to me, which they did; and out of spite and revenge, she had no better opportunity than to write to you. I own I was [so] foolish [as] to converse with her several [times], but it was merely by her informing me she was lately in the West Indies, and it being my native place, I was pleased to hear and to speak in [the] language of the country; I have seen my mother, who says, if the report is not down this week, it will not be till after next sessions; which is a dreary length of time to be kept in suspense in life or death. I must observe to you, though ignorant I may appear, I only wish I had affluence of tongue to express my real sentiments of heart more freely; but yet I trust that I am endowed with common sense enough to dictate a letter to my dear and valuable friends. I only wish I could handle my pen in a more proper manner; but it is more my misfortune that I cannot. I now conclude as your's with every mark of gratitude.

God bless you. Adieu.

E. F.

Fenning.

Letter 26.

Felons' side, Newgate.

[Written a short time before the report came down.]

Sir,

I have read your letter with attention and gratitude. I consider it my duty to reply; and am the more led to do so, in order to communicate a report that our summons is near at hand. It's highly gratifying to perceive the great change upon your soul. I confess, with pleasure, that my awful situation has made the like impression. I feel that, in one sense, if I die, I had better suffer innocently as I am. Yet life is sweet: to part with it in such an ignominious manner is hard indeed, not having committed a crime. Yet what concerns me most is the misery our dear parents must experience. My dear mother is almost comfortless, which distracts my heart. It's like a dream, for I know my innocence. I cannot prove it. Had my counsellor been properly informed, it would have been impossible to have pronounced me guilty: for, if even I had revenge against the family, to have been such a fool to poison myself! and besides, it was only a trifling quarrel. I can't help saying but I feel hurt at their taking such trouble to swear my life away: but, to be at peace with God, we must even forgive our enemies. Although I have not committed the crime for which I suffer, and could swear it before the Almighty Judge, yet I feel unworthy in his sight; and therefore call upon him for divine mercy, which I hope may be our happy lot, is the sincere prayer of your unhappy fellow prisoner,

Eliza Fenning.

Be careful of Mr. Cotton. Some one has made evil report to him about me; and I fear it has done me much harm. Some one must be guilty, and I still hope it will [be] strictly inquired into.

Mr. William Oldfield,
Condemned Cell, Newgate.

Letter 27.[194]

July 18, Felon's side, Newgate,

Sir,

With the greatest submission, I most humbly beg leave to return my grateful thanks and acknowledgements for your humane charitableness that has been

---

194 Fairburn, 20-21: 'The following letter was sent, by the prisoner, to the editor of the *Examiner* newspaper, and which appeared in that paper, on Sunday, July 23, 1815'. Fairburn amended the text slightly; the transcription provided here is derived from the *Examiner*, as per the clipping in Harvard Law School Library, MSS HLS MS 4130 (41).

Appendix VII.

extended towards me, an unfortunate victim; but God and his goodness has you to restore a lost and only child to her distressed and afflicted parents; and I trust and hope all those who help the afflicted in mind, body, or estate, will bear reward in heaven. Believe [me], cruel and pitiable is my distressing case to be even confined in the abode of wretchedness, much more to be continually warned of my approaching destination. Dear Sir, I do solemnly declare with firmness and perseverance of my innocence to God and man, I am innocent of the crime that [is] laid to my charge; but how can I convince the world when brought in guilty at the bar of man? Yet there will be a grand and great day when all must stand before the tribunal bar of God, then where will the guilty criminal stand or fly to secure [themselves] from the vengeance of Almighty Just God, who know [sic] the secrets of all hearts, and will reward all according to the work done in the body[?] What a pleasing consolation within my distressed mind to think I am clear of such [a] heinous and dreadful crime, and never hurted man or mortal, in thought, word, or deed. – My dear parents and myself will feel in duty bound to pray for your kind interference in my behalf in your Paper, as you have done. – I remain your much and injured humble servant,

Eliza Fenning.

Letter 28.

19 July.

Dearest and affectionate Father and Mother,

Let me entreat your immediate attendance to your lost child. Innocent, dear parents, I am, to God and man. Pray come soon. The report is come for me to be executed on Wednesday next. Judge what are my feelings in your distressed bosom. Don't grieve. No more from your unfortunate child,

Elizabeth Fenning.

Letter 29.

Let me beg and entreat of you to call once more to see me, before I leave this vale of tears, to go to glory, in a heavenly mansion of peace. You have been a dear friend to me, and will be more, if you comfort my dear and afflicted parents in this hour of distress. It's not a guilty character you see when you come, but an injured, and indeed innocent victim.

Yours with gratitude,
Eliza Fenning.

Fenning.

Letter 30.[195]

July 21, 1815.

Dear Charles!

I am so depressed with woe and affliction, that I scarce know how to direct my trembling and faltering pen. I did not expect I should have fortitude to direct my words to you. Oh, this blow is dreadful and distressing to me! It is impossible to describe to you my feelings in my awful situation. But time draws on a conclusion to my unfortunate case. I must bear the smart with patience and humble resignation, the closing scene of mournful and eternal parting farewell to my dear, oh unhappy, affectionate parents, whose breaking hearts tear my tortured breast. But God bless them, and give them consolation amidst that awful scene of oppressing woe. You have been a sincere and dear friend towards me, and I trust the Almighty will reward you for your kind endeavours in behalf to spare my life: but all is vanity and vexation of spirit. Oh I trust the God of all mercies will receive me in the heavenly mansions above, wherein sorrow and trouble will be no more. Oh believe I die innocent of the crime. I am sensible now what I am going to reveal to you, which is this, was I never to enter the kingdom of God, whose presence I must face, that I die innocent, and am a murdered person. Oh, Charles, what an unpleasant feeling to hear I am to die an ignominious death for the guilty person! How cruel that they should be screened from the laws of justice! But God will reward them according to their wicked deeds. Pray God forgive them, that they may never be destroyed in the world wherein everlasting burning must be endured, which is the portion of all wicked persecutors who take the life on the innocent. Pray comfort my dear parents, and God will bless you. Adieu, dear Charles. Pray call and bid me a farewell for ever. Adieu.

Your unhappy

Eliz. Fenning.

Pray keep these few lines, and this lock of hair, in remembrance of your Elizabeth Fenning, aged twenty-one years. God bless you for ever.

---

[195] Wansbrough, 11-12. 'Charles' was presumably Wansbrough's pseudonymisation of 'Edward'. Wansbrough (9) notes that Eliza, 'in the perturbation of her mind ... omitted to enclose the lock of hair to her lover. The letter, as usual, was opened by Mr Newman, who kindly gave it to me to have the omission rectified.'

Appendix VII.

Letter 31.[196]

Felons' side, 21 July, 1815,
Newgate.

Dear and affectionate Parents,

With heart-rending sighs and tears, I for the last time, and ever last time, write these solemn lines to you, hoping and trusting the Almighty to give you strength and fortitude to bear the distressing, awful, and dreadful scene, that is about to take place. Believe me, cruel and pitiable is my unfortunate and affecting situation; but God's will be done: and with humble resignation I must bear my untimely fate: but what pleasing consolation within my tortured breast, to suffer innocent! Dear parents, I do solemnly declare, was I never to enter the heavenly mansion of heavenly rest, I am murdered! Yes, dear father and mother, believe I am your only child, that speaks the sentiments of a breaking heart. Don't let me distress your breaking heart, I wish to comfort you, dearest of parents: be happy: pray take comfort: let me entreat of you to be reconciled, and I will be happy in heaven, and with my dear sisters and brothers, and will meet you by and by: pray read the blessed Bible, and turn your hearts, and live a religious and holy life, and then we shall be where sorrow and troubles will be no more. I grieve more to think I had an opportunity sooner, and did not make use of it; yet there's time, though short, to pray to my heavenly Father, to forgive me all my sins and offences in my life past: it's only the passage of death that I have [to] go through, which, I hope and trust, will soon be over. Oh my blest and beloved parents, think what are my present and distressed feelings, to part from you who gave me my being, and nourished me at that breast, and was my sole comfort, and nursed me in my helpless and infant years, and was always my directors, to keep me in [the] sacred path of virtue, which I have strictly kept, and will be one sin less to answer for, as a spotless frame will be acceptable in the eyes of God. I mention this, as I let you all [know] I have not done amiss. Oh dear parents, what an affecting scene, to part from you, which must endured by the laws of justice! but justice has not been shown at [the] bar. Man judges man: God will judge us all, who knows the secrets of hearts, and those who swore my life will never enter with me into rest. God bless you both, and may you live happy! Adieu from your injured and unhappy child.

Keep these few lines in remembrance of me, as that is all [the] comfort I can afford, with my imperfect prayers. Adieu, dear parents, God bless you both!

Eliza Fenning,
Aged 21 years.

---

[196] The same letter is transcribed, with trivial differences, by Wansbrough, 10-11. The transcription given in the pamphlet attributed to Watkins is preferred here. Wansbrough, 9, notes that Eliza enclosed a lock of her hair with this letter.

Fenning.

Letter 32.

23 July 1815. Newgate.

My dear Friend,

Out of love and respect I write these last and solemn lines to bid you an everlasting and eternal farewel[l] in this world of sorrow and woe. I have but a few hours before I leave this vale of tears to enter the heavenly mansion of rest but yet I never shall die happy till I communicate any secret that my dying heart contains – I die innocent of the crime I am to suffer such an ignominious death for. Pray tell my dear parents not to put a bit of black about me, as it will be a token of innocence. A very few leave this world a pure virgin: and when led to the gallows, I shall be led as a shepherd leadeth a lamb to the slaughter, or as a bride to her heavenly Bridegroom, and there to be united at the altar of God – and rest on the bosom of my heavenly Father, where parting shall be no more. Dear friend, pray lead a religious and holy life, and then I shall meet you in heaven with my dear parents, and enjoy everlasting felicity, with blessed saints and angels above. Please to grant me one request, if you possibly can, to see my body laid in the mouldering earth, in the early prime of youth; but I only go a little time before you all: we must all die, then why should I repine? It would be wicked to fly in the face of the Almighty, for God's will be done: the Lord gave, and the Lord hath taken away, and blessed is the name of God.

May God bless you, and all that may be yours in this world, and all your dear friends. Bless you once more, is my dying prayer – speak comfort to my poor unhappy parents, who will soon not have a single child to console them in the hour of distress, in their few remaining years of old age.

I once more bless you, and bid you an eternal farewel[l].

Eliza Fenning.
Aged 21 years. 1815.

Letter 33.[197]

23 – July – 1815   Newgate

Dear and Valuable Frind

I so deeply imprest with such a just sence of your unbounded and humane

---

197 Wansbrough, 16-17. This letter was transcribed by Wansbrough without corrections. Hone, writing as Watkins, admitted that, as Eliza had 'evidently penned them [her letters] without study or reperusal, it became necessary to supply words which she had omitted, by inserting them between crotchets, and to correct the spelling and punctuation' (1 [appendix numbering]).

Appendix VII.

Charitableness that I am at a Loss of words to Express my gratfull and humble thanks to you but yet trust and hope that all those who help the Afflicted in Body and Mind or Estate will Bear Record in heaven Dear Sir the Almighty has Extended his goodness far beyound Comprehension to give me such Fortitude to Conduct my trembling hand to paper and trust he will give me strenth to Bear my untimly fate like a Christian – but its hard and pitable and indeed interesting beyound discription to suffer such an ignomious Death innocent as I am bilive my words air the reale sentiments of a Diying heart or I may justly Call who has but a few hours when I shall Leave this world of sorrow and woe to Enter the heavenly mantions of Eternal Rest whaire troubles will be no more Oh you speak of taking a greate Charge to Conduct me to the Last yes Dear Sir Like a Shepherd that Leads a Lamb to the Slaughter or Like a Bride to her heavenly Bridegroom of my Beloved Redeemer whose arm will I trust will be open to receive me from all my labours – tho belive the End strike me and my dear Parents with Silent horrow – what a pity the guilty and dredfull Character should be Screned by the suffering of the innocent – wich remains in the house of Mr. Turner if they knew within thair Brests they was innocent why not Call and beg of me to forgive them wich injured as I am I freely forgive them and hope the Almighty will forgive them and trust this dreadfull Sin will never rise up against them in the grand and Awfull Day of judgment when Secrets of all hearts will be judgd before the tribunall Bar of an Almighty just God then whair will the guilty Criminall Stand before the presence of God who will Reward al according to deeds done in the Body – what a pleasing Consolation a Cleare Contions from all guilt as I have & in the meantime suffer me to remaine your humble Servent till Death

Eliza Fenning.

Letter 34.[198]

Condemned Cell (25 July).

Dearest Friend,

With heart-rending tears I address these melancholy lines to you. Don't grieve, dear girl, my time is but short in this troublesome world, and soon I shall be in eternal rest. Pray read the Bible, and make your peace with God and man. If you'll believe me, the parting with my parents is truly affecting; but it must be endured, though little expected when we ate our last supper together: but God bless you! and may God send you liberty soon. Here is a lock of hair for you, and another for Young,

From your much injured and distressed

---

198 To Mary Ann Clarke; written by Eliza on the day before her execution and 'thrown by her out of the cell window, with a gown' (Watkins, 20 [appendix numbering]).

Fenning.

Eliza Fenning.
Aged 21.

Letter 35.[199]

[Tuesday 25 July 1815.]

Wear my ear-rings, dear mother, for my sake. Don't part with them, dearest mother. I die innocent of the crime, indeed.

Letter 36.[200]

[No date.]

My dear Mrs. H—!

I feel deeply impressed with your sincere and affecting letter; and believe your good advice will not be lost on me, though placed in abode of wretchedness; for cruel and pitiable is my unfortunate case, for to just God I solemnly declare my innocence of the heinous crime laid to my charge; for there will be a great and grand day, when the secrets of all hearts will be known before the tribunal of an Almighty Saviour, and then where will the guilty criminal stand, who has nearly broke my dear parents' hearts, and driven them to distress, and has deprived me of every comfort? But what a consolation, if I suffer, to be received in the heavenly mansions above, where troubles will be no more. I feel in duty bound to pray for such a friend as you: and I trust all those who help the afflicted in mind, body, or estate, will bear record in heaven. I now conclude, with gratitude, your humble and penitent

E. F.

Letter 37.

[No date.]

Sir,

Mr. Davis is a very troublesome fellow – without feeling, or the least taint of goodness.[201] He saw me hanging out my linen to dry, and thought I had been washing there; and, it appears to me, any accommodation a prisoner can have,

---

199 Date as per Fairburn, 32.
200 Wansbrough, 29-30.
201 A reference to Samuel Davis, the Newgate turnkey. See Appendix IV.

Appendix VII.

gives him pain. But what can we expect from such illiberal characters? I set myself above the frowns of the steel-hearted gaolers and look to higher powers! When my dear father left me, Mr. Newman and Mr. Smart were at the gate. Mr. N. inquired who he was, Mr. S. informed him, but had no conversation, only bowed to my father. I hope you do not think I disregard your kind advice, as I think that would be a breach of gratitude: believe me, I peruse your letters so often, till I have them by heart. Mr. Cotton informed me the sacrament will not be administered till next Sunday, when I mean to prepare myself to take it. I have not heard from Mr. Oldfield, and I think it would be improper if I did. I mentioned Mr. — to father yesterday, and he required me not to see him. God bless you!

Your's, with due respect,

Eliza Fenning.

Letter 38.

[No date.]

Sir,

I am much obliged to you for your kind attention in respect to my health and spirits; but, as to exercise, where can I take it, excepting I was to intermix with those who are lost to every principle? There's a just God who knows the secret thoughts of all hearts; and, as I solemnly declare that I am innocent, I trust in God that he will extend his mercy to spare my life, that I may live a truly religious life. God bless you. Adieu.

Eliza Fenning.

APPENDIX VIII.

'Written in Newgate.'[202]

Editor's note.

This apparent cri de coeur is an amalgam of verses from The Book of Psalms, as 'fitted to the tunes used in churches' by Nahum Tate (poet laureate from 1692 until his death in 1715) and Nicholas Brady. Eliza's friends and supporters are known to have provided her with a number of books steeped in religious themes, so she may have copied the verses – albeit with some inaccuracies – from a volume in her extemporary library. The selection and arrangement of the verses is no doubt Eliza's own (and inarguably apt, taking into account her situation), but the work as a whole is not quite the independent creation that Thomas Wansbrough thought it was. 'During her confinement,' he wrote, 'she wrote some lines, which are here given; not that they possess any recommendation of themselves; but from a view that they may tend to show the character of her mind, contrasted with the limited education she had received'.[203]

The sources of the thirteen stanzas are as follows:

Stanza	**Source**
1	*Psalms 119:95*
2	*Psalms 119:84*
3	*Psalms 88:1-2*
4	*Psalms 88:3-4*
5	*Psalms 88:5-6*
6	*Psalms 88:7*
7	*Psalms 88:8*
8	*Psalms 88:9*
9	*Psalms 88:10*
10	*Psalms 70:1*
11	*Psalms 71:14*
12	*Psalms 55:18*
13	*Psalms 3:3*

---

[202] Wansbrough, 26-28.
[203] Wansbrough, 26.

Fenning.

the wicked have their ambush Laid
    my guiltless life to take
but in the midst of danger I —
    my God thy word thy study make

How many days must I endure
    of sorrow and distress
when wilt thow judgment excute
    on them who me oppress

To the my God and saviour I —
    by day and night address my cry
vouchsafe my mournfull voice to hear
    to my distress incline thine ear

For seas of trouble me invade
    my soul draws nigh to deaths cold shade
like one whose strength and hopes are fled
    they number me among the dead

Like those who shrouded in the grave
    from thee no more rememberence have
cast off from thy sustaining care
    down to the confines of despair

Thy wrath has hard upon me Lain
    afflicting me with restless paine
me all thy mountaines waves have prest
    too weak allas to Bear the teast

Removed from frinds I sigh alone
    in a loath'd dungeon laine where none
a visit will vouchsafe to me
confind past hopes of liberty

My eys from weeping never cease
    they waste but still my griefs increase
yet daily lord to the I prayed
    with out tretch'd hands invoked thy aid

Appendix VIII.

Wilt thou by mircals rivive
    the dead whome thou forsookes alive
from death restore thy praise to sing
    whome thou from prison woulst can bring

O lord to my relife draw near
    for never was more pressing need
for my diliverence Lord appear
    and add to deliverence speed

but as for me my stedfast hope
    shall on thy power depent
and I in gratfull songs of praise
    my time to come will spend

God has releast my soul from those
    that did with me contend
and made a numerous host of frinds
    my rightous cause defent

But thou O Lord art my defence
    on the my hopes rely
thou art my glory and shall yet
    lift up my head on high

Written by Eliza Fenning sutable for hir unfortunate Case Adue

APPENDIX IX.

Extract from F. W. Hackwood's Biography of William Hone.[204]

In the year following the Cochrane affair, having recovered his health, Hone took an intense interest in the case of Eliza Fenning, a poor innocent servant-girl who was hanged for a supposed attempt to poison her master, a law-stationer, in Chancery Lane. Her case has often been cited as one showing the danger of acting on purely circumstantial evidence.

As stated by Sir Samuel Romilly, this poor girl was tried at the Old Bailey in April 1815, before the Recorder of London, for administering poison to her master and mistress and her master's father. The only evidence to affect the prisoner was circumstantial. The poison was contained in dumplings made by her; but then, she had eaten of them herself, and been as ill as any of the persons whom she was supposed to have intended to kill, and her eating of them could not be ascribed to art or to an attempt to conceal her crime, for she made no effort whatever to remove the strongest evidence of guilt – if guilt there was. She had left the dish unwashed, and the proof that arsenic was mixed in it was furnished by its being found in the kitchen the next day, exactly in the state in which it had been brought from the table. No motive, moreover, could be found for so atrocious an act. Her mistress had reproved her about three weeks before for some indiscretion, and had given her warning, but had afterwards consented to retain her in her service.

This was the only provocation for murdering, not her mistress only but her master and her master's father.

A crime of such enormity produced by so very slight a cause has probably never occurred in the history of human depravity. The Recorder, however, appeared to have conceived a strong prejudice against the prisoner. In summing up the evidence he made some very unjust remarks and unfounded observations to her disadvantage, and she was convicted.

The victim was given a public funeral, which at once advertised her presumed innocence and appealed to popular sympathy. Not less than ten thousand persons assembled in and around the churchyard of St George the Martyr to see her buried. Hone published An Authentic Report of the Trial; and Charles Phillips wrote a brilliant rhapsody on 'the fate of one so young, so fair, so innocent, cut down in early morn, with all life's brightness, only at its dawn'. 'Little,' said

---

204 Hackwood, 98-102.

Fenning.

that facile writer, 'did it profit thee that a city mourned over thy early grave, and that the most eloquent of men – Curran, a fellow-countryman – did justice to thy memory'.

The singularity of the trial attracted the notice of many persons to her case, and they interested themselves in her favour, Hone being one who worked hard to obtain signatures to a petition in which they applied to the Crown for mercy. The master of the girl was requested to sign a petition on her behalf, but at the instance of the Recorder he refused. Every effort was unavailing; the sentence was executed, and the girl died, apparently under a strong sense of the truths of religion, and solemnly protesting her innocence.

Hone thus relates the scene of her execution:

I was going down Newgate Street on some business of my own. I got into an immense crowd that carried me along with them against my will; at length I found myself under the gallows where Eliza Fenning was to be hanged. I had the greatest horror of witnessing an execution, and of this in particular; a young girl of whose guilt I had grave doubts. But I could not help myself; I was closely wedged in; she was brought out. I saw nothing, but I heard all. I heard her protesting her innocence – I heard the prayer – I could hear no more. I stopped my ears, and knew nothing else till I found myself in the dispersing crowd, and far from the dreadful spot. I made my way to the house of a bookseller with whom I was very intimate; I asked him for a glass of water; I sat down and told him where I had been, and that people were saying the unhappy girl had 'died with a lie in her mouth'. 'Friend Hone,' said he, 'she is with her Almighty Father; I have visited her in prison, so have many of my friends, and we are satisfied of her innocence'. I was up immediately. 'Why, then, was she executed?' 'We made every possible exertion to save her life,' replied he, 'but we were not listened to'. 'The public must be roused about it,' said I. My friend replied, 'You are the man to do it, and I will print what you write'.

Hone continues:

I took lodgings away from my family, for I could do nothing among them, and for three weeks I was wholly engrossed on the case of Eliza Fenning. On the fourth Saturday evening my wife came to ask me for money – but I had none. I told my wife to go home, and that I would bring her money, but I had no idea where to get it; I had not sixpence. I went off to my friend the bookseller, and charged him with having made me neglect my family, asking him for the loan of a few pounds. Having obtained this, I walked through the turnstile into Lincoln's Inn Fields, and on, until a play-bill stuck up in large letters caught my eye: 'The Maid and the Magpie, repeated with unbounded applause to overflowing houses'.[205] An idea flashed upon my mind. I changed one of my notes and went to the play, in the pit, and saw The Maid and the Magpie.

---

205 See Appendix XI.

Appendix IX.

I went home and said to my wife, 'Give me a pair of candles and snuffers upstairs, and send for George Cruikshank'. He came; I said, 'Make me a cut of a Magpie hung by the neck to the gallows' – and I put my head on one side, and looked as like a dying Magpie as I could.

I walked to my printers, and by six o'clock in the morning The Maid and the Magpie was completed – and a thousand struck off. Cruikshank was ready with the frontispiece; and my wife sewed them. When the coaches drove up for the newspapers, we were ready with our pamphlets. 'Will you have this?' – 'How many?' – 'Half a hundred.' – 'A hundred.' So we effectually roused the public as to the case of Eliza Fenning, and I and my family lived for four months on The Maid and the Magpie.

That the case excited a great amount of public interest is evident from the amount of 'literature' which grew out of it. Hone, then at 55 Fleet Street (a small shop where he was twice robbed), published two works having rather formidable titles. One, at five shillings, was:

The Important Results of an Elaborate Investigation into the Mysterious Case of Elizabeth Fenning: being a detail of Extraordinary Facts discovered since her Execution, including the Official Report of her Singular Trial ... also a Memorial to H. R. H. The Prince Regent; and Strictures on a late Pamphlet of the Prosecutors' Apothecary; by John Watkins, LL.D.

The other, published at eighteenpence, was entitled:

Thirty Original and Interesting Letters written by the late Elizabeth Fenning whilst in prison and under sentence of Death, Declaratory of her Innocence ... Containing an Exposure of the Fabrications of the 'Observer' Newspaper, and other Falsehoods respecting the Case.

Hone also published a portrait of the poor girl, drawn by Isaac R. Cruikshank, father of George Cruikshank; while in the columns of the *Traveller* newspaper his pen was constantly busy in her defence.

APPENDIX X.

All the Year Round.[206]

Old Stories Retold.
Eliza Fenning. (The Danger of Condemning to Death on Circumstantial Evidence Alone.)

The background of this simple prosaic yet touching story is neither a palace nor a battlefield. The event we record was heralded by no stormy war-trumpets, and succeeded by no burst of national grief. Yet its catastrophe is the true basis of all tragedy – death, and, moreover, it is a story that is drawn, and will again draw, tears from eyes of all generous and warm-hearted people, who will here see a pure and, no doubt, entirely guiltless young creature entangled in a dreadful and irresistible destiny, and swept ruthlessly into another world without any further resistance than a piteous scream of despair, as she is dashed into the dark and pitiless gulf.

A third-rate London kitchen is perhaps the most unromantic of all places, the most dismal and dingy scene possible for any story. Everywhere it has more or less the same features – the smoky-faced clock ticking off the moments, the three rows of blue willow-pattern plates, the cat dozing on the scrubby hearth-rug, the ill-used blackbird in the willow cage in the cavernous area, the splashed and grimy windows dulling even the brightest sunbeam, the dusty bonnet on the nail behind the door, the jack-towel printed with black fingermarks, the great generous fire – the only joyous thing in the place, except the cook's reddened face, and the little square looking-glass hanging over the dresser, in which the housemaid reviews with approval her smiling face and bright eyes every three minutes before her sweetheart, the baker, raps at the back door. But dreary as the half-subterranean kitchen is, still more dismal are generally its subordinate rooms, its murderous coal-hole, its dark back wash-house, its sour smelling, mouldy beer-cellar, its dim lumber-cupboards, where black-beetles and rats alone hold holiday; and even more ineffably miserable than this part of the premises is the area itself, with often one crippled, dusty mottled-leafed Aucuba in an old red oil-jar, fighting for existence against soot, drought, and general misery and

---

[206] Thornbury, W., 'Eliza Fenning. (The Danger of Condemning to Death on Circumstantial Evidence Alone.)' in *All the Year Round* (ed. Charles Dickens), 13 July 1867. The text is presented without editorial interference.

Fenning.

destitution.

Probably not far unlike our rough picture was the kitchen of No. 68, Chancery-lane, on Monday, the 20th of March, 1815. No. 68 was then occupied by Mr. Robert Turner, a law-stationer, his apprentices and family. The shop was, of course, the usual congeries of blanched parchment, red tape, green ferreting ink, quills, blank law forms, penknives, almanacks, and other apparatus of law, and sometimes of justice. Eliza Fenning, a young cook, was bustling about the kitchen, getting a pastry-board ready to make some dumplings. The girl had been in the service of Mr. Turner only about seven weeks. Eliza was a good-natured, amiable girl; but three weeks before, her mistress had reproved her for romping with one of the apprentices, named Gadsden; but as the apprentice was clearly in the wrong, and had been rude to her, the mistress had withdrawn the warning she had threatened, and thought no more of the matter.

This unjust complaint had, however, preyed on the girl's mind, and she had been rather less respectful and somewhat sullen since the occurrence, and had told her fellow-servant, Sarah Peer, the housemaid, that she should never like the family any more; with several young man about, the mistress had been right in being particular; but the girl was sensitive, and thought that blame had fallen unjustly on her.

On the Monday morning early, there came a ring at the Chancery-lane door, and Eliza's fellow-servant, Sarah Peer, ran up to answer the bell. It proved to be Joseph Penson, a man from Mr. Edmonds's, the brewer, in Gray's Inn-lane. He had brought some yeast that Eliza had asked for some days before, to make some dumplings. The yeast had been taken out of the stilliards where the casks lay, and from the place from whence the bakers usually had it. Sarah emptied it into a white basin, thanked the man, chatted for one moment, flirted for another, then ran racing down-stairs with the yeast, and gave it to Eliza. The new cook instantly went up to Mrs. Turner in the dining-room, and reported triumphantly that the brewer had at last brought some yeast. The girl had repeatedly teased Mrs. Turner to let her make some dumplings, and she now again announced herself as a capital hand at making them. She seemed particularly anxious to show her skill, and the small vanity was in the eyes of the mistress rather commendable than otherwise. Mrs. Turner, however, informed Eliza that she did not on such occasions trouble the brewer's man, but always had the dough from the baker's, because it was thought the best; but having the yeast, she said, Eliza could now achieve her triumph, and make some dumplings next day; the poor girl retired to her own dominions delighted.

The next day (Tuesday), Mrs. Turner descends into the family vault to arrange the dinner and set the house in trim for the day. She orders the yeast dumplings, but tells Eliza to first make a beefsteak pie for the apprentices' dinner. Eliza is to go out and get the steaks in Brooks' Market, and afterwards carry the pie to the baker's, but when the dumpling dough is once made she is not to leave it

Appendix X.

till finished. Eliza is pleased and docile; so it shall be; she takes down the flour-dredger, the clean pastry-board, the rolling-pin, the flour-basin, and begins with a hearty good will, singing as she works. That is half-past eleven. At twelve, the pie ascends the area steps on its way to the baker's. The apprentices dine at two, the family at three. On Eliza's return, Mrs. Turner, a watchful housewife, now thoroughly roused on the question of dumplings, dives down again into the dim kitchen, and orders the dumpling dough to be mixed with milk and water. She then says:

'I suppose, Eliza, there is no occasion for me to stop?'

The girl replies: 'Oh, no, ma'am; I know very well how to do it.'

In half an hour, Mrs. Turner dives again, finds Eliza serenely triumphant, and the dough set in a pan before the fire, on the bright steel fender, to rise. Several times afterwards, Mrs. Turner returns to the charge, lifts the cloth from the pan, and eyes the dough, that, however, obstinately refuses to rise. It still lies in an unusual way, and in an odd shape. Before twelve, the six dumplings are divided ready to put into the pan; the other servant, Sarah Peer, who is going out for the day, has been up-stairs ever since a quarter-past eleven, mending a counterpane, and no one but Eliza and Mrs. Turner has seen the dough. Mrs. Turner merely remarks in a disappointed way to Eliza that the dough does not rise, and the young cook confidently replies:

'It will rise before I want it.'

At two o'clock the beefsteak pie was sent for; it returned savoury and hot, and Gadsden came rattling down, hungry as a wolf, after copying deeds all morning. Sarah Peer, the housemaid, was going out for the day to see her sister at Hackney, and the conversation was about her going. Sarah was not on very good terms with the cook. Their tempers clashed, Eliza considering Sarah as sly and artful, and Sarah having many causes of complaint (as she thought), especially a recent case of some apron of hers being taken by Eliza for a duster. There might, too, be a little rivalry for Gadsden. The girls were now, however, friends again, and the old difference had been quite forgotten, at least by Eliza.

Gadsden handed the dishes, and drank the girls' health in small beer, with the gallantry of the young law-stationer in good society. Presently, as it got towards three, Eliza asked the housemaid to run out and get a halfpenny-worth of milk, as there was not enough in the house left from breakfast, to make sauce for the dumplings. She went; then the sauce was made, and the dinner served up to the family. Having done this, the housemaid prepared to start for Hackney, and Eliza rested placidly after her labours, waiting for the bell that would be the order for clearing away.

Mr. and Mrs. Turner are dining, and Mr. Turner's father is with them. (Mrs. Turner, the law-stationer's mother, was at her house in Lambeth.) The dinner is steaks and potatoes, and the yeast dumplings. The appearance of the dumplings

Fenning.

is unsatisfactory; they are black and heavy instead of being white and light, and Mrs. Turner (vexed at the failure after Eliza's teasing) remarks the fact to the housemaid, who brought them up and removed the cover. Mrs. Turner helps her husband and father-in-law to some, and takes a small piece of the not very inviting spongy paste herself. The front door slams: that is Sarah Peer gone out for the day.

All at once, Mrs. Turner feels a death-like faintness come over her; a cold dew breaks out upon her forehead. The room seems to turn round. Then comes on a violent pain, an extreme excruciating pain, that increases every moment. Quietly she rises from the table, steals up-stairs, and throws herself on her bed almost insensible, and, as she thinks, about to die. A deadly vomiting begins, and lasts for hours. Her head and chest swell, her tongue becomes enlarged. She remains alone and in great torture, wondering that no one comes to her assistance, but on at last going down-stairs she finds both her father and husband also grievously ill, and apparently poisoned; but how, by what, and by whom, they have as yet no suspicion.

Almost immediately after Mrs. Turner left the room, her father-in-law, going down-stairs quietly to his own special parlour, met his son in the passage at the foot of the stairs. He had been very sick, and his eyes were swollen and staring. The old man was alarmed, and in a few minutes afterwards, he too began to violently vomit, and instantly an intolerable burning pain spread across his stomach and chest. In the mean time, Roger Gadsden, the apprentice, had gone down to the kitchen during the family dinner, perhaps in search of some tit-bit, perhaps to whisper a word of flattery to his new sweetheart, Eliza.[207] The untoward dumplings had just been brought down-stairs, and there was a dumpling and a half lying black and heavy on the plate. Gadsden took up a knife and fork, and playfully began to experiment on the cold dumpling, but only ate a piece about as big as a walnut. He then took a bit of bread and sopped up the white sauce in the boat. These young sedentary apprentices can eat anything and at any time. He then returned back to his high stool in the office. Ten minutes afterwards – that is, about half-past three – his master, Mr. Robert Turner, came to him, and leaning on one of the desks, complained of being frightfully ill. About ten minutes after that, the terrible epidemic, that had spread like wildfire from life to life, affected the apprentice; he, too, fell ill, but not so ill as his master, who had eaten a dumpling and a half. The family being all apparently dying, the apprentice volunteered to go off to Lambeth and fetch Mr. Robert Turner's mother. On his way, the apprentice became much worse, and thought that he too was going to die.

---

[207] There was never any suggestion that there had been a romantic connection between Eliza and Gadsden; in the interim between Eliza's death and 1867 when this article was published there may have been unfounded speculation and rumour.

Appendix X.

Old Mrs. Turner arrived in Chancery-lane about eight o'clock; she found her son, her husband, and her son's wife, stretched on their beds in agonising pain, and still tormented by sickness. Very soon after old Mrs. Turner's arrival, Eliza Fenning was also taken ill, and began to vomit and show the same symptoms as the rest. Mrs. Turner met her at the stair-foot, and, having already heard the story from the frightened apprentice, began immediately about the unfortunate dumplings.

'Oh, those devilish dumplings!' said the old lady.

Eliza replied, 'It was not the dumplings, but the milk, ma'am.'

'What milk?'

'The half-penny worth of milk that Sally fetched for the sauce which Mrs. Turner made.'

'That cannot be; it could not be the sauce.' Nor could it have been, because Mr. Robert Turner, who had not touched the sauce, was worse than any of the others.

But Eliza had her own theory (poor girl), although it slightly wavered.

'Yes,' she said; 'for Gadsden ate a very little bit of dumpling, not bigger than a nut, but he licked up three-parts of a boat of sauce with a bit of bread.'

The family had already sent for a friend and neighbour.[208] Now they sent for Mr. John Marshall, a surgeon. He arrived about a quarter before nine, and at nine Eliza's fellow-servant returned from Hackney. The family were already suspicious and alarmed, because Eliza, who had cooked the fatal dinner, had not evinced any interest in their illness or any desire to help them. How suspicion puts out the eyes even of honest people! The reason was obvious to any one but the frightened law-stationer and his family. The poor girl was found by the surgeon lying unheeded on the stairs, in great agony, and with exactly the same symptoms as the Turners. At that time Mr. Robert Turner and his wife were both in bed, complaining of violent and excruciating pain, and affected with irrestrainable sickness. The symptoms of all were unmistakably those following poisoning by arsenic.

The suspicion of the family had already fallen strongly and threateningly upon the poor young servant-girl. In the morning following that alarming day, the elder Mr. Turner began seriously to prosecute inquiries. He tried to ascertain if poison had ever been kept in the house, and if any traces of arsenic could be found in the kitchen, or in the relics of yesterday's dinner. All at once he remembered (in a flash) that there had been for a long time two packets of arsenic for mice, kept carelessly in an open drawer in the office, facing the fireplace. The poison had been in two flat packets, tied together very tight, and labelled:

'Arsenic – Deadly Poison.'

---

208   Mr. Henry Ogilvy, a local apothecary.

Fenning.

The drawer in which the poison had been kept, was a drawer in which wastepaper was also put. The girl had been seen to go to the drawer for paper. Eliza Fenning had access to the room after the apprentice unlocked it in the morning; but not at night, when it was kept shut. On inquiry, the poison had been seen by Gadsden on the 7th of March, but not since that date. That was mysterious, and must be traced further. The old gentleman then went into the kitchen to peer about. He looked into every pan for flour, yeast, or remains of dumpling. He found at last, a brown pan stuck round with some residue of the dumpling dough. Mr. Turner cautiously swilled the pan with water, and stirred it with a spoon until he had made the dough into a pasty liquid. Then, to his horror, he found, on setting the pan down for half a minute, and subsequently slanting the liquid, a suspicious-looking white powder trail slowly over the bottom of the pan.

Mr. Turner showed this to several persons, and then locked it up until Mr. Marshall, the surgeon, came. Mr. Marshall looked grave when he saw the white powder. He soon carefully examined the pan, and washed it round with a tea-kettleful of hot water. He stirred the liquid, let it subside, and decanted it off. He then washed it a second time. The result was the deposit of half a tea-spoonful of white powder, and that white powder was arsenic. In the fragments of pure yeast, and in the flour-tub, there was no arsenic. Mr. Turner also showed to Mr. Marshall, the knives and forks with which the dumplings had been eaten; they were quite black in the blades, and that blackness the surgeon attributed to their having touched arsenic. Mr. Turner then cross-examined the unhappy girl, on whom all faces now frowned and looked hard and condemning. The old man asked the girl sternly, how she came to introduce ingredients that had been so prejudicial to them? Eliza Fenning replied that it had not been in the dumplings, but in the milk Sarah Peer brought in. It was in the milk; must have been in the milk; that she persisted in. No one but herself, she said, positively and frankly, had (to her knowledge) mixed or had had anything to do with the dumplings.

The Turners' faces grew darker and sterner. The housemaid left Eliza alone, and was silent when she spoke. The old man looked pitying, but inflexible.

They whispered when she entered the room, then became gloomily silent till she left it. Even Gadsden avoided her when he came down to the kitchen. No one seemed inclined to take food from her hands. But worse was to come. On the morning of the 23rd, Mr. Turner entered the kitchen, followed by a dogged-looking man, who told her to put on her bonnet at once and follow him. Where? Why, 'to the Hatton Garden police-office.' Charge – attempting to poison the family of Mr. Orlibar Turner, on the 21st of March.

While sitting sobbing in an ante-room of that (to her) dreadful place, Eliza Fenning was asked by Thisselton, the officer who had apprehended her, and had examined her pockets and box, without finding anything suspicious, if she had at all suspected the flour? The poor girl said, in a simply unsuspicious way, that she had made a beefsteak pudding of the same flour with which she had made the

Appendix X.

dumplings, and that she and her fellow-servant and one of the apprentices had dined off the pie. Thisselton then said that if anything bad had been in the flour, it must have hurt them as well as her. She then said she had thought there was something in the yeast; she had noticed a white settlement in it after she had used it; or the other girl, who was very sly and artful, might have put something in the milk. Poor creature! She was evidently racking her brain for all possible causes of the intended crime, or of the accident, whichever it had been.

The witnesses were all strongly biased against this poor defenceless creature, and on the 30th she was committed for trial. Gadsden, when examined, mentioned that as he was cutting the dumpling, Eliza had said to him (a mere good-natured warning):

'Gadsden, don't eat that; it is cold and heavy; it will do you no good.'

The trial came on at the Old Bailey on Tuesday, April 11, 1815. The prisoner was indicted under the 43rd of George the Third, c. 58, which made it a capital offence (everything was capital in the then bloodthirsty state of the law) to administer a deadly poison with intent to murder. The recorder (a notorious hangman), John Silvester, presided as judge. Mr. Gurney (afterwards baron of the Exchequer) conducted the case for the prosecution. Mr. Ally (irritable Adolphus's irritable enemy) defended the prisoner, and was most painstaking and elaborate in his cross-examinations.

It was the savage and merciless custom of those days not to allow the counsel to speak for a prisoner upon the facts. No final recapitulation and appeal to the jury was permitted; the jury's often confused minds were allowed to grope for the truth amid all the prejudiced statements of interested witnesses, the violence of hurried prosecutors, and the natural difficulties of the case. In charges of misdemeanour in civil actions and where life was not involved, but property (far dearer to our Draconic lawgivers of the eighteenth century) was, the privilege was not withheld from the barrister for the defence. It was not till 1831 that this cruel and disgraceful anomaly was done away with.

From the beginning, Mr. Silvester inclined against the prisoner. At the close of his charge, his bias approached criminality. He decided that the poison was in the dough, because persons who had not touched the sauce had also been seized; therefore it was not in the milk; nor could it have been in the general mass of flour, because no one who had merely eaten the beefsteak pie had suffered. But in the following part of his remarks, he dwelt on Eliza's indifference to the sufferings of the family, suppressing all mention of the fact that she too was poisoned, and was at that very time in equal agony. He said:

'Gentlemen, you have now heard the evidence given on this trial, and the case lies in a very narrow compass. There are but two questions for your consideration, and these are, the fact of poison having been administered, in all, to four persons; and by what hand such poison was given. That these persons were poisoned

Fenning.

appears certain from the evidence of Mrs. Charlotte Turner, Orlibar Turner, Roger Gadsden, the apprentice, and Robert Turner, for each of these persons ate of the dumplings, and were all more or less affected; that is, they were every one poisoned. That the poison was in the dough of which these dumplings were composed has been fully proved, I think, by the testimony of the surgeon who examined the remains of the dough left in the dish in which the dumplings had been mixed and divided; and he deposes that the powder which had subsided at the bottom of the dish was arsenic. That the arsenic was not in the flour I think, appears plain, from the circumstance that the crust of a pie had been made that very morning with some of the same flour of which the dumplings were made, and that the persons who dined off the pie felt no inconvenience whatever; that it was not in the yeast, nor in the milk, has been also proved; neither could it be in the sauce, for two of the persons who were ill never touched a particle of the sauce, and yet were violently affected with retching and sickness. From all these circumstances it must follow that the poisonous ingredient was in the dough alone; for, besides that the persons who partook of the dumplings at dinner were all more or less affected from what they had eaten, it was observed by one of the witnesses that the dough retained the same shape it had when first put into the dish to rise, and that it appeared dark and was heavy, and, in fact, never did rise. The other question for your consideration is, by what hand the poison was administered; and although we have nothing before us but circumstantial evidence, yet it often happens that circumstances are more conclusive than the most positive testimony. The prisoner, when taxed with poisoning the dumplings, threw the blame first on the milk, next on the yeast, and then on the sauce; but it has been proved, most satisfactorily, that none of these contained it, and that it was in the dumplings alone, which no person but the prisoner had made. Gentlemen, if poison had been given even to a dog, one would suppose that common humanity would have prompted us to assist it in its agonies; here is the case of a master and a mistress being both poisoned, and no assistance was offered. Gentlemen, I have now stated all the facts as they have arisen, and I leave the case in your hands, being fully persuaded that, whatever your verdict may be, you will conscientiously discharge your duty both to your God and to your country.'

The prisoner's defence was extremely touching, because it contained no oratorical cant, no quibbles, no counter-charges, no cowardly accusations, but merely a few simple-hearted remarks denying malice against the family, which was supposed to be her motive, and explaining that she had been too ill on the Tuesday to assist her master. She said:

'I am truly innocent of the whole charge. I am innocent; indeed I am! I liked my place. I was very comfortable. Gadsden behaved rudely to me; my mistress came and saw me; she said she did not like it. I said, 'Ma'am, it is Gadsden that has been rough to me.' The next morning I said, 'I hope you do not think anything

Appendix X.

of what passed last night.' She was in a great passion, and said she would not put up with it. I was to go away directly. I did not look on Mrs. Turner, but the old lady, as my mistress. In the evening the old lady came to town. I said, 'I am going away to-night.' Mrs. Turner said, 'Do not think any more about it; I don't.' She asked Mrs. Robert Turner if she was willing for me to go. She said, 'No, she thought no more about it.' As to my master saying I did not assist him, I was too ill. I had no concern with that drawer at all: when I wanted a piece of paper, I always asked for it.'

The prisoner called five witnesses, who gave her the character of a good-natured and amiable girl; but they were heard most impatiently by the partial judge, and one of them he summarily put down. William Fenning, the prisoner's father, greatly agitated, stepped up into the witness-box, and said: 'I am the father the unfortunate girl, my lord; if you won't hear her, I hope you will hear me.'

He was proceeding to relate, amongst other circumstances, his having been denied access to his daughter when she was lying in great agony below stairs in Turner's house, from the effects of the poisoned dumplings; but the recorder would not let him go on, and put his hand out, motioning him to leave the witness-box, exclaiming that he could not hear him – it was too late. He must go down. The father left the box, tears streaming over his face.

The jury were quiet, dull, respectable people, who did not by any means wish to see servants trying to poison their masters with impunity. In a few minutes after retiring, they returned to their box, and, in answer to the mechanically put but portentous question, the foreman stood up and uttered the fatal word 'Guilty'.

The unhappy girl fell back in convulsions and was carried, screaming, from the court. She was soon brought back, pale, dazed, and stunned; the recorder put on the black cap and passed judgment of death upon her in a cool business-like way. That was over. Not a sort of girl one would have suspected of such a thing as this; but there was never any telling! So perhaps chatted the hanging recorder that evening over his Madeira. Mr. Ally, keen and subtle, had perhaps other feelings on the subject as that night in solitude he mused over the subject; but he was powerless, except to urge petitions to government.

In a very able article, entitled Legal Puzzles, in *Blackwood's Magazine*, some years ago, the 'learned and able writer' sums up the convincing (as he thinks) arguments of the guilt of Eliza Fenning. They are these:

1. That she was convicted, despite of the defence of able counsel (who was not allowed to speak in her favour).
2. That from the 11th of April to the 26th of July the case was repeatedly investigated by the law officers of the crown, but nothing fresh transpired in her favour. (The hanging recorder was present at these consultations, and his vanity would be of course roused not to let the verdict be reversed. That is human nature.)

Fenning.

3. That though the girl ate a portion of the dumpling after she had warned Gadsden of its heaviness, she did so when old Mrs. Turner was expected, to cunningly disarm suspicion. (Killing one's self is an odd way of disarming suspicion.)
4. That she made different and contradictory statements as to the food in which the poison was mixed. (How could a frightened innocent girl, who was merely guessing, do anything else but make tentative remarks?)

The arguments for her innocence are, we think, incontrovertibly stronger.

1. There was no adequate motive for the crime, nor was the girl by any means one of those sullen malignant tempers who kill for mere revenge. A month before she had been rated, justly or unjustly; she then had expressed momentary anger, perhaps exaggerated by her evidently hostile fellow-servant. She herself said in court that she liked her place, and was comfortable.
2. No poison was traced to her, and she was never seen with any poison.
3. Her caution to Gadsden was only kind, professional, and natural, and her own sufferings from the poison were most strongly in her favour. Moreover, let us remember that no one had then told her that the family had suspected the dumplings.
4. Still stronger in her favour is the fact that she made no effort to remove the pan, which still contained poison, and which, after all, furnished the only positive proof that arsenic had been mixed with the food which had been eaten.

A little imagination could conceive a thousand ways by which the poison, kept with such criminal carelessness in an open office drawer, had got mixed with waste paper, and been thoughtlessly taken down into the kitchen. Let us suppose the girl went, as she was allowed, to the office drawer for waste paper to light the fire; had more than she wanted; and carried the residue down-stairs for the use of the kitchen. The poison, a year and a half tumbled about unheeded in the drawer in a tight flat packet pinched with twine, might have leaked at one corner, and have sprinkled the paper to the extent of a spoonful, at least, without necessarily being noticed. That paper may have been used to rub out the pan, or to put the flour in, or for some purpose connected with the fatal meal.

The popular mind has a keen sense of injustice. That excellent and unswerving man, Sir Samuel Romilly, boldly and generously recorded his belief in Fenning's innocence. In Lord Sidmouth's time such an impugnment of the governing wisdom was not without its dangers. The people had borne pretty well for some centuries being hanged for stealing five shillings, for stealing a strip of cloth from a bleaching-ground, for passing a bad shilling; old men and children had gone to the gallows in hundreds for the smallest felonies; but now a terrible conviction seized people that judges, in their anxiety to purge the commonweal of perilous stuff, often leaned so much towards the gibbet that they sometimes

Appendix X.

forgot justice. There had been in this case palpable and cruel prejudice or folly; innocent facts had been willfully distorted into proofs of guilt. The public is but a grand jury, and it refused to consider the girl as a would-be murderess. She had not sufficient motive – so many unaccountable accidents it was clear might have led to the apparent crime. The friends of the poor girl almost compelled Lord Eldon to rouse himself in the matter. What was etiquette when a human life was depending on the turn of a moment? The lord chancellor, the recorder (now Sir John Silvester, Bart.), and Mr. Beckett met at Lord Sidmouth's offices. They decided that nothing had occurred that should stay the hangman's eager hand. The bias of government then, was to resent with arrogance all popular interference. The servants had got into the bad habit of defying the masters who paid them. The lawyers were, in fact, so certain of the justice of the verdict, that Lord Eldon, to satisfy his own – seldom satisfied – mind, and to put a stop to the doubts of irritated and alarmed people, held another meeting the night before the execution, and came again, singularly enough, to the very determination to which they had long since determined to come. To negative a recorder's sentence would be to confess that the sentences of that good servant of the crown had been often unjust. That would never do.

The unhappy victim of some unaccountable accident was put to death on Wednesday, July 26th, 1815. It is a sorry sight even to see a bull-necked murderer, with ape's forehead and cruel cretin eyes, appear upon the scaffold before the Debtors' Door, trembling as he unconsciously repeats the prayer. How agonising is the shuddering look as the sickly eye is raised involuntarily and falls on that one horrible object that seems to fill heaven and earth – the gallows! But there was a young and probably innocent girl to be lifted up and killed before ten thousand pitying people. No feverish hatred, no screams of delight, as the poor girl, dressed in white (at her own desire), ascended the steps firmly. The interest was intense, because it was fervently expected that she would make in public a final and decided denial of the crime of which she had been found guilty. So it proved.

Mr. Peter Burke, who has taken great interest in the innocence of this victim of bad law, says that she ascended the scaffold about a quarter-past eight.

'A few minutes before she ascended the scaffold, the Reverend Mr. Cotton, the Ordinary of Newgate, asked her whether she had any communication to make; she paused for a moment, and then said with firmness and strong emphasis, "Before the just and Almighty God, and by the faith of the Holy Sacrament I have taken, I am innocent of the offence with which I am charged." She afterwards said, in an indistinct tone of voice, what seemed to the bystanders to be, "that the truth of the business would be disclosed in the course of the day."

The Reverend Mr. Cotton, anxious to learn precisely what she uttered, requested her to repeat her words. She then said, "I am innocent, and I hope, in God, the truth may be disclosed in the course of the day." She prayed fervently, and

Fenning.

seemed perfectly resigned to her fate. On being asked in the last awful moment to confess her crime, she unhesitatingly declared, as she had done throughout her imprisonment, in the most solemn manner, her perfect innocence. She also expressed her resignation, and her confidence of entering the kingdom of Heaven. This she repeated while the executioner was preparing for his fearful office. The last words of Eliza Fenning, on being addressed by the attendant clergyman, were, "I know my situation, and may I never enter the kingdom of Heaven, to which I feel confident I am going, if I am not innocent."

'A thrill of agony ran through the hearts of that vast crowd when the bolt fell, and the slender form in white swayed in the wind and rain. For her, elsewhere there was mercy; we do not doubt it.'

The executioner, after demanding fees oppressive to poor people, although in this instance no more than fourteen shillings, was allowed to surrender the body of Eliza Fenning to her friends. They resolved on a public funeral, as at once an assertion of innocence and an appeal to popular sympathy. She was buried on the 31st of July, at St. George's-the-Martyr. There were ten thousand persons in the churchyard, as the coffin, inscribed,

ELIZA FENNING,
Died July 26th, 1815, aged 22 years,

was lowered into the grave. To that grave-side, there had followed the body, a long procession. Six young women dressed in white had supported the pall. The coffin was preceded by a dozen constables, and followed by about thirty more. There were several hundred mourners. Many thousand persons succeeded them. The windows, and even the tops of the houses, were thronged by spectators. The people of London wept for her, and the great generous heart of London is seldom in the wrong in such a case.

As usual, however, when partisan feeling is excited, the recorder party set afloat many hasty, unsifted, and cruel calumnies. It was reported that Eliza Fenning had, when a child, been turned out of the schools in Lincoln's Inn-fields for dissolute conduct; that, at Mr. Turner's, she had nightly visited the apprentices' bedroom; that, even in Newgate, she had fallen in love with some of the prisoners, and written to them in terms of the grossest licentiousness. With these things we have nothing to do; the question is simply, did she intentionally mix poison with the Turners' food? We are filled with a deep conviction that she was entirely innocent. With many persons the case will, perhaps, always remain a problem. In the Annual Register for 1857, it is stated, on the authority of Mr. Gurney, that Eliza Fenning, on the morning of her execution, confessed the crime to Mr. James Upton, a Baptist minister. If this statement were true, it would authoritatively end the matter, but we disbelieve it in toto. Weak ministers, unaccustomed to give spiritual advice to persons condemned to death, get flurried and confused

Appendix X.

in a prison cell. Importuned to confess, the poor girl, no doubt, made some general confession of her utter sinfulness; and this the Baptist minister, perhaps previously prejudiced, may have mistaken or exaggerated. We implicitly believe that he did this (it may be, with some little unconscious touch of vanity in his own powers of working repentance, but we do not think, wilfully). The evidence of Mr. Cotton, a man of tried experience, is expressly contrary to any such testimony. Curran used to declaim glowingly on the unhappy fate of Eliza Fenning; Hone, the ardent politician and author of the Every Day Book, published an authentic report of her trial, as an antidote to the garbled summary of it put forth in the Old Bailey Sessions Paper, with curious letters from the prisoner herself, and, in our own time, Mr. Charles Phillips wrote a brilliant rhapsody on the fate of one – 'so young, so fair, so innocent' – cut down in the morning, with all life's brightness only in its dawn. 'Little,' says the writer, 'did it profit thee that a city mourned over thy early grave, and that the most eloquent of men (Curran, a fellow-countryman) did justice to thy memory!'

We reserve for our concluding paragraph, the statement that the Judge who tried this case was an Advocate against the girl, and was unfeeling, and unfair.

APPENDIX XI.

La Pie Voleuse.

THE NARRATIVE OF THE MAGPIE;
Or the Maid of Palaiseau.
Being the History of
The Maid and the Magpie.
Founded upon the Circumstance
Of an Unfortunate Female
Having been
Unjustly Sentenced to Death,
On Strong Presumptive Evidence.
With a Preface.

The romantic Drama of the MAID and the MAGPIE has excited the deepest and most extraordinary Interest, and is received with
UNANIMOUS AND REPEATED SHOUTS OF APPLAUSE.

LONDON:
Printed by J. Swan, 76 Fleet Street,
For William Hone, 55 Fleet Street.
1815.
(PRICE SIXPENCE.)

TO THE READER.

In the *Recueil des Causes celebre*, a Collection of celebrated Trials, is recorded the case of a servant girl who was accused of robbing her master of plate and jewels, to a considerable amount, and, *upon presumptive evidence, found guilty and executed*. It was discovered, some time afterwards, that the real thief was a Magpie who conveyed the articles missing to its nest, in the belfry of a neighbouring steeple. The prosecutor, to atone for the dreadful error, of which he was the cause, founded a daily mass for the repose of the poor girl's soul, and it was regularly celebrated until the Revolution swept away the endowment.

Upon the above incident is founded a melo-dramatic piece, intitled, *La Pie Voleuse*, which has nightly attracted all Paris, and, being adapted to the English stage, under the title of *The Maid and the Magpie*, is now received with extraordinary sympathy by the crowds who anxiously witness its representation.

The basis of the plot appears almost too simple and too improbable, but genius renders trifles important, and experience proves what appears improbable to have been true. With slender materials the talent of the dramatist has constructed an elegant piece, in which the dialogue is kept up with spirit, and the interest never subsides. There is little to attach us to the victim of injustice beyond the simple fact of her oppression; but innocence suffering the punishment of the guilty seizes with firm grasp upon the feelings, and the combination of the attendant circumstances produce an effect truly astonishing. Upon the representation of the Drama of *The Maid and the Magpie*, 'many incidents were seized on by the audience, who thought proper to apply them to the case of Eliza Fenning.'* The piece proceeded amidst tumultuous bursts of feeling, and, when the curtain fell, the shouts of approbation were repeated and unanimous. Every subsequent performance has been seen with equal admiration, and been received with similar vociferous applause.

'In ENGLAND, where every part of the population may become, as jurors, the arbiters of the lives of their neighbours, it is highly important that the habit of DECIDING WITH THE GREATEST CAUTION *should be cultivated*; and that suspected innocence should have everything to hope from an *investigation* into the untoward circumstances which have first sullied its reputation.'†

With these views, this *most interesting* story, as it is dramatised, has been put into narrative, in the following pages of this little publication, and in doing so, the variations from the drama are very trifling. The sentiments principally applauded by the audience are printed in *Italics* and CAPITALS.

M. E. – Sept. 6, 1815.

* See Mr Louis Goldsmith's Anti-Gallican Monitor, Sept. 3, 1815.
† *Morning Herald*, Sept. 4, 1815.

*

THE NARRATIVE OF THE MAID AND THE MAGPIE, &C. &C.

In the window of the farmhouse of the rich Gerard, a farmer at Palaiseau, hung a magpie, in a white wicker cage.

Blazeau! Blazeau! called the knavish magpie.

Blazeau, the good Gerard's godson, ran into the courtyard, and, meeting Annette, the maid servant, enquired if she called him.

Blazeau! Blazeau! vociferated the magpie.

Blazeau and Annette laughed when they found who had occasioned their meeting; and Blazeau related how he had been alarmed from the immorality of encroaching on a bottle of his godmother's delicious wine, by 1the mischief-loving magpie loudly screaming Blazeau! Blazeau! just as he had lifted the bottle

Appendix XI.

to drink. Blazeau was proceeding to account for his godmother's keeping the bird, on account of its loquacity being similar to her own, when the bustling Dame Gerard entered, anxiously calling for her lazy godson, Blazeau.

Annette was quickly despatched by her mistress, and Gerard luckily came in and saved Blazeau from his wife's resentment, by good humouredly rallying her on her domestic qualifications for scolding the servants; the dame, in return, charged her husband and Blazeau with turning Annette's head, by praising her person, and expressed her belief, that even the Justice himself had been such an old fool as to fall in love with the girl.

Blazeau protested the Justice should not have her.

Gerard declared that although misfortunes had reduced Annette's father to serve as a soldier, yet, as she was well educated and deserving, she merited protection.

Dame Gerard said, she could not talk all day; she called – Annette!

The farmer declared his wife never allowed a moment's peace to --

Annette! cried the magpie.

Annette came in with some articles of plate, in a basket, enquiring if she was called.

The dame charged Annette to take care of the plate, reminding her that, on the good farmer's birthday, a silver fork was missing.

Annette declared her sincere concern at its loss.

Blazeau believed that Old Nick must have carried it off.

The farmer requested that the unceasing lamentations over the fork might be ended.

His wife went away in dudgeon; Annette was in great distress the uneasiness the loss of the fork had occasioned: but Gerard consoled her with the intimation, that he wished an union between her and Blazeau, to whom she was attached, and who, in return, loved her sincerely, and, conjuring-her to bear with his dame's infirmity of temper, he left her.

Scarcely had the good Gerard departed, when Isaac, a Jew pedlar, solicited Annette's attention to his box of wares. She had sent her father all her money a week before, and, declining to become the Jew's customer, he went his way.

A man now approached the farm house, wearing a large cloak over a military uniform, with his hat pulled over his eyes. He seemed distressed. Annette viewed him with pity --

It was her father!

Annette was holding in her hand a spoon and fork, which she had taken from Dame Gerard's basket of plate: in her agitation, she threw them on the table, instead of into the basket, and flew to embrace her father.

After the first emotion, he informed her that, on his regiment arriving at Paris, he

Fenning.

had solicited two days' leave of absence, to visit her; had been refused – entreated again – was again refused – had charged his superior officer with cruelty, who, lifting hls cane at him, the indignant father drew his sabre and was disarmed by his comrades, but having, by military law, thus incurred death, he had purchased a disguise, had fled to embrace his daughter, and, having now succeeded in clasping her in his arms, intended to quit the village at daybreak. The wretched father obtained a solemn promise from his daughter, that she would not disclose his error to anyone, and being known in the regiment by the name of *Evrard* only, purposed to conceal himself by his real name, *Grandville*.

Annette proposed to fly with her father.

Whilst negativing her affectionate but imprudent proposal, Annette, with vexation beheld the Justice approach. She had no time to conceal her beloved parent, but she entreated him to cover his uniform and sit quiet, and, as the odious Justice entered the gate, she filled her father a glass of wine.

When the Justice arrived, he smirkingly wished her good morning, and enquired who that man was: she said, a poor traveller whom she was refreshing. The Justice told her that he required her charity himself. She offered him a glass of wine. He chid her for not comprehending his meaning, and her father affecting to be asleep, the dotard proceeded to make love to her.

The Justice's servant entered with a letter, which had just been left by an officer of the *Marechausee*.

The Justice, not having his spectacles, with difficulty read the commencement – it was a description of a deserter – he entreated the terrified Annette to read it for him – trembling she suggested his return home – he repeated his wish. In dreadful agitation, she took the paper: it was the description of her father! Compelled to read it, she glanced her eye towards her father's dress – he sat in speechless agony. She beckoned him to seem sleeping, and then, affecting to read the contents of the paper, she gave a description of his person and dress exactly opposite to that which he wore. The paper concluded by ordering the Justice to cause Evrard's arrest, if he was in his jurisdiction, and requesting him to transmit copies of the description to the different stages of the *Marechausee*.

Evrard still appearing to sleep, the Justice clapped him on the shoulder and desired him to stand up. He was double the age of *Annette*'s description, and, in other respects, wholly unlike it. The Justice caused him to depart. Annette, suspecting the Justice's motive, entreated his permission to withdraw to finish her work – he proceeded to rudeness.

Villain! cried Evrard, who had, in ambush, watched the Justice's behaviour.

Annette rapidly motioned her father to retreat.

The Justice looked fearfully round – he saw nobody.

Annette pointed at the magpie!

Appendix XI.

Again the Justice was rude.

Annette in a tone of proud disdain admonished him – he persisted – she desired him to desist, or he would suddenly repent. She felt secure in the presence of her beloved father, who continued from his hiding place to behold the scene – the Justice was not sufficiently repulsed, he laughed in scorn. Annette threatened him with the vengeance of one who should chastise his insolence. He became irritated: she answered him with disdainful irony. The Justice, maddened into rage, bade Annette tremble, and rushed homewards, threatening her with revenge, with bitter, with terrible revenge!

Poor Evrard, agitated by what he had been compelled to witness, came forward and embrace[d] his daughter: there was no time to be lost; it was necessary they should part. Evrard had no money, he had told his daughter he had expended all her little savings in purchasing his disguise. They were alike destitute; but he had preserved a silvery fork and spoon, the only memorials he possessed of his dear Annette's mother; he gave them to his weeping daughter, and entreated her to sell them immediately and privately, and to hide the money she got for them in a hollow willow tree, which he described at the entrance of the village, from whence, at nightfall, he would fetch it. Annette put them in her pocket, and parted from her father in an agony of distress.

Whilst the unhappy father and his daughter were embracing, the magpie, whose cage door was open, came down on the table, where Dame Gerard's fork and spoon lay, which had been thrown there by Annette, on her father's first appearance. The magpie flew off with the spoon, unperceived by Annette, who hastily caught up the fork, without missing the spoon, and, putting it into her basket, carried the plate indoors.

The poor girl, whilst pondering in the farmhouse *parlour* how she should dispose of her father's fork and spoon, recollected the Jew. Luckily he made his appearance: she sold them to him, received the money, and, whilst putting it in her pocket, was accosted by Blazeau, who, when he learned she had been selling to the Jew, whom he had seen leave the parlour, instead of having purchased of him, affectionately remonstrated with Annette, for not sharing with him his little hoard. She excused herself on the ground of not wanting what she sold.

Annette, anxious to deposit the money in the hollow tree, for her father, was prevented by the entrance of the worthy Gerard, who seeing Blazeau with her, proposed that his dame should be immediately made acquainted with their views as to marriage. The poor girl, not being in spirits to talk on that theme, was leaving the room, when Madame Gerard met her with her usual complaint of, nothing having been done whilst the mistress was absent.

The farmer and Blazeau withdrew.

The good woman was not in a bad humour *for her*: she began to talk of a fête the day before, at the same time counting the spoons. Only *eleven*? said she. She proceeded with counting them again – two – four – six – eight – ten – *eleven*! Why, where's the other spoon? why it's lost! She desired Annette to count them herself, Annette counted the spoons – Eleven! – no more! she was thunderstruck!

Madame Gerard called her husband and Blazeau. She desired Blazeau to look for the spoon – the spoon that was *lost*! Annette had been earnestly seeking it: Her mistress saw she was unsuccessful, but still she enquired if she had found it. She had not. Blazeau returned to report, that he could not find it, notwithstanding Dennis, the Justice's servant, had helped him to look for it. Blazeau jocosely supposed the spoon was gone to look after the fork. The dame became seriously enraged at its loss. In vain did Annette's deep distress plead for her. The spoon was lost and it must he found – there had been a. fork lost before! – they could not have gone without hands! – the only question was, who was the thief? --

Annette! screamed a voice.

Annette's heart died within her.

Dame Gerard and Blazeau enquired together – who spoke?

Gerard laughing, pointed to the magpie, and observed that their bird had called her favourite.

Blazeau exclaimed against the rascally mag.

Madame Gerard thought that there was something *very extraordinary* in what the bird said, notwithstanding.

Annette's distress increasing, the good farmer asked her if she supposed they minded the chattering pie.

Annette, in tears, with deep sobs pointed to his wife.

Dame Gerard said, she accused nobody, but suspected everybody.

Her suspicions, though not expressed by words, were evidently against Annette. She was determined, she said, to get to the bottom of it.

In vain did Gerard entreat no more might be said on the subject: his wife would only be pacified by the assurance, that nobody should go out until the spoon was found, or until after the Justice had been.

At this moment the Justice came in: he had been informed of the loss of the spoon by his man, who had assisted Blazeau to look for it. He brought his clerk, he said, to take the examinations of everybody. Gerard protested against such a general investigation, but his wife thought it would be best, and, whoever might turn out to be guilty, she consoled herself that --

-- The culprit would be hanged, and there's an end on't – said the Justice.

Gerard solemnly conjured his wife to consider --. In vain did he entreat: the good woman was vociferous for her lost spoon, and the Justice was determined that *justice* should take its course!

The examination was made to state, that a silver fork was stolen a fortnight

Appendix XI.

before, and a silver spoon that day; that they *having been in Annette's custody*, SHE *must of course be suspected*; in short, *there was* STRONG PRESUMPTIVE PROOF *against* HER.

In vain did Blazeau protest, *if that was* THE LAW, it was *villanous*!

Annette, drowned in tears, in drawing her handkerchief from her pocket, drew out the money she had received from the Jew: – it fell on the ground.

The farmer's wife suspiciously enquired what it was.

As Annette hastily picked up the purse, she said it was her own.

Dame Gerard declared that Annette, not a week before, had sent all her money to her father.

The farmer himself solemnly enquired of Annette how she came by the money. Annette, horror-stricken at the good farmer's manner, vowed the money was her own.

Blazeau; hoping to explain in Annette's favour, related that he knew Annette had come honestly by it: — she had received it from the Jew that morning.

For what?

Annette, in a stupor of grief reproached herself, that she had not sold her cross from her neck.

The Justice exulted in the turn the enquiry was taking: — the cruel Justice ordered her to deliver up the money.

In vain did Annette, thinking of her father's necessities and danger, fall on her knees, and, lifting her eyes to heaven, declare the money her own – that what she sold was her own. *I am innocent!* – she cried – *I am innocent!*

The Justice desired his clerk to write that Blazeau said he had seen Annette receive payment of the Jew for the *stolen* property.

Blazeau exclaimed that he had not said so, that it was a shame to TWIST WORDS AND MEANINGS.

The Justice attempted to intimidate Blazeau.

The good Gerard DECLARED BROWBEATING to be *unnecessary to the ends of justice*.

Blazeau ran out in search of the Jew.

Annette anxiously desired his appearance, that he might produce the articles she sold him.

Gerard believed the Jew would clear Annette.

The Justice, who had been accustomed to delinquency, to the evasions and arts of the vile, said his *knowledge of the world* enabled him to decide upon her guilt.

The farmer knew little of the world, but believed Annette innocent, and protested against further proceedings.

Fenning.

The Justice declared the matter must go on upon the PROOFS before him.

Proofs! said Gerard — *grounds of suspicion*, if you please; but SUSPICION IS NOT PROOF.

Dame Gerard was terrified at the severity of the justice: she lamented the mischief occasioned by her precipitancy.

Blazeau entered, dragging in the Jew, who was immediately interrogated. The Jew looked wistfully at Annette: she desired him instantly to declare the *truth*.

The Jew said he had bought of Annette a silver fork and spoon!

Dame Gerard and her husband were astonished.

Reveal the *whole* truth, cried Annette; *produce* the fork and spoon, and — save my life!

The Jew had sold them to another travelling Jew, whom he had met, passing through the village!

Annette asserted her innocence.

She was requested to explain how she came possessed of any other fork and spoon but her master's. Spellbound by her promise to her father, and by the recollection of his dreadful situation, she could explain nothing.

I am the victim of CIRCUMSTANCES — said the miserable Annette.

The Justice ordered that the soldiers, whom he had taken care to have in waiting, should conduct her to prison.

The farmer's wife, rushing to her *beaufet*, took out a fork and spoon of the same set to which those missing belonged: her husband motioned her to be silent.

Gerard required the Jew to describe the fork and spoon he had bought of Annette. — The Jew's description corresponded with Gerard's lost articles. — Had they any cypher, or letter? — The Jew said they had — a *G*!

It was the initial of Grandville – the real name of Annette's father – as well as of Gerard.

The farmer showed the fork and spoon to the Jew, who thought them very like those he had bought. He could not swear positively to the exact resemblance; but, to the best of his recollection and belief, they were similar.

The Justice said that was sufficient, he would hear no more.

Blazeau quitted the room in deep sorrow.

I am INNOCENT! *I am* INNOCENT! said the overwhelmed girl.

Gerard, in distraction, entreated .her to prove it.

Annette energetically exclaimed — *Impossible*. I am INNOCENT! INNOCENT!

Her head fell upon her bosom, which heaved convulsively as she groaned to herself in bitter agony. Oh, my poor father! Once more she loudly shrieked, I AM INNOCENT!

Appendix XI.

She was hurried off by the soldiers to await her trial before the Grand Provost, who was on his circuit, and expected soon at the village.

The worthy Blazeau, faithfully attached to Annette, recovering from the first-effects of grief, visited the poor girl in prison. He brought sad tidings – the arrival of the terrible Grand Provost, whose judgements were alarmingly rapid, and executed as soon as pronounced. Annette was to be tried almost instantly.

Annette could only appeal to heaven. She might suffer here, she said, but *there* she was certain of her innocence being manifest to the great Judge of ALL. She asked Blazeau if he would serve her in an affair, without asking questions. He promised her he would: she put into his hands her cross to sell, and requested him to place its produce immediately in the hollow tree. The excellent creature promised he would, and, rapidly returning the cross, fled to execute her commission, but not before Annette had caught hold of him and insisted that, as he would not sell the cross, he should accept and keep it for her sake. The poor fellow took it, and, placing it next his heart, vowed never to part with it.

Gerard and his wife now appeared at the prison, where they expected to find the Justice. The poor woman was incapable of bearing the reproaches of her own mind, and came with her husband to see if anything could be done to save poor Annette. Gerard expressed his assurance of her innocence, notwithstanding circumstances had so rapidly increased against her, and entreated his wife to speak little and cautiously to the Justice whilst he unmasked the motives of *that obdurate man with an* IRON HEART.

The Justice entering, overheard honest Gerald's expressions, who perceived it; and, instead of explaining them away, demanded the restoration of Annette. Dame Gerard, who had a good heart, said that the universe would not tempt her to shorten the existence of a human being on account of such trifles. The Justice said it was too late, the *Grand Provost* was already trying Annette! The Justice was in no way to be mollified. Gerard indignantly charged upon the Justice his designs upon Annette: they each parted enraged against the other; and the Justice, more than ever determined on vengeance, ordered the gaoler instantly to carry Annette into court.

In the meantime, Blazeau had placed the money in the hollow tree: unable to muster courage to proceed directly to the prison, he had wandered towards Gerard's house.

Blazeau! Blazeau! called the Magpie, as she hopped towards him.

Blazeau sat down on a seat near the green hedge, and taking Annette's cross from his bosom, laid it on the bench, and fixing his eyes on it, in deep melancholy, endeavoured relieve his heart by expressing his thoughts.

Dennis, the Justice's man, came up with a heavy countenance. Poor Annette is found guilty, said he, she is condemned to die!

Blazeau wept in bitter grief, and exclaimed against the sentence.

Fenning.

See! Blazeau! cried Dennis, look at the Mag!

The Magpie flew off to the church steeple with Annette's cross.

Blazeau, in despair at the loss, ran to the church, to get up into the belfry.

The procession, conducting Annette to the place of execution, appeared. She was strongly guarded by soldiers, who kept off the crowd assembled to behold her. As she approached the church, she looked in at the door, and, kneeling down, implored a blessing upon her poor father.

Blazeau, from the belfry, suddenly shouted out, Stop! — stop! – go no further! – she's innocent l – she's innocent! – Look here! – See! – See! He held something shining in his hand.

The people shouted their surprise.

Blazeau pulled the bell rope, as rapidly as possible.

The confusion increased.

The rapid sounding of the alarm bell, and the acclamations of the crowd, which rent the air, reached the worthy Gerard and his repentant and afflicted wife: they hastened to enquire the cause.

Blazeau saw them approaching: he called out from the belfry window, ANNETTE'S INNOCENT! – The Mag was the thief! – Here's the spoon! and the fork too! and my dear Annette's cross which she gave me! The Mag flew away with it whilst I was talking to Dennis, and here I found it with the fork and spoon! Hold up your apron, Godmother! hold up your apron! here they are!

Blazeau threw them down, and the rejoiced dame, receiving them in her apron, she and Gerard identified them with screams of joy. Blazeau returned to ring the bell, which went *dong-dong*, as loud and as quick as he could make it, and heightened the rapturous tumult of the rejoicing crowd below.

The Justice rushed into the midst to know the meaning of what he beheld, which was soon explained to him.

Gerard, addressing him, said, Heaven has saved poor Annette from the effects of your experience of the world; from your suspicious proofs which were only proofs of suspicion; from your presumptive evidence, which was only evidence of presumption. You are feared as a magistrate, for you have the power to do much mischief and your office demands respect; but you are hated as a man, for if you have a heart, it is insensible to the feelings of humanity. The guilty and the accused are, in your eyes, alike deserving of punishment. The accused are suspected, and the suspected you treat as guilty. May such a magistrate never again sit in the seat of justice; never again have the power to obstruct the streams of mercy.

The unhappy Evrard, who had heard of his beloved daughter's misfortune, rushed amongst the multitude. My dear Annette! he cried, as be pressed her to his heart. My father! said the agitated girl; Oh my father! --

Appendix XI.

The Justice ordered the guards to seize Evrard, the deserter.

An officer, who followed Evrard, produced his pardon. The king had granted it upon the earnest solicitation of Evrard's captain, who generously acknowledged his conduct to Evrard to have been wrong.

Foiled in his attempt to seize Evrard, the Justice demanded explanation as to the spoon and fork sold to the Jew.

Evrard declared that they were his, and the purpose for which he put them in his daughter's possession.

The Jew opportunely arrived, in great haste; he had just succeeded in recovering the articles from his friend, who bought them of him: he now produced them.

The *counter-circumstantial evidence* was complete.

The *worthy* magistrate had no more to say: he could neither object to the evidence, nor suppress it. He was silent and dissatisfied. The case had 'slipped through his fingers' in a way he did not expect. Nothing remained for him but – to hang the magpie.

APPENDIX XII.

The Harvard Papers.

Editor's note.

On 15 May 1900, a bound volume in cinnamon covers arrived at the Harvard Law Library. The volume contained the collected papers of Basil Montagu, an English lawyer – or rather, those of his papers which related to the case of Eliza Fenning. They remained largely unseen until they were accessed during the preparation of this book, and are now available to all, digitally, via the link which can be found in the bibliography.

Montagu's own life had been touched by crime at an early age. He was the illegitimate son of John Montagu, the fourth Earl of Sandwich, and a popular entertainer of the Georgian stage named Martha Ray. In an event which was nothing if not a Notable British Trial in waiting, his mother was shot and killed in 1779 – a few weeks before young Basil's ninth birthday – by a jealous lover named James Hackman. Hackman was tried at the Old Bailey, and hanged at Tyburn. Twelve days elapsed between the murder and the execution.

Following a privileged education at Charterhouse and Christ's College, Cambridge, where he made the acquaintance of Wordsworth and Coleridge, Montagu was called to the bar. Professionally, he pursued a radical political agenda, advocating for the reform of bankruptcy provisions, keeping a firm eye on the death penalty, and, in 1824, becoming a founder member of the Society for the Prevention of Cruelty to Animals. He died in France in 1851.

His Eliza Fenning papers open with a modified quotation from Virgil's Aeneid, Book 2, lines 5-6, 8: *'Quae ipse miserrima vidi et quorum pars magna fui. Quis talia fando temperet a lacrimis?'*[209] It may be argued that Montagu's part in the Fenning affair was not quite that of Aeneas at Troy, but no doubt he felt the agony of Eliza Fenning's cruel treatment at the hands of British justice, and did not withhold his tears.

---

[209] Harvard Law School Library, MSS HLS MS 4130 (13).

Fenning.

Document 1.[210]

On the 24th July [illegible] I received the following letter from G. Houston to whom, by the recommendation of my friend William Allen, I had been enabled to do some small acts of kindness and who, at that time, was a prisoner in Newgate for a libel.

*

State Side, Newgate
July 24th 1815

My Dear Sir,

There is now in this prison a girl named Eliza Fenning, who has been left for execution on Wednesday morning, who, I am strongly persuaded, is innocent of the crime with which she is charged.

Independent of no direct proof having been brought against her on her trial, there are circumstances connected with her case which lead me to suspect, that she is the victim of a foul conspiracy. As these circumstances, however, are of a nature which I cannot, with propriety, state in this note, I have to entreat you to call on me, without a moment[']s delay, and I shall disclose them to you verbally.

I am, Sir,
Your faithful and obt servant
Geo. Houston

B. Montagu Esq.

---

[210] Harvard Law School Library, MSS HLS MS 4130 (51-55). Montagu annotated some of the paperwork in his collection, including this example, introducing the circumstances in which he received the letter. He had had no involvement in Eliza's case before this, and apparently took no immediate action upon receiving the letter itself. Its sender, George Houston, had been imprisoned in November 1814 for 'a libel on the Christian religion' after translating and publishing *Ecce Homo!*, an atheistic tract of 1778 by Paul-Henri Thiry, Baron d'Holbach, which had originally been written in French (under the title of *Histoire Critique de Jésus-Christ, ou Analyse Raisonée des Évangiles*) and published in Amsterdam. Houston's reasons for believing that Eliza Fenning may have been the victim of a conspiracy are not known to us.

Appendix XII.

Document 2.[211]

July 25, 1815

On the 25th of July I received the following letter.

*

Sir,

My esteemed friend Mr Forster having allowed me to enclose his letter to you Respecting Eliza Fenning, I take the Liberty of adding that I can produce, if time be granted, most Respectable evidence to prove the insanity of Mr Turner the Prosecutor – the witness, at least[. A] Mr Gibson will this night prove his having known him more than once perfectly insane, and not only so, but his having heard him say that he would murder himself & all the Family[. T]his Gentleman is a Medical man & knows the Turners intimately, so much so that Previous to the Trial, he went to the Elder Mr Turner & urged him not to think of Prosecuting, knowing as he did the State of Mind of the younger Mr Turner; the fear of hurting his Son in his Business if it was known he was insane, induced Mr Turner Senr to conceal all knowledge of the Circumstance & a false Delicacy of the same kind has kept the Respectable witnesses which can be adduced from coming forward at a more early period. Surely Sir, When it is on evidence that Mr Turner Junr bought the Poison, for a Purpose (that of destroying Rats, as he says) to which however he never applied it, & it had been a considerable time in his Possession, it must be Impossible that a Young Person, a Female of 20 years of age of a Character which (I state it advisedly) has been hitherto irreproachable, can be put to Death in London, while her Prosecutor is charged not only with insanity, but of meditating, undoubtedly under the influence, the dreadful crime of Murdering his own Family. I know nothing of Eliz. Fenning whatever, but I know well all the Respectable Witnesses to whom I allude and I feel certain that it is impossible she can be guilty of the crime laid to her charge.

While writing this I happened to name the circumstance to Mr Chas. Druce, eldest son of Mr Druce Respectable Solicitor[212], and he instantly stated that it had ever been the impression upon his Mind that the Turners['] Maid was not perfectly

---

211 Harvard Law School Library, MSS HLS MS 4130 (68, 59-60). This letter and the next one (Document 3) apparently arrived together. Hone, writing as Watkins, 82, states that Richardson wrote to Montagu on the morning of Tuesday 25 July, but this is apparently disproved by the substance of the letter and its arrival together with Mr Forster's letter, both of which indicated that the meeting at the Recorder's house had already been arranged for 8.00 pm on the Tuesday evening. This meeting was not set up until Tuesday afternoon, when, 'between three and four o'clock in the afternoon, Mr J. B. Sharp, Mr Ogle, Mr Blathwaite, Mr Aberdour, and Mr Gibson waited upon Mr Beckett [the Under-Secretary of State for the Home Department] at the Secretary of State's office' (Watkins, 84).

212 Charles Druce joined his father (also named Charles) in the family firm in 1823. The business is still in operation, and a little over 250 years old at the time of writing, although the last Druce partner retired in 1958.

correct; the whole of the circumstances added to that of its being in evidence that the young woman was absent from the Kitchen more than a sufficient time for any person to add any thing they might chuse [sic] to the puddings she had been making, induce me to trust confidently that a Respite may yet be obtained, in the event of which such additional Evidence will be produced, as will I flatter myself incontrovertibly prove the young woman's Innocence. I would apologise for the liberty I have taken, & I did not feel as if I should be insulting you by so doing. I therefore only say that I am

Sir

Your Much Obliged Serv

J. M. Richardson

Booksr

No 23

Cornhill

23 Cornhill

July 25, 1815

To Basil Montague [sic] Esq

Document 3.[213]

Tuesday 25 July 1815

Dear Sir,

I understand there is to be a meeting at the Recorder's house (Bloomsbury Sq.) this evening at 8. ocl. respecting the young woman Eliza Fenning, convicted of intending to Poison a family in Chancery-Lane. As Mr Richardson of Cornhill has informed told me there is respectable evidence which will be brought forward at the Recorder[']s, that one of the principal witnesses against the woman has been Insane, and that great doubts have arisen of her the woman's guilt [illegible] I think you might be of some service if you could be at the Recorder[']s and share what you know of the principal prosecutor as I am just now informed you are acquainted with him. I hope you will excuse my writing to you as I do.

I remain,

B. M. Forster.

---

[213] Harvard Law School Library, MSS HLS MS 4130 (43). This letter and the previous one (Document 2) apparently arrived together. Benjamin Meggot Forster (1764-1829) was a botanist and natural scientist who advocated for (among other things) the emancipation of slaves, the abolition of the slave trade, and animal welfare.

Appendix XII.

Document 4.[214]

Mr Saml. Godfrey
41, Lant Street
Boro'

If Mr Godfrey will call upon the Recorder in Bloomsbury Square at Eight O'Clock this Evening, the Recorder will hear any thing He has to say about the fate of Eliza Fenning.

Whitehall
25 July
1815

Document 5.[215]

I attended at the Recorder. The result of my interview is partly contained in a letter contained in the tract which was published by Mr. Hone.[216]

The Recorder, presuming, possibly, upon my acquaintance, and irritable, perhaps, from repeated applications was, at first, rather hasty. He soon recollected himself. I regret that I did not at once go to the Lord Chancellor, always patient and always kind.

Document 6.[217]

I immediately went to Newgate but was satisfied that, whether the poor creature was innocent or guilty, I could not so possess myself of the facts as to be able to render her any assistance.

I was in the next room to hers, but, convinced that I could not be of service & she not knowing that I was there, I did not see her. I went to the Secretary of State and added my application to many applications which had been made. The consequence was that a meeting was appointed at the Recorder[']s on that evening at which it was understood the Lord Chancellor would attend.[218]

---

214 Harvard Law School Library, MSS HLS MS 4130 (47). An outlier in Montagu's collection, this letter was apparently neither written by him nor sent to him. The addressee, Samuel Godfrey, is not mentioned in the various publications about Eliza Fenning, and no more is known about him, or whatever he may have had to say about Eliza's fate. He did not attend the meeting at the Recorder's house that evening. This letter was presumably written on the afternoon of Tuesday 25 July by one of the delegation to the Secretary of State's office in Whitehall.
215 Harvard Law School Library, MSS HLS MS 4130 (49-50).
216 The same letter is reproduced from Montagu's own copy as Document 7 in this appendix.
217 Harvard Law School Library, MSS HLS MS 4130 (64).
218 Hone, writing as Watkins, 84, states coyly that, at the Secretary of State's office, it was arranged that

Fenning.

Document 7.[219]

Copy

Sir,

I am to apologize for my apparent inattention to your letter, respecting Elizabeth Fenning, by stating that the instant I received it, I waited upon the Recorder, and informed him of the communication which you had kindly made to me, and as I was wholly ignorant of the merits of the case, I requested the Recorder to inform me whether any alteration could be formed, in the opinion respecting the propriety of her Execution, if satisfactory evidence were adduced that there was an insane person in the Turners['] House, who had declared that he would poison the Family, as it appeared by your letter that such evidence could be produced. The Recorder assured me that the production of such evidence would be wholly useless. I therefore retired. I had not at that time read the trial of this unfortunate young woman: and she was executed early the next morning.

I am very sensible of your kind exertions, and I trust you will forgive my apparent neglect.

I am Sir

Your faithful Servant

B. Montagu
Lincoln[']s Inn
August 10th 1815

Addressed
Mr J. M. Richardson
Bookseller
23 Cornhill

'one other person should attend' the meeting at the Recorder's house that evening. It was clearly Montagu's understanding that the Lord Chancellor would attend the meeting; as Document 4 shows, a Mr Samuel Godfrey was invited to attend; and Forster invited Montagu himself to attend – so 'one other person' seems to be an underestimate. The same text notes that 'it is highly essential that the statements asserting that the Lord Chancellor was present at the meetings on Tuesday should be contradicted. The Lord Chancellor was not present at either of the meetings above mentioned.' (Watkins, 85.)

219   Harvard Law School Library, MSS HLS MS 4130 (92).

Appendix XII.

Document 8.[220]

August 15th, 1815
Letter from Dr Parr.

*

Alcester Augt 9th 1815

Dear Basil Junr

I thank you for sending me a long letter, & I wished it to be yet longer, because the subject was important, the narrative was clear, & the remarks were judicious. Your father's very active[,] discerning & humane Heart will, I am persuaded, explore the truth, & both his Arguments & his Observations will be of signal use. His professional Habits will come to the Aid of his natural Sagacity, & the Character which he has deservedly acquired as the advocate of Mercy will give additional weight to his Statements. From the very beginning I laid little or no Stress upon the words imputed to the poor Father of the Girl, they were straggling Expressions, they were equivocal, they were compatible with Innocence in the Girl & with the Father's conviction that she was innocent.

If the Father was sufficiently infatuated & sufficiently depraved to prefer his own worldly Character to the Salvation of a dying Child, the only one left him of ten, he would have said more, and, more being said would have been overheard, and being overheard, would have been reported[.] But the Turnkey's affidavit destroys that Evidence which was so hastily revealed & so fatally acted upon. The Contents of the Vessell [sic] are with me nearly decisive, it was in the Girl's Possession, it was under her Controul [sic], and is it probable either that having a large Quantity of Poison, she should imploy [sic] only a small Quantity, she should leave a proof of her Guilt by the large Quantity which remained[?] Such Folly is not of a piece with the imputed Cunning which led her to take a portion of the impoisoned Dumpling for the purpose of Concealment.

If some of the Stories in circulation be true the Girl herself was not perfectly sane and the want of sanity will account for her prattling Answers and her lascivious Letter to her fellow Sufferer, but did she really write them? Letters may be easily forged when the Hand writing is known and the writer is dead. When did Oldham[221] mention these letters, to whom did he mention them[,] for what purpose and how was it possible for the Girl to have an Intrigue with him in

---

[220] Harvard Law School Library, MSS HLS MS 4130 (98-102). Basil Montagu's son, Basil Caroline Montagu (1792-1830) had enjoyed an education with Dorothy and William Wordsworth, and was busy readying himself for the law; Dr Parr's letter is a reply to the younger Basil's letter. Dr Samuel Parr (1747-1825) was an educator and doctor of law, an enthusiastic flogger, and, as Richard Porson apparently noted, 'a great man but for three things – his trade, his wife, and his politics'.

[221] *Sic* in letter. Read: Oldfield.

Fenning.

Newgate[?] Oldham[222] had No Chance of a respite[;] Fenning was not without Hope & the Discovery of her Letters tended to disappoint that Hope.

Who bought the Poison[? D]id Fenning know where it was[? D]id others know as well as Fenning[? W]as she for one Minute absent while the Dumplings were preparing[? W]as there any other Person known [lacuna] suspected to be at Hand[?] She was [lacuna] did she ever intimate Her wi[lacuna. D]id Her Mistress often catch her in Lies before the Poison was administered[?] That she had been provoked and that she made the Dumplings are Circumstances which might justly produce strong suspicions, but this is not enough. She told her Fellow Servant not to eat them[. W]hy then did she herself eat them[?] Did she give this warning to the Servant Boy before she eat [sic] them[?] If from their Taste or their Look she found any thing offensive[,] she might discourage the Boy[,] especially if she had any liking for him.

What are the Circumstances of the warning as to the time & the words[?] I hope the Trial will be published and that the Publication will be a faithful one, for this is very material.

Basil[,] I hear with great Distrust the Eulogies bestowed upon circumstantial Evidence. They who have veracity enough to shrink from a strong Lye are negligent & precipitate in stating small Circumstances of which they do not See the Bearing. I am [lacuna]leased when those [lacuna] produce

---

Document 9.[223]

Sir,

Several most Respectable friends, who have taken the trouble of investigating the circumstances connected with the case of Eliza Fenning are very Desirous that the 10th instant, which you did me the honor [sic] of writing in reply to my application to you on behalf of that unfortunate young woman, should be published along with the other information which they have been able to collect upon the subject, I therefore take the liberty of entreating your permission to lay it before the Public. Your Compliance will much oblige.

Sir
Your Able Servt
J. M. Richardson
No 23
Cornhill
August 22d 1815

To Basil Montague [sic] Esq

222 *Sic* in letter. Read: Oldfield.
223 Harvard Law School Library, MSS HLS MS 4130 (113).

Appendix XII.

Document 10.[224]

Sir,

If it appears to you to be necessary to publish your letter, I think it would be wrong in me to withold[225] [sic] my consent from your publishing my answer: but I earnestly and affectionately entreat you to deliberate upon the expedients[226] of such publications.[227] The justification of Eliza Fenning is a very different consideration from the censure of the Recorder. I am aware, there are various reports[228] in circulation, respecting the indelicate conduct of the Recorder to the different members of society who thought it their duty to interest themselves in this sad case and respecting his interference with the prosecutor to prevent the Prince from extending mercy to this young woman. If these facts can be substantiated, if as a Judge he has so far forgotten himself as to pollute or close the fountain of mercy, I submit to you that the proper mode of proceeding is not by inflaming the public mind, but by petition to the House of Commons either by the parents of this young woman or by those who feel the wound which justice has sustained and are conscious that the most grateful act of our Sovereign has ever been in attending to the gracious promise in his coronation oath[:] 'that he will execute justice with mercy'.

It could not be the wish of the Recorder to execute innocence under the forms of law. He may have erred in his judgment: he may have suffered himself to be shaped by power, [illegible] but there is a respect due to his office which calls upon every well regulated mind to proceed with caution and, in censuring judicial intemperance, to put act itself with moderation.

I am Sir with very kind feeling

Your faithful

[B. Montagu][229]

L. I.[230] Aug. 30 1815

---

224 Harvard Law School Library, MSS HLS MS 4130 (115-124). Montagu's copy of his reply to Richardson's letter of 22 August (Document 9). The original is in the British Library, Add MS 41071, ff. 56-57.
225 British Library, Add MS 41071, ff. 56-57 gives 'withhold'.
226 British Library, Add MS 41071, ff. 56-57 gives 'expediency'.
227 British Library, Add MS 41071, ff. 56-57 gives 'publication'.
228 British Library, Add MS 41071, ff. 56-57 gives 'There are, I am aware'.
229 Signature given in British Library, Add MS 41071, ff. 56-57.
230 British Library, Add MS 41071, ff. 56-57 gives 'Lincoln[']s Inn'.

Fenning.

Document 11.[231]

Elizabeth Fenning

There seem to be some important considerations attendant upon the trial of Elizabeth Fenning from which the community may, sooner or later, be enabled to extract some good.

1st, ought there not to be some regulation with respect to the publication of the trials at the Old Bailey, the annual register & there [sic] eventful proceedings which, badly as they are executed, are under the superintendance [sic] of the magistracy.

2nd, why is a prisoner indicted for a capital offence deprived of the privilege to which every British subject is, in every other case, entitled to resort, the privilege of Counsel to address the jury[?] In the smallest controversy respecting property; in an action on an indictment for a common assault, the Defendant is entitled to be heard by Counsel. Why, when a prisoner is tried for his life, is this privilege witheld [sic][?] Is this a moment when a young woman should be defenceless? The reason said to be assigned for this peculiarity of the English law is the supposition that the Judge is counsel for the prisoner: a supposition as delusive in theory as it is unfounded in fact. It is not theoretically true that a judge should be counsel for either party. He is an impartial arbiter, standing between the sovereign and his people; to a judge it ought to be indifferent how the beam turns. When, indeed, after a careful estimate, the balance preponderates against a fallen brother, the feelings of his nature may influence him.

Avenging Angel – See Sandys[,] [illegible] & Shower[.][232]

---

231 Harvard Law School Library, MSS HLS MS 4130 (235-245). These incomplete and undated notes may or may not represent Montagu's views on the legal aspects of the case: occasionally, in his Eliza Fenning collection, he wrote out by hand parts of letters or newspaper articles which he could not otherwise clip or paste onto the page, but since there is no complement to this fragment within the collection, it is probably best understood as Montagu's personal reflection on the matter.

232 These three scarcely-legible words have defied certain interpretation. The first one – tentatively read here as 'Sandys' – may be a reference to the speech made by Sir Samuel Sandys in the House of Commons on 23 February 1739:

As to criminal Causes, I know that those who were accused of Treason or Felony, were not of old allowed Counsel, unless some difficult Point of Law happened to be started upon the Tryal; because, as our Lawyers say, the Judges are to be of Counsel for the Prisoner, But every Man will, I believe, grant, that this was a Severity, introduced in favour of the Crown, nor very favourable for the Subject. Our Volumes of State-Trials will make it appear, how seldom the Judges have acted the Part of being Counsel for the Prisoner. They often appear rather to have acted the Part of being Counsel against him … With respect to Felonies, 'tis true, Sir, the antient Custom still remains; but I am surprised it has not in this Case likewise been altered by Statute. 'Tis better twenty Guilty escape than one Innocent suffer; and I am convinced, this Custom has been the Occasion of many an innocent Man's being condemned, who, if he had been allowed Counsel, would have made his Innocence as bright as the Sun-shine.

The third one – tentatively read here as 'Shower' – may be a reference to Sir Bartholomew Shower, and in particular his *Reasons for a New Bill of Rights*, published in 1692:

In the Name of God, what Harm can accrue to the Publick in general, or to any Man in particular, that in

Appendix XII.

The virtuous and pious Sir Matthew Hale in the rules for the regulation of his judicial conduct says[,] 'Let me not be biased with compassion to the poor or favour to the rich. In business capital, though my nature prompt me to pity, yet let me consider that there is also a pity due to the country: but if in criminals it be a measuring cast[,] let me incline to mercy and [sic]

It is not true in fact that the Judges are counsel for the prisoner.

Case of State Treason Councel should be allowed to the Accused, what Rule of Justice is there to warrant its Denial, when in a Civil Case of a Halfpenny Value the Party may plead either by himself or Advocate: That the Court is Councel for the Prisonner can be no effectual Reason, for so they ought to be in every Action, unto each Party, that Right may be done.
The second word cannot be interpreted at all.

APPENDIX XIII.

The Hone Papers.

Editor's note.

William Hone's retained correspondence on the subject of Eliza Fenning consists of five letters and a personal note. Of these, one letter – sent by Basil Montagu to J. M. Richardson – is given in transcript with editorial notes in Appendix XII (Document 10) above, from Montagu's copy in the Harvard Law Library. The remaining four letters and the personal note appear in the British Library, Add MS 41071, ff. 43-50, and are reproduced here.

Document 1.[233]

Sept 24/15

Dr Sir,

I have been from day to day anxious to hear of your progress and to confess the truth had wrought my mind into a state of painful suspense being apprehensive that the result of your Inquiries had been unfavourable to the principles which were common with us both at the outset of the business. This day's *Observer* has revived my ideas to the Subject and the extract from Marshall's publication instead of shaking my faith has served to confirm it – with a still stronger abhorrence of the Recorder's conduct as developed in an observation said to have been made by him at the Trial.

There is another recent case of a somewhat similar nature in [sic] the other side of the water, which in my mind is as palpable an accident as the other, and yet a wise Coroner (whom I know to be an arrant fool) and a literal Jury have sent a girl to prison on a charge of wilful murder.[234] Where are these things to end, and what will become of our trusted securities if they are thus suffered to be tampered with by Prejudice and abused by Ignorance?

You will greatly oblige me by letting me know whether your Collection is suppressed, or when it is likely to appear. Should the former be the case you have no doubt very substantial reasons for the measure, but without troubling you with too many questions I hope to be favoured with a brief report of the state of the

---

233 British Library, Add MS 41071, ff. 43-44.
234 See Appendix XV.

Fenning.

Proceedings and as far as proper with the grounds of the delay.

I am with great esteem
Yours truly
J Watkins
Hampden St[235]
Sep. 24, 1815

P. S. Should your narrative be forthcoming some notice ought to be taken of Marshall's Pamphlet which by [lacuna – probably 'chance'], if you have got I shall [lacuna – 'be'] glad to see.

Document 2.[236]

55 Fleet Street
27 Sepr, 1815

Sir,

As by your pamphlet you appear to be in possession of the ~~Charg~~ Recorder's Charge to the Jury in the Trial of Elizabeth Fenning, the copy which I have of it is incomplete & as I am very anxious to render the my forthcoming pamphlet ~~as complete~~ on her Case as perfect as possible I ~~will thank you if you can~~ take the liberty of saying I shall feel myself under much obligation to you if you ~~will please to~~ can favor [sic] me with a Copy of that Charge or intimate to me ~~in what way~~ how I can procure a Copy of it. ~~A line in answer will further oblige~~.

I am, Sir,
Yr very obed
hble servt
W H

[Addressee] John Marshall
27 Sept 1815
To Mr Marshall

Document 3.[237]

27 Sept

Sir,

~~To enable me to make~~ I will thank you to ~~inform you me what~~ give me an Estimate of the Expense of Printing the Fenning Pamphlet at per sheet according

---

235 Now Polygon Road.
236 British Library, Add MS 41071, ff. 45-46.
237 British Library, Add MS 41071, f. 47.

Appendix XIII.

to its sorts – also to say how much of the Pamphlet you have already set up – i.e. ~~how muc~~ what quantity it makes in the metal – The sooner you can do this the more satisfactory it will be to me & you will therefore perhaps tell the bearer how soon I can have this at what hour

I am, Sir
Your obedt servt
W Hone.
27 Sept
To Mr Moyes[238]

Document 4.[239]

4 5 Letters

This poor girl was executed after a conviction shockingly obtained. *I wrote* the work intitled an *Elaborate Investigation into the Case of E. F.* – on the title page John Watkins L.L.D. [sic] appears as the author – He had intrusted himself to save her, and lent me his name.

Document 5.[240]

Mr B. Montagu Junr is extremely sorry he did not meet with Mr Hone at Lincoln[']s Inn, [on either of] the two mornings he was kind enough to call upon him respecting the trial of Harvey[,] and still more so that Mr H shd have been disappointed by the person he has engaged to take it for him in shorthand as he much wished for a correct statement of what passed upon the trial[241] – His object

---

238 The pamphlet was printed by J. Moyes of Greville Street, London.
239 British Library, Add MS 41071, f. 48.
240 British Library, Add MS 41071, ff. 49-50.
241 'On Monday, Mr Francis Harvey was brought to Bow Street, in the custody of Westcote, charged with committing a violent outrage and assault on the body of Harriet Stratford, a girl who has just attained her sixteenth year, who was in his employ as a servant; she stated that on Thursday the prisoner ordered her to go into the garret, where he wanted her; she accordingly went there, and after waiting some time, he entered the garret with a cord and a new birch broom, which he had sent her to purchase for the occasion. He ordered the girl to strip, which she refused to do. He then proceeded to take off her clothes by force, and continued to do so till he had stripped her entirely naked; afterwards he tied her wrists together with the cord he had brought with him, and then tied her up by the cord to an iron staple at the top of the room, and began to flog her with a large rod, and continued to flog her most severely for about a quarter of an hour or twenty minutes; the excruciating pain inflicted by such continued violence caused her to twist and turn her body about very much, till her hands worked through the loop of the cord with which she was tied up, which caused her body to fall on the floor, the noise of which, together with the girl's cries, brought the lodgers in the house to her assistance. The prisoner then left off his flogging. The defence set up for this extraordinary violence, and the explanation given by the girl, is that some days since the prisoner's wife gave the girl some meat for her dinner, which had been kept till it had become so bad that she could not swallow it. Her mistress told her she should have no more victuals till she did eat it, and she kept her

Fenning.

in mentioning it to Mr Hone arose from a wish that a correct statement should be put into the hands of the public, and from conceiving it came entirely within the line of publications Mr H had marked out to himself, but of this Mr H must be the best judge as to the probability of its repaying him for his trouble &c, as Mr M. had much rather appropriate any money he might have to spare to the service of the poor girl to enable her to obtain some situation hereafter, than incur any expense in publishing an account of the trial however anxious he might be that it should be as widely diffused as possible, in the hopes that it might benefit that most to be pitied class of our fellow creatures parish apprentices, and servants who have places procured them by the parish, by deterring those from acting in the same way who are only to be restrained by the fear of punishment not from the love of what is right.

If upon deliberation Mr Hone thinks fit to publish the trial, and there is anything Mr M Jr can assist him in he will be happy to forward his views in any way he will point out and will be happy feel obliged by a call in Bedford Square from Mr H any time on Saturday the 9th after 10 and before 1 o'clock in the morning – He wd call on Mr H [but he] is unable to go his way.

25 Bedford Square, Friday Evening
Post Paid
Mr Hone
Bookseller
Fleet Street
Dec. 1815
B. Montagu Esq. Junr.

---

threat. On the following day the girl was sent out with sixpence to purchase some cat's and dog's meat, when the girl being extremely hungry, having been kept without food for such a length of time, was tempted, instead of buying the cat's and dog's meat with the sixpence, to purchase some rolls and butter for herself. On this being discovered by the prisoner, he applied to a magistrate to prosecute the girl as a felon for stealing the sixpence, but the magistrate refused to take up the business in such a serious manner, but observed that he thought he had better give her a flogging and turn her out of doors, not of course suspecting that he would resort to such an outrageous act of violence.' (*Kentish Weekly Post*, 22 August 1815.) Other reports add Harvey's address – 13 Tavistock Row, Covent Garden – and the fact that Harriet Stratford was an orphan. Harvey was 'convicted at the Middlesex sessions of violently assaulting Harriet [and] sentenced to three months' imprisonment in the House of Correction. … The unhappy girl was extremely ill from the dreadful castigation she had received; and the sentence passed on the defendant gave great satisfaction to the court.' (*Salisbury and Winchester Journal*, 18 December 1815.)

APPENDIX XIV.

Trial of Henry William Wyatt.[242]

Editor's note.

In 1806, Peter Alley was involved in a case that was strikingly similar to that of Eliza Fenning. Fifteen year old Henry William Wyatt, one of two young apprentices to a London watch-finisher, James Goldsmith, was charged at the Old Bailey with having attempted to poison Goldsmith, his wife, Maria, and their four year old daughter, Louisa, by adding arsenic to the coffee which he served for breakfast on the morning of Sunday 6 April.

As with the case against Eliza Fenning, evidence was purely circumstantial; no person had seen the lad add arsenic to the coffee grains (which he had fetched from the chandler's shop in Benjamin Street). Furthermore, the arsenic, used to kill rats, had been kept in an unlocked drawer. Wyatt had also drunk some of the same coffee he had served to the family, and had become ill.

At his trial, Henry Wyatt was represented by Peter Alley and acquitted. Nine years later, many who supported Eliza Fenning when she faced a similar charge at the Old Bailey must have hoped that she, too, would be found not guilty. However, as we have seen, this was not to be and, despite concerted efforts to save her from the gallows, she was executed on 26 July 1815.

Henry William Wyatt was indicted for, that he being a person of wicked mind, feloniously did intend to poison, kill, and murder, one James Goldsmith, and Maria, his wife, and Louisa Goldsmith, spinster, on 6 April, with force and arms, feloniously, and unlawfully, did administer to the said James Goldsmith, Maria Goldsmith, and Louisa Goldsmith, and caused to be administered and taken by them a certain deadly poison, to wit, white arsenic, intending thereby to kill and murder them, against the statute, and against the king's peace; and three other counts for like offence, with like intention.

---

242 Transcript from www.oldbaileyonline.org, version 8.0, accessed 9 December 2018, April 1806, trial of Henry William Wyatt (t18060416-63).

Fenning.

JAMES GOLDSMITH, sworn.

I am a watch wheel finisher. I live at number nine, Pear Tree Street, Goswell Street The prisoner was my apprentice. He had been with me about nine months.

How old is he? — He is near fifteen years old.

Had you done anything to him? — There was nothing to affront him as I know of.

What happened to you yesterday se'nnight? — On yesterday se'nnight, I sat down on that Sunday morning, as I usually do, to breakfast with some coffee.

Had you sent the prisoner out? — I was not at home. My wife had.

How many does your family consist of? — My wife and three children.

What is your wife's name? — Maria.

Is your daughter's name Louisa? — Yes. She is four years old.

You drank your coffee. Did you find yourself very ill afterwards? — I found myself very ill afterwards, after the first cup that I drank.

Did you see the prisoner drink any coffee? — I did not. My wife did. He was downstairs.

Did you drink any more afterwards? — I drank two cups afterwards; I began to complain after I drank the first cup of my inside being very bad, and my head.

Your wife went out? — Yes, she went out to fetch some spinach, just before church time.

What time did she go out? — Near eleven o'clock.

What time did you breakfast? — A little after ten o'clock.

Your wife returned again? — Yes. While she was gone, I was taken very sick, and when she returned, she was taken very sick.

Was either of your little children ill? — My little girl said she was very sick indeed. She said, 'Daddy, Daddy!' I then said to my wife, 'I suppose the child is sick'.

On seeing her sick, do you know whether there was anything in the coffee? — I went over the way to the chandler's shop, where we have the coffee.

Did you examine the coffee pot? — I examined it, and took it to the doctor's, in Wilderness Row. I saw two or three white specks at the bottom of the saucers.

Did you find anything at the bottom of the coffee pot? — Yes. I took out all I could find with a knife, and carried it to Mr Field, the apothecary.

You did not carry the coffee pot to Mr Field? — No.

What did you find at the bottom of the coffee pot? — White arsenic. I knew it was arsenic because I had some in my shop myself. My shop was about ten yards from my house, at the bottom of the garden.

Was it locked up? — No, the arsenic was in a drawer, where I am always using things for my business.

Appendix XIV.

Was your shop locked up then? — Yes, on Sunday morning it was locked up, but if any person got into the shop, they could get at the drawer where the arsenic was. The drawer was not locked, but I forewarned him of it when he first came apprentice to me, and my errand boy and all. I told them it was poison, and never to touch it. It was what I had to kill rats.

Did you perceive any difference in this arsenic? It was in a lump? — Yes.

Did you find any part of it gone when you looked at it? — Yes, one third of it nearly.

How big was the piece of arsenic? Have you got it here? — Yes [witness producing it].

There had been a piece taken from this? — Yes. I had it in my shop for two or three years.

How long was it since you had seen it before? — I had not looked at it since I told the two boys of it – that is, near nine months ago.

So that when it was broken off, you cannot tell? — No.

Cross-examined by Mr ALLEY.

How many boys have you in the house? — Two: this little boy has been with me the same time as the other.

You say it was nine months since you saw the arsenic? — Yes.

The boy went home to his mother? He did not come to you the next day? — No.

Did you see the boy sick? — He told me he was sick; I did not see him sick.

MARIA GOLDSMITh, sworn.

I am the wife of James Goldsmith.

You drank of the coffee – so did your daughter Louisa? — Yes, I was taken ill.

Did the prisoner drink any? — About half a cup – or rather better – of a middling-sized cup.

Did he drink it at the same time that you did? — Afterwards.

Was it after you was [sic] taken ill? — Before I was taken ill.

Your husband was taken ill immediately? — He was taken ill while I was gone for some spinach for dinner.

Your boy was not ill with you, but after he left you? — Yes.

Was your daughter taken ill before the prisoner drank? — No, after.

Then the boy was not aware that any of you were ill when he drank it? — No. He drank the bottom of the coffee, what was left. I put some more water in it, and boiled it up.

Fenning.

Did he drink as much as usual? — He never drank as much as one cup.

Did he drink as much as you poured out? — No, he left about a quarter of it.

That quarter that he left there was a great deal of grounds in? — Yes.

Did he drink as much as might be expected, leaving the grouts? — No. He left a little coffee in with the grouts.

A middling-sized cup, you say? — Yes.

Was the boy taken ill? — Yes.

How soon? — He went downstairs; my husband called me up. When I went down again, he said he had been exceeding sick.

You turned something out of the coffee pot, and found something white? — No, I did not.

Then you did not turn out the grounds of the coffee pot? — No, my husband did.

Cross-examined by Mr REYNOLDS.

You saw the boy the next day? — No. His mother sent word the next day that he was very ill; he could not come.

He seldom drank any more than one cup? — No.

He drank out of the same pot that you drank out of? — Yes.

FRANCES LEE, sworn.

I live in Benjamin Street, where I keep a chandler's shop.

Do you know the prisoner at the bar? — Yes.

Did he come and buy coffee of you? — Yes, a little after nine on the Sunday morning.

What did you sell him? — Half an ounce of coffee.

You gave it him, did you? — Yes.

Did you grind it? — Yes.

Do you know whether there was anything but coffee in it? — There was nothing else in it but coffee.

Had you ground any other coffee at that mill that morning? — No, nothing before.

Did you afterwards? — Yes.

Did you grind this for the prisoner while he was in the shop? — Yes.

And you had not used the mill before that morning? — No.

How lately before had you used that mill? — On the Saturday morning.

To grind what? — Coffee.

Are you the only person that attends the shop? — My sister does.

Appendix XIV.

Is she here? — No.

Then you cannot tell what was ground in the mill? — I was not out of the shop.

Are you sure there was nothing ground in the mill before, on Sunday morning? — There was nothing on Sunday morning.

Any other person in the shop? — My father; he never does anything in the shop.

Is he here? — No.

Then you ground this coffee first? — Yes.

Did you grind anything after, on that day? — Only some coffee for our own breakfast; that I ground at the same time.

Did you find any bad effects from the coffee? — No.

Did you drink any? — Four cups, and my sister drank four cups.

You all breakfasted on coffee? — Yes.

You had some left, had you? — Yes, in the mill.

Then when this boy came for half an ounce, how came you to grind so much? — We wanted some for our own breakfast.

You ground more than enough for that. — Yes, there was some in the mill afterwards.

How came you to leave any in the mill? — We mostly do.

Then when the prisoner came in the morning, there might be some in the mill? — No, there was none at all.

How came that about? You commonly leave coffee in the mill. — No.

You tell me you do. — We did on the Sunday morning.

Do you commonly leave it in on Sunday morning, or on every morning? — On Sunday morning, we generally have customers come in one after another.

And there was some left? — Yes.

THOMAS FIELD, sworn.

I am an apothecary, living in Clerkenwell.

The witness brought you some coffee? — Yes, in the morning of 6 April, about half after eleven o'clock, he brought some coffee grouts mixed with a white substance.

Did you examine it? — I examined it at the time. It was in such a situation as is unusually to be met with: it is generally in a large mass. As you may have seen it, it was irregularly powdered.

What was it? — White arsenic. It is generally made use of in a fine powder.

Mr Goldsmith and his wife and child were all very ill? — They were all very ill and sick.

Fenning.

What quantity of white arsenic did you see? — I saw six or eight grains in irregular lumps.

Was the quantity that you saw sufficient to make the people sick? — It was more than sufficient to make them ill, that which I saw in the saucer.

You tell us it is white arsenic. How do you know that? — I examined it on a burning iron, which is one of the best tests: it evaporates in a white fume, with a strong garlic smell.

Then have you any doubt of its being arsenic? — Not any.

You impute the sickness from this arsenic to these persons? — To the suspending of the arsenic that they drank. When you boil arsenic up, it impregnates the water: the arsenic itself is not soluble in water.

If this arsenic was boiled up again and again, it would have been the same to all the water? — Not if it was not suspended – held up – in the water.

[NAME NOT GIVEN], sworn.[243]

I live with my mother, who lodges on the ground floor in the same house.

Do you remember when the prisoner returned with the coffee? — Yes, I suppose then it was about half past nine o'clock. After the breakfast, I met Mr Goldsmith on the stairs. He looked very bad. I asked him if he was not well. He said, 'No'. He believed he was poisoned with the coffee, and his wife and child too. He requested me to go upstairs, which I did. I found Mrs Goldsmith and his daughter retching very much. Afterwards, Mrs Goldsmith desired me to look at the coffee, and I did. I observed a white substance.

JONATHAN THORN, sworn.

How old are you? — I am twelve on 5 August.

You are errand boy to Mr Goldsmith? — Yes. I have been with him very near a year.

Do you remember the prisoner asking you what was in the drawer? — Yes.

Was that before or since he was taken ill? — A week, almost, before that.

How lately were they all taken so ill? — Yesterday se'nnight.

How long was it before that? — Three days. He said he wondered what stuff that was master called poison.

Did you tell him? — I said I did not know what stuff he called it. He asked me what it would kill, or poison. I said it would kill rats or anything.

Is that all that passed? — Yes.

---

243 The name of the witness is not given in the Proceedings.

Appendix XIV.

Did you see the stuff in the drawer then? — Master showed it us both about nine months ago, and told us never to touch it. It was poison.

Cross-examined by Mr ALLEY.

Do you know the nature of an oath? — No.

Were you ever examined before in a court? — No.

VERDICT.

Not guilty.

First Middlesex Jury, before Mr Justice Rooke.

ADMINISTERING POISON.[244]

Henry William Wyatt, a boy only fifteen years of age, was capitally indicted for administering white arsenic to James Goldsmith, and Maria and Louisa Goldsmith, the wife and daughter of the former, with intent to poison and destroy them.

This was a very singular case. — The prisoner was an apprentice to Mr Goldsmith, the prosecutor, a watch-finisher, in Goswell Street, and on Sunday week was sent out for coffee to make the family a breakfast. After the family had taken it they all, one after the other, became extremely ill, and were obliged to have medical assistance. The accustomed remedies to expel poison were used with effect, and the prosecutor and his family were saved from death. The prisoner also drank some coffee, about half a cup, but left the whole of the sediment in the cup. It was subsequently discovered that a quantity of arsenic had been mixed with the coffee, and had occasioned the sudden illnesses of the family. The prisoner was himself affected in a slight degree. In order to prove that the prisoner mixed the arsenic with the coffee, Mr Goldsmith stated that he had nine months before pointed out some arsenic to him, which was deposited in the workshop, for the purpose of killing rats, and on his searching for the same after the above affair, he found that one third part of it had been taken away. A lad about thirteen years of age, who also lived in the house of the prosecutor, deposed that the prisoner asked what else the arsenic would kill, besides rats, and he told him it would kill anyone if they swallowed it. This was only two days before the affair. It appeared, however, that the prisoner had had no previous quarrel with his master, nor did there appear any motive to influence the commission of so horrid an act, if malignantly and wilfully done.

244 *Morning Advertiser*, 22 April 1806.

Fenning.

The judge did not call upon the boy for his defence, and left it to the jury to say whether, without any direct evidence of the prisoner's administering the poison, and in the absence of all inducement to effect so wicked a purpose as that of destroying his master and his family, together with his having drank part of the coffee himself, it would be safe to find a verdict of guilty? It might be accidentally, it might be wantonly done; or it might not have been done at all by the prisoner. In such a case therefore they would do well to acquit the boy.

The jury immediately pronounced the prisoner Not Guilty. He was a smart looking lad, and bowed very respectfully when he left the bar.

APPENDIX XV.

Trial of Elizabeth Mary Miller.

There is another recent case of a somewhat similar nature in [sic] the other side of the water, which in my mind is as palpable an accident as the other, and yet a wise Coroner (whom I know to be an arrant fool) and a literal Jury have sent a girl to prison on a charge of wilful murder. Where are these things to end, and what will become of our trusted securities if they are thus suffered to be tampered with by Prejudice and abused by Ignorance? [John Watkins to William Hone, 24 September 1815.]

Editor's note.

A report of the inquest upon the body of Elizabeth Ann Newman – the 'recent case of a somewhat similar nature' to which Watkins referred in his letter to Hone – had been widely syndicated. At least one newspaper carried the story under the potentially provocative headline, 'Another Family Poisoned'; this was a symptom of the popular hysteria which gripped the upper echelons of society in late Regency England.[245] People thought that their servants – and the underclasses in general – were not to be trusted and were intent on doing them harm. The following account is taken from the London Courier and Evening Gazette, 18 September 1815.

*

Saturday morning [16 September 1815] an inquest was held at the White Hart, facing Kennington Cross, before Charles Jemmett, Esq., Coroner for Surrey, on the body of Miss Elizabeth Ann Newman, whose death was occasioned by giving her arsenic in some gruel for supper. The jury was composed of the most respectable inhabitants in the neighbourhood. After viewing the body, the first witness examined was

Mary Eades, who being sworn said, I am servant to Mr Richard Newman, butcher, no. 8, Kennington Cross; I have lived with the family three years. Last Wednesday

---

[245] *Bristol Mirror*, 23 September 1815. The *Globe* used the same headline to report the death of Elizabeth Ann in its edition of 15 September 1815, but described the event as a 'calamitous accident' which had occurred 'through the carelessness of families keeping arsenic in open places', and said that Elizabeth Miller had 'thickened the gruel with the arsenic, mistaking it for flour'.

Fenning.

evening, the 13th instant, about six o'clock, I accompanied my mistress and her two children, Elizabeth Ann, the eldest (now dead), and Mary, the youngest, to take a walk; we returned home about half past seven o'clock; I took the youngest babe, Mary, and undressed her, and gave her to my mistress, who carried her to her bedroom in her arms, and a cup of gruel in her hand, that my fellow servant, Elizabeth Miller, made for the children's supper. My mistress ordered me to get some magnesia and rhubarb to give her; I accordingly went to the cupboard in the parlour, I took a teaspoonful of the magnesia out of a blue paper, and put it in a wine glass, and then took a lump of rhubarb out of the same cupboard, and grated part of it into the wine glass with the magnesia, and I then carried it into the bedroom to my mistress. She desired me to mix it with a spoonful of the gruel with which she was feeding the child, Mary, which I did out of the cup, which was about half a coffee cup full.

My mistress gave the baby, Mary, a large teaspoonful of the mixture, and in about three minutes afterwards she was taken very ill, and vomited dreadfully. The deceased, Elizabeth Ann, came to the room door, crying in a most dreadful manner. My mistress desired me to let her in, which I did. She came in crying, with a cup of gruel in her hand, and a spoon in it. My mistress asked her what was the matter with her, or had her father been beating her? She answered, 'No'; but desired me to rock her in her chair. I took her in my lap, and I had her not ten minutes before she began vomiting most dreadfully. I said to my mistress, 'Sure there can be nothing in the gruel'. My mistress answered, 'I hope not, Mary'.

Both the children kept vomiting constantly, and I called my master in. When he came, he called my fellow servant, Elizabeth Miller, and when she came up, my master asked her what she had been doing to the gruel. She said she had done nothing to it, and then she began crying. My mistress then ordered her to bring up the basin with all the gruel in it. She went down and brought up the basin with a little gruel in it, and gave it to my mistress. This was about half past seven or eight o'clock. I swallowed about two desert spoons full; I did not find anything amiss with the taste, but soon after I found a burning heat in my stomach and throat. My master, seeing that, said to her, 'Elizabeth Miller, now to show you put nothing into the gruel, and to prove your innocence, take and eat it up yourself'. She stood still, and did not touch it.

Mr James Cross, a neighbour, then came into the room, and having seen the children, he tasted the gruel with the point of a knife, and he said it made his mouth very dry and hot. Mr Wilkinson, another neighbour, came in, and seeing the children very ill, he said to my mistress that she should have some advice. My master and mistress sent Elizabeth Miller for Mr Dixon, the surgeon at Newington. Elizabeth returned first, and Mr Dixon shortly afterwards.

Mr Dixon inquired how long they had been ill, and examined the saucepan the gruel was made in, and ordered what was left of the gruel, with the saucepan, spoon, and some remaining grits, to be locked up until he had more leisure to

Appendix XV.

examine them minutely. Mr Dixon then stated his opinion that the children had been poisoned, and desired the servant (Elizabeth Miller) might be sent with him to bring back some castor oil, which he ordered to be administered as speedily as possible. This was accordingly done, and caused increased vomiting. I then found myself exceedingly ill, and gave my mistress the child; I then went to the back door, where I vomited dreadfully, and my mistress ordered me some castor oil, which I took.

The children and myself continued ill until five o'clock next morning, when I remarked about that time to my mistress that I thought the child Elizabeth Ann appeared better; in about a quarter of an hour after, the deceased asked for drink, of which I gave her, and observed she had changed countenance. I called to my master from an adjoining room; she was then in a fit. My master sent again for Mr Dixon. Before Mr Dixon came, she had recovered from the first fit. He gave her a little white wine; sent home again for medicine, which he gave to both children and myself. Mr Dixon stayed nearly two hours; after he was gone, the child had three more fits, and expired about nine o'clock. About eight o'clock I found myself much worse, much swelled, and very sick.

To a question put by the coroner – if she knew of any poison in the house? – she replied: About two months since she saw something in a paper on the kitchen window, which one of the young men said was poison, and cautioned her not to touch it, as it was to be put with chopped beef upon cabbage leaves, to be put into the slaughterhouse to poison rats. She did not know of poison in the kitchen, or any part of the house, after that time. She did not observe anything particular in the conduct of Elizabeth Miller to induce her to suspect that she would or could have given poison to them. She appeared at times cross to them. Shortly after the death of Elizabeth Ann, the witness went up to Miller's bedroom, and found her locked in. She opened the door, and witness told her the child was dead, upon which she stamped her foot upon the floor, and raved out, 'What shall I do with myself'?

Mr Dixon, the surgeon, corroborated the evidence of Mary Eades, and further deposed that when he took Miller with him home to fetch the castor oil, he particularly questioned her: if she prepared the gruel, and what it was made of. She said that the grits she got at Mr Holland's, the corn chandler's,[246] and she thickened it with nearly a tablespoonful of oatmeal, which oatmeal was part, she said, of some that was left about a month ago by one of the young men, who had some gruel made for his cold. She denied any knowledge whatever of poison being put into the gruel. Mr Dixon further stated that he had analysed the gruel in the basin, and also what was in the teacup, in the presence of four philosophical gentlemen, and that it was evident it was strongly impregnated with arsenic.

---

246   The report in the *Globe* (15 September 1815) gives, 'Mr Hollands, a corn chandler in White Hart Place'.

Fenning.

He also examined the remaining grits, and they appeared to be free from any poisonous ingredient. He further deposed that on opening the body of the child, he ascertained she died of poison; but that he had not yet analysed the contents of the stomach.

Mrs Newman deposed nearly the same evidence as Mary Eades, and said it was not her intention to keep her but a few days longer; but she had not acquainted Miller with such intention; that she was a bad tempered girl, and appeared cross to the children; and the deceased child (not four years old) did not like to go out or be with her; it was the first time she ever made gruel for the children; and to a question from Mrs Newman why she made so much, she said, 'I supposed you might want some for yourself'. Last Monday, Mrs Newman scolded her twice for suffering the men in the shop to take improper liberties with her.

Henry Walker, hairdresser, deposed that about two months since he prepared some minced meat, mixed with it a quantity of arsenic, and, assisted by Mr Newman and his two journeymen, Mills and Allen, stopped up the holes with it in the slaughterhouse and shop, and about five weeks since he again repeated it, but is not aware that he left any behind him.

Henry Allen, journeyman to Mr Newman, deposed that he had a cold about two months since, and that he bought a halfpennyworth of oatmeal at Mr Cooper's, and used the whole of it.

Mr Newman deposed that he did not know of any poison whatever being in the house. About two years and a half since he bought some stuff to kill rats, all of which he used for that purpose.

Brown, the Beadle, on conveying Miller to the workhouse as a place of security till the decision of the inquest, deposed that she said she made the gruel of grits, but not finding it thick enough, she took nearly a tablespoonful of oatmeal from a paper that was in a jar in a cupboard in the kitchen; that she mixed it up in a butter-boat, and put it in the gruel, throwing the paper, with a little oatmeal that was left, into the fire; and said that there was in the same jar oatmeal and poison – both in separate papers.

Henry Hill, journeyman to Mr Newman, deposed that Mr Walker, the hairdresser, came with stuff to kill the rats, and that some of it was left in a paper which the witness took into the kitchen when the maids were at tea; he opened the paper, and said it was poison to kill rats; he does not recollect what became of it.

The jury, after consulting near an hour, gave their verdict, finding Elizabeth Miller guilty of wilful murder; when the coroner issued a warrant for her committal to Horsemonger Lane Prison, for trial at the next Surrey assizes. – She is about seventeen years of age, and had lived in Mr Newman's family about four months.

Appendix XV.

Editor's note.

The trial of Elizabeth Mary Miller took place at the Surrey Assizes on Friday 5 April 1816. This account is taken from the Evening Mail, 8 April 1816.

*

ELIZABETH MARY MILLER, aged nineteen, was indicted for the wilful murder of Elizabeth Ann Newman, by administering to her certain deadly poison, called arsenic, in the parish of St Mary, Lambeth, on 13 September last.

Mr ESPINASSE stated the case on the part of the prosecution.

MARY EADES deposed that she lived in the service of Mr Newman, a butcher, at Lambeth, three years. Was there in the month of September last. Her master had two children, one of which (the deceased) was two years and a half old. On 13 September, she and her mistress had been out walking with the children, and they returned about half past seven o'clock in the evening. Her mistress ordered her to get some magnesia and rhubarb for the children, and the prisoner brought up the gruel for their supper, which had been prepared by her for that purpose. Her mistress then gave the children some of the gruel and medicine, and witness afterwards proceeded to undress the youngest. The prisoner was engaged to undress the deceased. Soon after, the youngest child exhibited symptoms of sickness, and in a short time the deceased child came running to her mother, crying bitterly; and being asked by the latter whether her father had been beating her, she said not, and asked to be rocked in her mother's lap. Shortly afterwards, the deceased was taken violently ill with a vomiting; and soon after, the younger child was affected in a similar manner.

The father of the child then came in, and the prisoner was called, when the former said to her, 'What have you been doing with the gruel?' The prisoner replied, 'Nothing'; and the question being repeated, she still denied, but burst into tears. A basin containing part of the gruel which had been made was then brought into the room from the parlour, and Newman said to the prisoner, 'Here then, if you have done nothing to the gruel, drink some of it yourself'. The prisoner again cried bitterly, but refused to drink the gruel. Witness then took two dessert spoonfuls of the gruel herself; soon after felt a burning heat in her mouth and stomach, and a disposition to vomit. The prisoner was then ordered to go for Mr Dixon, an apothecary, which she did, and returned soon after with him – the distance she went was about half a mile, and she must have gone with great expedition.

Upon the arrival of the apothecary, the prisoner was ordered to bring the basin which contained the gruel that had not been used, also the remainder of the grits. These, together with the cup and its dregs, were locked up by direction of Mr Dixon. The latter, after remaining a short time, desired some person to be sent with him for the necessary medicine for the children. The prisoner accordingly went, and returned without much delay. The children, however, got worse; the eldest particularly, whose sickness increased to a violent degree, and who

Fenning.

languished in great agony until the following morning, when she died. At this time the prisoner had locked herself up in her bedroom; and upon being informed of what had happened, she exclaimed, in bitter terms – 'Good God, what shall I do?'

Cross-examined by Mr NOLAN. – The prisoner was deeply affected, and wept much, when she heard the child had died. Witness knew her master's house was infested with rats. A person named Skinner, a rat-catcher, was in the habit of coming there with parcels and papers for their destruction. There were several jars in the kitchen, and in these were kept parcels, in paper, of rice, spices, etc. There were similar parcels in the cupboard. Witness could not say precisely what they contained. She slept with the prisoner, who had only an open box in her room, to which any person might have had access. Remembered a person of the name of Shaw, who also frequented the house of her master as a rat-catcher, and used certain parcels.

ANN NEWMAN deposed that she was mother of the deceased child. On the evening of 13 September, she went out with her children to walk, having previously ordered the prisoner to get money from her master to buy grits, and make some gruel. Upon her return home, she desired the last witness to bring a little magnesia and rhubarb in a wine glass. The prisoner had brought up the gruel in a basin. Some of this was put into a coffee cup with the medicine, and administered to the children. Soon after, they were affected violently; and upon the entrance of her husband into the room, and seeing the state of his children, the prisoner was called up, and asked about the grits she had purchased. Witness had bought no arsenic herself, nor did she know of any being in the house.

Mr DIXON deposed that he was an apothecary. The prisoner came to his house on 13 September in the evening, and stated that he was wanted immediately. Upon his arrival at Newman's, he found the two children dreadfully ill. He immediately ordered the gruel and other things to be locked up. One of the children died the following morning, and he in consequence analysed the gruel, and found in it ingredients of arsenic.

The prisoner was the person who came home with him for the medicine from the house of Mr Newman. He asked her if she was the young woman who made the gruel, and of what it was made. The prisoner answered she was, and had made it of grits. He then asked whether or no she had added anything to the gruel. She replied she had thickened it with oatmeal, which had been in the house a month before for one of the men who had got a cold. The symptoms he had perceived were those uniformly arising from arsenic in the stomach; and he was of opinion that, in the present case, the death of the child was produced in this way.

Cross-examined by Mr NOLAN. – The prisoner was most importunate in begging his attendance to repair to the house when the children were affected. White arsenic, generally used for destroying rats, might easily be mistaken for oatmeal.

Appendix XV.

Richard Newman was father to the deceased child. His dwelling and slaughterhouse were very much infested with rats; but he did not think there was any arsenic in or about his house when the accident happened. About two years ago, he saw a powder exposed in a window for the destruction of rats; he purchased several papers of it, and placed it about. Finding no good effects from this, he employed a person named Skinner, and afterwards one Walker, in June or July, who undertook to destroy the rats as he pleased, but was not aware that that person had left any of his papers or ingredients about the house.

Cross-examined by Mr NOLAN. – Skinner, the rat-catcher, had laid some of his papers in the kitchen as well as other places; remembers Walker being employed in that way about two months before the accident: his preparations were like white paste, and were rolled in white powder.

HENRY WALKER, rat-catcher and hairdresser, obtained of last witness putrid meat, which, being chopped fine, was mixed with arsenic and rolled together in one body, till it presented the appearance of flour. This composition he afterwards divided into several parcels of paper, and distributed them behind the wainscots, the holes under the stones, and in the suet-drawer. Some of the parcels were rolled up, and some were laid open. He frequently called at Newman's to see the effect, but found the parcels as he left them; any person might carry them away.

HENRY MILLS, a servant to Newman, remembers being told by another person that one of the rat-papers was lying in the dust of the shop, when he went and took it out, and then placed it in the kitchen window; did not know what became of it afterwards.

There was no defence; and Mr JUSTICE ABBOTT having shortly addressed the jury, attributing the unfortunate death of the child to accident merely, the girl was instantly acquitted.

Editor's note.

The London Courier and Evening Gazette, reporting on the trial in their edition of Monday 8 April 1816, said that 'the prisoner continued totally senseless during the trial, and was frequently seized with convulsive fits. She was carried from the bar in a state of insensibility.'.

INDEX.

15th Regiment of Foot, 1, 2, 21

Abbot, Richard, 9 & n26, 71n154
Adams, Abraham, 30 & n71, 36, 37
Addington, Henry *see* Sidmouth, Henry Addington, 1st Viscount
Adolphus, John, 5n21
Affecting Case of Eliza Fenning (Fairburn), 18, 19, 30–2, 33, 34, 35n85, 36n91, 38–9, 39n97, 39n98, 40, 62n141, 144n194
All the Year Round (magazine), 39, 57, 161–73
Alley, Peter: defends Henry Wyatt, 203, 205, 209; defends Eliza Fenning, 5, 11, 94n175, 97; cross-examinations: Charlotte Turner, 87; Orlibar Turner, 90; Roger Gadsden, 91; Sarah Peer, 93–4; Joseph Penson, 95; examination of character witnesses, 96–7; disinterested in outcome of trial, 11; fights duel with pistols, 5n21
anti-Catholic prejudice, 50n122, 70, 72
arsenic: availability and use, 3n7, 67, 74; criminal cases, 26n62, 53n130, 67n149, 74n159; effects on metal, 10, 17, 20, 29n68, 49, 65, 120 & n185; effects on yeast dough, 17, 20, 28–9, 49 & n120, 119–20, 120n184; in Eliza Fenning case, 8, 17, 19, 23, 64–7, 64n145, 68, 88–9, 90, 94, 95, 98; poisoning symptoms, 10n28; sale restricted by law, 3n7; tests for, 3n8, 10n29, 67; Wansbrough's experiments with, 17, 20, 28–9, 120n184, 120n185
attempted murder: as capital offence, 12n31

Barbados: slave insurrection (1816), 71n153
'Barran, F. M.', 19–21
Beckett, John, 27–8, 171, 189n211
Berry, James, 36n91
blackening of knives *see* arsenic: effects on metal
Blathwaite, Mr, 26, 27, 189n211
bodysnatching, 39n96
Bristol Mirror, 37, 211
British Critic, The (newspaper), 50
British Press (newspaper), 19–21
Bury and Norwich Post, 52
Buxton, Fowell, 75

'C.A.' (letter-writer), 30–1, 62n141
Caledonian Mercury, 39–41
capital punishment, 74–5; *see also* executions

child pickpockets, hanging of, 75n161
Circumstantial Evidence: The Extraordinary Case of Eliza Fenning (London, 1829), 50–2, 70 & n152
Clarke, Mary Ann, 5 & n18, 139; letter from Eliza, 149
Clerkenwell Prison and infirmary, 4–5, 12–13, 66; Eliza's letters from, 129–30
coal delivery (21 March 1815), 43n107, 60, 87, 93, 109–10; coal merchant's records, 110–11
Coldbath Fields, 73
confessions, 27n66, 56–7, 72
Corderoy, John, 75n161
coroners: medical qualifications, 17n46
corpses: dissection and atomisation, 38n94
Cotton, Reverend Horace: as hell-fire chaplain, 27n66, 32n73, 43; distrusted by Eliza, 141, 142, 144; witnesses Thomas King's declaration of innocence, 43–4; condemned sermon, 32n73; meeting at Mr Newman's house, 27; attends Eliza during execution, 35, 36, 37, 116; collusion with the Turners, 58; and Mr Fenning's affidavit, 46, 113, 117; interviews child pickpocket, 75
crime rate, 2
criminal journalism, 76n163
Crockford, Mr, 28
Cruikshank, George, 48n117, 159
Cruikshank, Isaac R., 159
Curran, John Philpot, 76n162, 158

Davis, Samuel: affidavit, 45–6, 113–14, 115; retracted, 46n112, 117; Eliza Fenning on, 150–1
Day, The (newspaper), 62n141
defendants right to counsel, 11–12, 12n30, 196–7, 196n232
Dickens, Charles: on Eliza Fenning case, 57–8; opposed to public hangings, 74
dissection and atomisation of corpses, 38n94
dolly-mop, as pejorative term, 70n152
Dominica, West Indies, 1
Druce, Charles, Snr, 189–90
Dundee Courier, 71

Eagle Street, Red Lion Square, 38–9, 40, 45, 46
Edmonds, Mr (brewer), 6, 63, 94
Edmunds, Christiana: poisoning case (1871), 3n7

219

Index.

Edward (Eliza's fiancé): identity unknown, 4n15; character, 70; relations with Eliza, 1, 35n85; letters from Eliza, 4–5, 12–16, 129–32, 133–4, 135–6, 146

Eldon, John Scott, 1st Earl of, 22n; Eliza writes to, 22–3, 136–7

Essex Herald, 52

Evening Mail, 71n153, 215–17

Examiner, The (newspaper): early concerns about Eliza Fenning case, 18–19; publishes letter from Eliza, 24, 144–5; support from Leigh Hunt, 73; letter of protest from Corbyn Lloyd, 30; contests Silvester's summing up and after behaviour, 46–7; reviews *The Important Results,* 19n51; on Robert Turner's confession, 51–2

executions: as deterrent, 75; as public spectacle, 34 & n82, 74–5; hanging method, 36n91; of Corderoy and Fellowes, 75n161; of Elizabeth Fenning, 35–7, 36n91, 38n93, 158; of Catherine Foster, 74n159; of Catherine Hayes, 12n31; of Elizabeth Wollerton, 35n85

Fairburn, John, *Affecting Case of Eliza Fenning,* 18, 19, 30–2, 33, 34, 35n85, 36n91, 38–9, 39n97, 39n98, 40, 62n141, 144n194

Fellowes, John, 75n161

FENNING, ELIZA

Before the trial: birth and family background, 1–2, 41; attempted murder of mother story, 41n104; schooling, 41; appearance, 1 & n1; portrait by Cruikshank, 159; literacy, 8, 21, 73, 127; character, 41–2, 60, 73 & n157, 128; alleged lewdness and immorality, 42, 43, 70 & n152; in service of Mr Hardy, 42, 70–1; alleged attempts to poison Hardy family, 121–6, 128; relations with Edward, 1, 35n85; employed as cook in Turner home, 1, 42; quarrels with Sarah Peer, 9, 93; in boys' bedroom, 6, 58–9; threatened with dismissal, 6, 96; relations with Charlotte Turner, 7, 9, 51–2, 59, 69; orders yeast, 6; makes dumplings for servants' supper, 8; actions on day of poisoning, 6–7, 22–3; watched by Mrs Turner, 59; prepares dinner for Turner family, 2, 6, 7, 61; leaves kitchen to take coal delivery, 43n107, 60, 109; samples leftover dumpling, 8, 62, 66; warns Gadsden from eating dumpling, 8, 62; taken ill, 2, 66; believes milk adulterated, 8n25, 10, 48, 74, 90, 91, 105; confined to sick-bed, 3n9, 62–3; arrested and charged with attempted murder, 3–4, 94; box searched, 48, 105; committal hearing at Hatton Court, 4, 103–5; in Clerkenwell Prison, 4–5, 12–13; trial (*see* trial)

After the trial: in Newgate, 4 & n15, 5, 5n18, 12; conduct and behaviour in prison, 16–17, 43–4; her letters, 4–5, 4n15, 12–18, 21–6, 76, 129–51; relations with William Oldfield, 16, 43, 142, 193–4; Privy Council review, 42; lack of motive for poisonings, 65, 69–70; agitation by her supporters, 26–30; public support for, 30; press coverage, 18–19, 24, 30–1, 41–6; character assassination, 41–6, 48, 49–50, 72; and closing of ranks by Establishment, 58, 69; petition for royal clemency, 21, 23, 29, 52, 55, 107–8; appeals to Lord Eldon, 22–3; date of execution fixed, 25, 30; receives sacrament and hears condemned sermon, 32 & n 73; continues to declare her innocence, 32, 33; supposed confession and retraction, 54–7, 58, 71–2; visited by Mr and Mrs Turner, 32–3; tests King's innocence, 43–4; writes verse lines ('Written in Newgate'), 153–5; final visit from mother, 33; sends ear-rings to mother, 33–4; last hours, 34–5, 35n85; no last-minute confession, 72; outfit for execution, 35 & n85; execution, 35–7, 36n91, 158; last words, 36 & n91; public reactions to her death, 38; spared dissection, 38n94; body on view, 38–9, 45; funeral procession and burial, 39–41, 39n98; martyrdom, 76; sanctified in death, 76–7, 76n162; posthumous reputation, 52–3, 53n130, 77; divided opinions on case, 41, 46–8; and political disenfranchisement, 2n5, 71, 73; supposed confessions to crimes ascribed to Eliza Fenning, 53–4, 71; *Eliza Fenning's Own Narrative,* 33

Fenning, Mary (*née* Swayne; mother), 1, 2, 18, 21, 41; pays for Eliza to share cell, 5; letters from Eliza, 132–3, 145, 147, 150; last prison visit to Eliza, 33; receives ear-rings from Eliza, 33–4; at daughter's funeral, 41 & n102

Fenning, William (father), 1–2, 18, 21, 41; pays for Eliza to share cell, 5; written statement ignored at trial, 11, 94n175, 97; refused as witness, 69, 98; letters from Eliza, 132–3, 145, 147; redeems daughter's body for burial, 38; financial hardship, 38–9; slurred by Davis, 45–6, 46n112, 113–14; affidavit, 114–16

Fielding, Henry, *Amelia,* 48

220

Index.

Fleet, River, 74
Fletcher, Dr (minister of Finsbury Chapel), 53–4, 71
food poisoning, 73, 74
Force, Reverend Mr, 40
Forster, Benjamin Meggot, 190 & n213, 192n218
Foster, Catherine, 74n159
Freemasonry: links to judiciary, 69n150
Fry, Elizabeth, 4n14

Gadsden, Roger: apprentice, 1 & n2; 'takes liberty' with Eliza, 59, 62, 96; warned by Eliza not to eat dumpling, 8, 62; samples leftover dumpling, 8–9; taken ill, 2, 9, 61; fetches Margaret Turner from Lambeth, 9, 61; evidence at committal hearing, 4, 104; evidence at trial, 90–1, 97–8; as witness, 11; wild stories concerning, 45; epileptic seizures, 45n110; and missing arsenic, 68; later life, 90n169
Gate Street Charity School, 41
George IV, King (*formerly* Prince Regent), 31
Gibson, Mr (chemist): statement about Robert Turner's disturbing behaviour, 26–8, 68, 189; urges Orlibar Turner not to prosecute, 28
Globe, The, 4, 211n245, 213n246
Godfrey, Elizabeth: execution of (1807), 34n82
Godfrey, Samuel, 191 & n214
Great Fire of London (1666), 50n122
Grieg, Reverend Mr, 32n74
Gurney, John: legal career, 5n20; prosecutes Eliza Fenning, 5; examinations: Charlotte Turner, 85–7; Orlibar Turner, 88–90; Roger Gadsden, 90–1; Margaret Turner, 91–2; Robert Turner, 92; Sarah Peer, 92–3; William Thiselton, 94; Joseph Penson, 94–5; John Marshall, 95; re-examinations: Roger Gadsden, 91; Sarah Peer, 94
Gurney, Reverend J. H., 54–7, 71
Gurney, William Brodie, 54–7

Hackman, James, 187
Hackwood, F.W., *William Hone: His Life and Times,* 157–9
Haggerty, Owen: execution of (1807), 34n82
Hale, Sir Matthew, 197
Hardy, Mr (grocer), 42, 70–1, 73n157, 123–8
Hardy, Mrs, 124, 125–7, 128
Harland, Edward, 43
Harvey, Francis: assault case (1815), 201–2, 201n241
Hatton Garden Police Office, 3, 4, 49; committal hearing, 59, 70, 103–5; affidavit not sworn for Mr Fenning, 114
Hayes, Catherine: execution of (1726), 12
Hickson, Mr (oilman), 123–4, 125
Hinchcliff, Elizabeth: poisoning case (1810), 26n62
Hinson, Mrs: evidence at trial, 96
Holloway, John: execution of (1807), 34n82
Holmes, John, 39n96
Hone, William: radical journalist and political agitator, 48n117; possible letter to *British Press,* 19–21; attends Eliza Fenning execution, 36, 38n93, 158; edits Eliza's Newgate letters, 76, 159; correspondence on case, 199–201; 'The Maid and the Magpie' (prose narrative), 158–9, 175–85; interest in Francis Harvey assault case, 201–2; *see also Important Results of an Elaborate Investigation, The*
Horsemonger Lane Gaol, 73
Houston, George, 188 & n210
Hume, Joseph, 3n8, 10n29
Hunt, John, 73
Hunt, Leigh, 73 & n155
Hutchinson, Mrs: evidence at trial, 96
hygiene and sanitation, 73–4

Important Results of an Elaborate Investigation into the Mysterious Case of Eliza Fenning, The (Watkins): Hone as author, 19n51, 201; writing, 76; publication, 48, 159, 200–1; marketing hype, 76; critical reception, 50; trial evidence questioned, 10n27, 48–9, 49n120, 58–9, 61, 63–5; defamations rebutted, 49–50; condemned sermon, 32n73; meeting at Silvester's house, 189n211, 191n218; Eliza's last hours, 34n84; execution, 35–6; her scaffold outfit, 35n85; spared dissection, 38n94; dismisses *Observer* article, 41, 44n109; on attempted matricide story, 41n104; coal merchant's records, 109–11; affidavit of Samuel Davis, 113–14; affidavit of William Fenning, 114–17; Effects of Arsenic Upon Yeast Dough, 119–20, 120n184; Effects of Arsenic Upon Knives, 120 & n185; opinions of Mr and Mrs Hardy, 121–8
Inglis, John, 53n130, 54
Ivimey, Reverend Mr Joseph, 32n74

Jones, Alice, 74n159
judges, as counsel for the defendant, 196–7, 196n232
juryman, deaf, 19, 84n166

Index.

Kentish Gazette, 34n82
Kentish Weekly Post, 35n85, 201n241
King, Mr (Thomas's father), 122–3
King, Thomas: apprentice, 1; loiters in kitchen, 7, 23, 66, 136–7; fetches John Marshall, 3; prevents Eliza's escape, 3n9; Eliza seeks to call as witness, 11, 97–8; not called as witness, 3, 11, 59, 61, 65–6, 98; visits Eliza in prison, 32–3, 43; swears innocence on Bible, 43–4; as culprit, 66
Kinnaird, Mr (magistrate), 114

La Pie Voleuse see 'Maid and the Magpie, The'
Lancet, The, 17n46
L'Angelier, Emile, 53n130
Langley, John (hangman), 35n85, 36, 72
Lloyd, Corbyn, 26, 30, 47
London Courier and Evening Gazette, 211–14

'Maid and the Magpie, The': play, 158; prose narrative (Hone), 159, 175–85
Marsh test, 3n8, 67
Marshall, John: medical qualifications, 3n6; treats Turner family, 2–3, 10; delay in calling out, 10n27, 68–9; detects arsenic in leftover dumplings, 3, 9n26, 10; evidence at committal hearing, 4, 103–4; seeks second opinion from Joseph Hume, 10n29; evidence at trial, 95; dismissive of Wansbrough's arsenic experiments, 29; trial evidence flawed, 49, 64–5, 66, 67; collusion with the Turners, 29–30, 58, 69; letter from Hone, 200; *Fives Cases of Recovery,* 3n9, 4n12, 32n75, 33, 45n110, 47–8, 51n126
Marshall, Tim, 76
Maybrick, Florence: trial of (1889), 67n149, 71
Maybrick, James, as arsenic eater, 67n149
Maze, Richard: evidence at trial, 96
milk, contaminated, 74 & n158
Millar, Mr, 38–9
Miller, Elizabeth Mary, 199; inquest on body of Elizabeth Ann Newman, 211–14; trial (1816), 215–17
Montagu, Basil: background, 187; urged to intervene in Fenning case, 188–90; interview with Silvester, 26–7, 191, 192; application to Secretary of State, 191; advises caution over censure of Silvester, 195; personal reflections on legal aspects of case, 11–12, 196–7; Harvard Papers, 187–97
Montagu, Basil Caroline, 193n220, 201–2
Montagu, John, 187
Morning Advertiser, 32n73, 209–10

Morning Chronicle, 19
Moyes, J. (printer), 200–1

New Clerkenwell Prison *see* Clerkenwell Prison and infirmary
Newgate Calendar, 27n66, 50n122, 94n175
Newgate Prison: conditions, 4n14; Eliza Fenning in, 4 & n15, 5, 5n18, 12, 16–17, 32 & n73, 45–6, 70
Newman, Mr (Newgate gaoler), 4n15, 27, 43, 146n195, 151
Newman, Elizabeth Ann, 211–14
Norfolk Chronicle, 39
Observer, The, 41–6, 199
Ogilvy, Henry: called out to Turner family, 2, 20, 23; not called as trial witness, 10n27, 49
Old Bailey, 5
Oldfield, William: child rapist, 30n71; relations with Eliza Fenning, 16, 43, 142, 193–4; letters from Eliza, 134–5, 138, 144; execution, 36, 37
Oxford National Dictionary of Biography: entry for Eliza Fenning, 77

Palmer, William, 55 & n134
Parr, Dr Samuel, 193–4
Patch, Richard, 55
Peck, Mr (grocer), 122–3
Peer, Sarah: housemaid, 1; quarrels with Eliza, 9, 93; takes delivery of yeast, 6; servants' supper, 8; collects milk, 9; serves meal to Turner family, 7, 8, 9, 62; visits sister in Hackney, 9; returns to Chancery Lane, 9; lies about Eliza's illness, 11, 94n175, 97; evidence at committal hearing, 4, 104–5; accused by Eliza of adulterating milk, 10, 74, 90, 105; in court before giving evidence, 61; evidence at trial, 92–4, 95; on grudge between Eliza and Mrs Turner, 59, 98; lies about coal delivery, 43n107, 60, 93, 109; as culprit, 66, 67
penal reform, 4n14
Penson, Joseph, 6; evidence at trial, 94–5
Perkins, Mr (bootmaker), 77n164
Perkins, Reverend Dr, 27
petition for royal clemency, 21, 23, 29, 52, 55, 107–8
Pharmacy and Sale of Poisons Act (1868), 3n7
Phillips, Charles, 76n162, 157–8
pickpockets, at public executions, 75 & n161
Pierrepoint, Albert, 37n91
Pitt, William, the Younger, 21n55
Prisoners' Counsel Act (1836), 12n30

222

Index.

Ray, Martha, 187
Raynsford, Mr (magistrate), 3
Redit, Mr (solicitor), 128
Reinsch test, 3n8, 67
Richardson, J.M., 26, 189–90, 189n211, 194
Roman Catholics, prejudice against, 50n122, 70, 72
Roughead, William, 53
Royal College of Surgeons, 38n94

Sale of Arsenic Regulation Act (1851), 3n7
Salisbury and Winchester Journal, 202n241
Sandys, Sir Samuel, 196n232
scalding the yeast, 61
servants, domestic, 12n31, 70–1, 73, 121, 211
Shearman, Mr (magistrates' clerk), 4, 49, 59, 69; refuses to swear William Fenning's affidavit, 114–15
short drop (execution method), 36n91
Shower, Sir Bartholomew, 196n232
Shuter, Mr (solicitor), 50, 71
Sidmouth, Henry Addington, 1st Viscount, 17, 21n55, 26; Eliza writes to, 140–1
Silvester, Sir John: character and reputation, 5n19; tries Eliza Fenning case, 5; disregards trial evidence, 11, 94n175, 97 & n178; refuses to hear witnesses, 98; summing up and sentencing, 98–100; declines to petition Prince Regent, 12n31; ignores plea for respite, 26, 30; claims Eliza's supporters swayed by her looks, 26, 30; interview with Basil Montagu, 26–7, 191, 192; meeting at Silvester's house, 189n211, 190, 192n218; learns of Robert Turner's insanity, 28; deters Turner from signing petition, 29–30; criticised, 46–7, 49; collusion with the Turners, 29–30, 49, 58; on hanging miscreant children, 75n161
slave insurrection in Barbados (1816), 71n153
Smith, John: affidavit, 59; evidence at trial, 20, 96–7; testimony curtailed by judge, 59–60, 97n178
Smith, John Gordon: experiment on arsenic, 29n68
Smith, Madeleine, 52–3, 53n130
St George the Martyr, Bloomsbury, 39 & n96, 40, 157
Stamp Act (1712), 2n5
Stratford, Harriet, 201n241, 202
Stratmann, Linda, 10n28, 77
suffrage, 2n5, 71, 73

Thiselton, William: arrests Eliza, 3–4, 48; evidence at committal hearing, 4 & n12, 10, 63, 70, 105; evidence at trial, 9–10, 94
Thornbury, Walter: Dickens writes to, 57–8; 'Eliza Fenning. (The Danger of Condemning to Death on Circumstantial Evidence Alone.)', 39, 57, 161–73
Times, The: quotes Marshall, 48; Eliza Fenning's supposed confession, 53–7, 71; on public executions, 74–5; death of Alice Jones, 74n159
trial: indictment, 5–6, 83; judge and legal teams, 5; jury, 19, 84 & n166; case for the prosecution, 6–11, 85–95; previous inconsistent statements by prosecution witnesses, 10, 59; collusion of witnesses, 49, 61, 69; witnesses not called, 3, 10n27, 11, 49, 59, 61, 65–6, 98; case for the defence, 11–12, 95–8; Eliza Fenning gives evidence, 95–6; evidence ignored, 11, 94n175, 97 & n178; witnesses refused, 69, 98; judge's summing up, 12, 98–100; verdict and sentence, 100; Eliza's reaction to verdict, 12; evidence omitted from official transcript, 49; trial evidence questioned, 10n27, 18–21, 48–9, 49n120, 58–63, 68, 193–4
Turner, Charlotte (*née* Churchman): household, 1; marriage to Robert Turner, 51n125; reproves Eliza for lewd behaviour, 6; relations with Eliza, 7, 9, 51–2, 59, 69; permits Eliza to make dumplings from scratch, 6; noses around in kitchen, 7, 59, 60; instructs Eliza to add milk to dumpling mixture, 8n25; comments adversely on quality of dumplings, 7, 62; taken ill at lunch, 2, 7; and ingestion of arsenic, 74; evidence at committal hearing, 4, 104; indisposed from pregnancy, 4n12; evidence at trial, 6, 85–7, 89, 92; testifies to Eliza's literacy, 8; lies about coal delivery, 43n107, 60, 87, 109; contradictions and mistakes in her evidence, 22–3, 59, 60; visits Eliza in Newgate, 32–3; birth of daughter Sophia, 51n126
Turner, Margaret: intercedes on Eliza's behalf, 6, 96; arrives at Chancery Lane, 9; evidence at committal hearing, 4, 104; evidence at trial, 91–2
Turner, Orlibar: law stationer, 2 & n5; notices arsenic missing from office, 8, 68; taken ill at lunch, 2, 7–8; suspects Eliza of attempted poisoning, 3, 8; repeatedly questions Eliza, 62–3; orders Eliza confined to house, 3n9; evidence at committal hearing, 4, 103; apprised of son Robert's threatening tirade, 68; urged not to prosecute, 28, 189;

Index.

evidence at trial, 88–90, 94; withholds knowledge of coal delivery, 60, 109–10; inconsistencies in trial testimony, 48–9, 61; collusion with Silvester and Shearman, 49, 69; spreads vicious rumours about Eliza, 49–50, 71; Eliza writes to from prison, 23–4, 134; persuaded of Eliza's innocence, 28–9; deterred by Silvester from signing petition, 29; procures Davis affidavit, 117; criticised for keeping arsenic in open place, 19, 63; later life, 51n125

Turner, Robert Gregson: household, 1; taken ill at lunch, 2, 9, 10n28; evidence at committal hearing, 4, 104; evidence at trial, 9, 63, 92; not stringently questioned in court, 68, 69; public protests outside his house, 38, 44–5, 46, 69; panic attacks, 45n110; refuses to sign petition for clemency, 21; Eliza writes to from prison, 23–4, 134; visits Eliza in Newgate, 32–3; evidence of his insanity and homicidal disposition, 26–8, 51, 68, 189; wild stories concerning, 45; dissuaded by Silvester from signing petition, 29; later life, 51n125; supposed deathbed confession, 51–2, 71; as culprit, 68, 74

Turner, Sophia Gregson, 51n126

Upton, Rev. James: Fenning confession story, 55–6, 57, 71–2; Dickens repugns, 58

Vasey, Reverend Mr Thomas, 35

Wakley, Thomas, Dr, 17n46
Wansbrough, Dr Thomas William: career, 17n46; describes Eliza, 1n1; experiments with arsenic, 17, 20, 28–9, 120n184, 120n185; visits Eliza in prison, 30n70, 33; acts as intermediary, 32n75; lock of hair incident, 4n15, 146n195; letter from Eliza, 17–18, 137–8; with Eliza on eve of execution, 34–5, 34n84; at execution, 36n89; on 'Written in Newgate' (verses arranged by Eliza), 153–5; campaigns for coroner medical qualifications, 17n46; *An Authentic Narrative,* 1, 17n46, 34–5, 34n84, 140n192

Waterloo, Battle of (1815), 73
Watkins, John: on John Marshall, 3n6; letter to Hone, 199–200, 211; *see also Important Results of an Elaborate Investigation, The*
Wesley, Charles, 32n73
white arsenic *see* arsenic
white blackbird, 52n128
Williams, Reverend Mr Griffith, 32n74
Williams, Robert, 39n96
Wilson, Ben, 5n19, 19n51, 76
Wollerton, Elizabeth, execution of (1815), 35n85
Wood, Mr (Pimlico coal merchant), 109–11
Woodderson, John, 97; evidence at trial, 96
Wyatt, Henry William: trial (1806), 203–10

NOTABLE BRITISH TRIALS SERIES.

Trial	Date of Trial(s)	Editor(s)	Volume No.
Mary Queen of Scots	1586	A. Francis Steuart	30
Guy Fawkes	1605-1606	Donald Carswell	61
King Charles I	1649	J. G. Muddiman	43
The Bloody Assizes	1685	J. G. Muddiman	48
Captain Kidd	1701	Graham Brooks	51
Jack Sheppard	1724	Horace Bleackley	59
Captain Porteous	1736	William Roughead	9
The Annesley Case	1743	Andrew Lang	16
Lord Lovat	1747	David N. Mackay	14
Mary Blandy	1752	William Roughead	22
James Stewart	1752	David N. Mackay	6
Eugene Aram	1759	Eric R. Watson	19
Katharine Nairn	1765	William Roughead	38
The Douglas Cause	1761-1769	A. Francis Steuart	8
Duchess of Kingston	1776	Lewis Melville	42
Deacon Brodie	1788	William Roughead	5
The 'Bounty' Mutineers	1792	Owen Rutter	55
Eliza Fenning*	1815	Kate Clarke	88
Abraham Thornton	1817	Sir John Hall, Bt.	37
Henry Fauntleroy	1824	Horace Bleackley	34
Thurtell and Hunt	1824	Eric R. Watson	26
Burke and Hare	1828	William Roughead	27
James Blomfield Rush	1849	W. Teignmouth Shore	45
William Palmer	1856	Eric R. Watson	15
Madeleine Smith	1857	A. Duncan Smith (first edition)	
		F. Tennyson Jesse (second edition)	1
Dr Smethurst	1859	L. A. Parry	53
Mrs M'Lachlan	1862	William Roughead	12
Franz Müller	1864	H. B. Irving	13
Dr Pritchard	1865	William Roughead	3
The Wainwrights	1875	H. B. Irving	25
The Stauntons	1877	J. B. Atlay	11
Eugène Marie Chantrelle	1878	A. Duncan Smith	4

Notable British Trials Series.

Kate Webster	1879	Elliott O'Donnell	35
City of Glasgow Bank Directors	1879	William Wallace	2
Charles Peace	1879	W. Teignmouth Shore	39
Percy Lefroy Mapleton*	1881	Adam Wood	86
Dr Lamson	1882	H. L. Adam	18
Adelaide Bartlett	1886	Sir John Hall, Bt.	41
Israel Lipski*	1887	M. W. Oldridge	84
Mrs Maybrick	1889	H. B. Irving	17
John Watson Laurie	1889	William Roughead	57
The Baccarat Case	1891	W. Teignmouth Shore	56
Thomas Neill Cream	1892	W. Teignmouth Shore	31
Alfred John Monson	1893	J. W. More	7
Oscar Wilde	1895	H. Montgomery Hyde	70
Louise Masset*	1899	Kate Clarke	85
William Gardiner	1903	William Henderson	63
George Chapman	1903	H. L. Adam	50
Samuel Herbert Dougal	1903	F. Tennyson Jesse	44
The 'Veronica' Mutineers	1903	Prof. G. W. Keeton and John Cameron	76
Adolf Beck	1904	Eric R. Watson	33
Robert Wood	1907	Basil Hogarth	65
Oscar Slater	1909-1928	William Roughead	10
Hawley Harvey Crippen	1910	Filson Young	24
John Alexander Dickman	1910	S. O. Rowan-Hamilton	21
Steinie Morrison	1911	H. Fletcher Moulton	28
The Seddons	1912	Filson Young	20
George Joseph Smith	1915	Eric R. Watson	29
Sir Roger Casement	1916	George H. Knott (first and second editions)	
		H. Montgomery Hyde (third edition)	23
Ronald Light*	1920	Sally Smith	87
Harold Greenwood	1920	Winifred Duke	52
Field and Gray	1920	Winifred Duke	67
Bywaters and Thompson	1922	Filson Young	32
Ronald True	1922	Donald Carswell	36
Herbert Rowse Armstrong	1922	Filson Young	40
Jean Pierre Vaquier	1924	R. H. Blundell	47
John Donald Merrett	1927	William Roughead	46
Browne and Kennedy	1927	W. Teignmouth Shore	49

Notable British Trials Series.

Benjamin Knowles	1928	Albert Lieck	60
Sidney Harry Fox	1930	F. Tennyson Jesse	62
Alfred Arthur Rouse	1931	Helena Normanton	54
The Royal Mail Case	1931	Collin Brooks	58
Jeannie Donald	1934	J. G. Wilson	79
Rattenbury and Stoner	1935	F. Tennyson Jesse	64
Buck Ruxton	1936	Prof. H. Wilson	66
Frederick Nodder	1937	Winifred Duke	72
Patrick Carraher	1938-1946	George Blake	73
Peter Barnes and Others	1939	Letitia Fairfield	77
August Sangret	1943	MacDonald Critchley	83
William Joyce	1945	J. W. Hall	68
Neville George Cleveley Heath	1946	MacDonald Critchley	75
Ley and Smith	1947	F. Tennyson Jesse	69
James Camb	1948	G. Clark	71
Peter Griffiths	1948	George Godwin	74
John George Haigh	1949	Lord Dunboyne	78
Evans and Christie	1950 & 1953	F. Tennyson Jesse	82
John Thomas Straffen	1952	Letitia Fairfield and Eric P. Fullbrook	80
Craig and Bentley	1952	H. Montgomery Hyde	81

* New series.

In preparation:
Henry Hunt and Others (ed. Caitlin Kitchener)
The Mannings (ed. Linda Stratmann)
Frederick Baker (ed. David Green)

www.ingramcontent.com/pod-product-compliance
Lightning Source LLC
Chambersburg PA
CBHW031140160426
43193CB00008B/195